CW01090861

AN ACTOR'S RESEARCH

Investigating Choices for Practice and Performance

Tamsin Stanley and
Dr Philippa Strandberg-Long

Routledge
Taylor & Francis Group

NEW YORK AND LONDON

Cover image: Sergey Nivens/Shutterstock

First published 2023
by Routledge
605 Third Avenue, New York, NY 10158

and by Routledge
4 Park Square, Milton Park, Abingdon, Oxon, OX14 4RN

Routledge is an imprint of the Taylor & Francis Group, an informa business

Library of Congress Cataloging-in-Publication Data
A catalog record for this book has been requested

ISBN: 978-1-032-12370-7 (hbk)
ISBN: 978-1-032-12368-4 (pbk)
ISBN: 978-1-003-22613-0 (ebk)

DOI: 10.4324/9781003226130

Typeset in Bembo
by Apex CoVantage, LLC

AN ACTOR'S RESEARCH

An Actor's Research: Investigating Choices for Practice and Performance presents an accessible and highly practical guide to the research approaches required of the actor. It aims to establish the precision and rigour of the actor's craft that is intrinsic to a compelling acting performance, explore a range of research activities surrounding and emerging from practical work in the studio, and enable the actor to evolve a multifaceted skillset in researching for performance.

The chapters focus on different research areas such as the self, character, relationships, circumstance, and context, providing accessible and practical guidance to developing a personal research practice. Each aspect is explained and engaged with as practice, rather than study – offering helpful hints and advising against common pitfalls – ultimately enabling the actor to locate the necessary knowledge to shape and inform their performance in both text-based and devised scenarios. Additionally, as the actor's self is a personal instrument that is drawn on in terms of expression, impulses, and imagination; the self also becomes a source for creative appraisal and research. This book therefore offers comprehensive advice and strategies for self-evaluation and reflection, connecting research investigation with self-exploration in making expressive performance choices, making it a practice highly applicable to the actor's needs.

An Actor's Research closely follows the training actor's needs in terms of performance-based research; however, its practical research activities for text and character creation and strategies for the development of critical thinking and self-reflective skills support the ongoing development of the actor and their craft in both training and professional circumstances.

Tamsin Stanley currently teaches contextual studies across various UK drama schools, and provides project, event, and communication support to the Federation of Drama Schools. She sits on the board of various theatre companies, including 53/Two in Manchester and Lighthouse Theatre in Swansea.

Dr Philippa Strandberg-Long is an acting teacher, director, and researcher, originally from Stockholm, Sweden. Philippa is also the Head of Actor Training at LAMDA (the London Academy of Music and Dramatic Art).

CONTENTS

ACKNOWLEDGEMENTS

This book would not have arrived without the support and encouragement of Heather, Gemma, Rob, Ellie, Charlie, and all the staff and practitioners we've worked with who have shared our interest in evolving this as a resource.

Many thanks to Guy Stanley for the cartoons, Robert Shaughnessy for the pre-read, and all the talented students and actors we have worked with, who never fail to surprise and inspire with their imaginative research for practice.

And thanks also to those who have patiently explored with us in developing exercises and research activities even when they went nowhere. Those exercises are the ones that didn't make it into this book – we *hope* . . .

INTRODUCTION

What is Actor's Research?

Research often gets a bad rep in acting work and it's true that it isn't always used effectively. We tend to have quite anecdotal ideas about it – usually at the extremes of activity (these are the ones journalists like to write stories about). Often this ranges from horror stories about weird and impractical *method* activities like *living as the character for months* – to the reverse:- I *don't need to do research* because *acting is all just pretending; I just use my instinct and intuition.*

We can end up making an artificial distinction between *proper acting* in *practical rehearsal* and the *intellectual* work that we are suspicious of, because it's too *academic*, it's not *creative*, it *keeps us in our heads*. We want to avoid overthinking or being *intellectual*. Had we wanted to do a history or psychology course, presumably we would have signed up for one; and many of us carry the sneaking belief that spending too much time and effort researching and analysing somehow makes us less authentic and instinctual as creative and imaginative actors.

While sometimes we can be resistant, lazy, or just unconfident about the research work we *ought* to do, quite a lot of the time this is often because we don't recognise the work we already do quite naturally in the process *as* acts of research – let alone explore other approaches – and so we don't effectively develop our skillset, engage with research comprehensively, or explore it as a methodology that is intrinsic to our practice. We get (or want to get) the tablework *done* and then start rehearsal.

It is a truth, pretty much universally acknowledged, that actors SHOULD do some kind of research. Almost every book on acting will recommend this activity as part of the process of developing a character and preparing for performance, whether you are an amateur afficionado, a student, or even a seasoned professional.

DOI: 10.4324/9781003226130-1

But we have found that there's much less guidance about what exactly that research should be in practice. How and what do we research for useful information that helps us make choices for an acting performance (as opposed to, say, a survey, project, or essay)?

Our objective in developing this book was to really explore the nature of an actor's research; the research that needs to be done FOR the practice of acting. What are the methods and activities that help actors in any context really use relevant research to inform their expressive choices in performance, and also recognise and develop the thinking skills and acts of research that are intrinsic within the rehearsal process?

Who Are We Talking to in This Book?

We came to this book through working with students in fulltime acting training courses in UK drama schools, alongside our professional work in directing, dramaturgy and writing, producing, and design.

You may be engaging with this book while you are undertaking formal acting training, theatre studies, or theatre making of some kind; perhaps you are an emerging director wanting to enrich your rehearsal room practice, or a working actor wanting to refresh or expand your process or a teacher looking for practical ways to encourage specific research skills in your students to support and inform their practice. Whatever your context, and your aspiration, we hope this book offers some insight into researching for creative choices.

We've found that often in formal acting/directing training or study of drama or theatre (from school to higher education), artefacts of this kind of creative research, such as reflective evaluations or proposals for a production, working process notebooks, research presentations and projects, or even performance programme notes are often elements which are used for assessment purposes. We do hope this book will suggest some practical ways for engaging with that kind of activity, as well as give developing and curious actors (professional or otherwise) the confidence to really expand and celebrate the capacity to be a creative researcher in their practice as well as an actor, director, or performance maker.

Establishing Some Common Ground and Starting Points

We are working on the basis that if you are reading this, you are interested in really evolving your craft as an actor. We're assuming you are probably already undertaking some form of practical rehearsals, workshops or classes, or study which focuses on practical skills, exercises, and techniques. So, this isn't a comprehensive *how to do acting* handbook (of which there are many excellent ones already around).

However, it has been our observation that quite a lot of the research activity that supports the making of creative choices for performance can be based in practical activity, rather than just reading and note making. So, you may find that many of our suggested activities we think you can use and appraise as research feel very similar to rehearsal exercises and practical classwork; we're inclined to view this as a feature, not a bug!

For the most part, this kind of research-informed, *realistic* or *naturalistic* making of creative choices meshes well with the practices and approaches which emerge from the work of Konstantin Stanislavski. While we would be a bit reluctant to suggest our ideas are directly connected to his work (he's been dead for quite a while now . . .), we have used terminology and concepts that, at least initially, were coined and articulated by him and his translators, and which more recent practitioners have continued to use, redefine, and reimagine. We have found Sanford Meisner, Uta Hagen, Stella Adler, and Dee Cannon, among many others, to be useful acting practitioner references who built on and form some of his foundational ideas and terms, and we've flagged some of their acting books as further reading in various chapters.

Many of the terms and ideas are used flexibly by more contemporary practitioners and teachers, but they remain a useful shorthand in a lot of cases, and so we have included a glossary of the key terms we use throughout this book which are drawn from this context.

However, twenty-first-century performance is multifaceted with huge variations of texts, processes, and contexts. Not every text the actor works on is going to be a finely drawn psychological portrait of real human beings in realistic or naturalistic situations, that benefits from a classical Stanislavski model of engagement and is judged according to Western European models. While much of his approach (and those who developed his precepts subsequently) still holds good in respect of detailing human interaction *truthfully* in a *realistic* performance style, actor's research often needs to be more plural than that. And we are not suggesting that there are not other valid and insightful routes to creative investigation, that draw on different performance cultures and aesthetics.

Where possible we've included exercises that can be applicable in different ways, if the text for example might evolve from a more collaborative, devised process, or offers a more stylised expression or abstracted aesthetic than conversational dialogue interactions. However, this is not intended to be a handbook for the devising (or writing) process – again there are many excellent texts already – even if there are some potential intersections.

Redefining Research Approaches for the Actor

If we had to research in order to write an essay about the causes of the First World War, our methodology would be relatively straightforward; we would probably focus our attention on considerable reading, balancing primary and secondary sources, evidencing some readily tested facts from material data, weighing effective arguments or potential bias, exploring ideas drawn from multiple perspectives, and using critical analysis in order to infer and construct our own conclusions based on more than just what we feel, assume, or think we know.

In a history essay or scientific research, the use of imaginative interpretation, personal intuition, or sheer invention is rarely an acceptable approach to filling in gaps in the information or *evidence*, and distilling research *findings* into a subjective, individual (often fictional!) character perspective in imaginary circumstances and action is unlikely to persuade as an argument. **Yet for an actor both of these ideas are essential.** What might be right or wrong in history or science doesn't always apply consistently in performance. Sometimes something completely counterfactual is what gives you insight to find something specific and truthful in your expressive choices.

Actors do use skills such as critical thinking, analysis, evaluation, problem solving, source appraisal, inference, and evidence-based *argument*, even if sometimes these feel more intuitively applied. But these skills cannot stand on their own in this context. There are few if any universal techniques, consistent knowledge bases, or established methodologies; and the actor's critical judgement of the choices which *work* often relies at least in part on subjective self-knowledge rather than objectively framed subject knowledge.

As an actor, you demonstrate your understanding of your research in your performance. Your research outcomes are not your notebook, your historical or psychological knowledge, or your massive bibliography. Your research, fundamentally, is presented through selecting embodied vocal, physical, and mental choices that, synthesised through the action and circumstances of the text, communicate to the audience the recognisable experience of a human being/character.

If all your diligent research and reading doesn't come through in your acting work, then it's the same as handing in the notes for your history essay in school, not the essay itself.

The Scope of the Activity

If the actor's job is to be able to investigate and then potentially embody the whole gamut of human experiences, there is simply no limit to the amount of research that is possible. We've all managed to lose hours disappearing down internet wormholes, gathering vast amounts of information and ideas, only for these to slip through our fingers when we're back in the rehearsal studio. While knowledge is never a waste and being interested in the myriad details that shape and nuance human endeavour is creatively vital, in practice we do need to be able to focus our research, answer our questions with details that specifically inform our acting choices, and be able to do this swiftly and accurately.

Our intention was to offer some practical approaches for evolving your own practice and skillset for engaging effectively with actor's research. It's not a study guide for plays or rehearsal processes and it's certainly not a gold-standard blueprint you should learn and reproduce consistently; we aren't trying to provide you with answers, but to offer some directions of travel for the questions it can be useful to ask. We have avoided giving specific examples from texts in most cases, so you don't judge your investigation according to an external reference, and can freely shape your own ways of seeing.

Many of the exercises and activities we suggest are not new, and we're certainly not the first people to come up with all of them; what we're aiming to present are methods of exploring research as an activity that really reflects the critical thinking and creative judgement that lies underneath great performance choices and encourages you to be able to turn your mind to engaging with almost anything as an active source of practical insight. Your own self and your subjective experience are vital sources, requiring evaluation, appraisal, and interrogation perhaps, but not to be eradicated or neutralised. Your self is your art, and so the evaluation of this is central.

No actor is ever the same as another, and even if they are preparing the same part, each actor will need to investigate their own lines of enquiry to develop their own performance of it. Every actor brings their own unique self to the process, their own instincts, references, and imagination; the research that each will need to do may have the same objective (find the detail that supports great performance), but the journey, the questions, and the insights will need to be as individual as the actor. There's no universal *right way* to develop performance as an actor; only the continuous drive to develop skills and practices that generate what *works* for the individual actor in each and every text they encounter.

Navigating This Book

We've separated each chapter in terms of having a particular focus, but, in reality, there's a fair amount of overlap (where is the line between researching character and researching a character relationship?), and while some chapters offer some logical starting points (it's likely that any process should probably start with reading and unpicking the play text), they are not intended to suggest a directly linear progression. There may very well be texts or processes that need to start with unpicking or evolving a world, rather than identified characters, or it can be helpful to engage with the self as research outside a specific project.

Chapter 1: Actor's Research Mind Set – Creative Critical Thinking

We introduce some of the critical thinking, investigative skills, and appraisal practices for sources an actor might need to engage with.

Chapter 2: Self Evaluation as Research – Starting With the Self

We consider the use of the self as a source, and how unpicking and evaluating our own instincts, experiences, and habits can provide insights and obstacles in investigating for character and performance.

Chapter 3: Interrogating the Text – Close-Reading the Play

We get to grips with the nuts and bolts of text analysis as a route into identifying questions to research for practice and evidencing choices for performance.

Chapter 4: Investigating the Character – Shifting From Self

We focus on the idea of character research to underpin the specific, embodied, and complex representation of a character as a living, breathing person.

Chapter 5: Character Into Relationship – Investigating Interaction

We apply the character research into investigations that support the development of relationships between characters that are live, connected, and rooted in action.

Chapter 6: Character Into World – Exploring Given Circumstances

We consider the *world* within the text, the circumstances of the scenic action and unpick how these need to be investigated to detail, ground, and focus scenic action in a live dramatic present.

Chapter 7: World of Production – Context of Creative Choices

We expand our investigation to consider the contexts of production, the world in which the performance takes place, and how these can impact and nuance our research and performance practice.

Chapter 8: Repurposing Actor's Research – Different Applications

We consider the wider potential applications of the research actors undertake, and how the skills can be used to shape and inform activity beyond the immediate rehearsal process.

Chapter Structure

Most chapters are organised into sections in order to help frame and direct the suggested research investigations within. Depending on the thematic focus, some sections are more or less substantial.

Defining the Challenges and Objectives

Because actor's research can be incredibly wide-ranging and varied, we have aimed to provide a focus for each chapter that articulates the purpose and contexts of each line of enquiry within, and then to be specific about the skills objectives we are aiming for. We hope this provides a more targeted starting point than *I need to research why people are like that* . . .

Prep and Tools for the Job

Where relevant we have suggested prep activities and potential resources that may be useful to pull together for yourself or to have access to for the exercises within the chapter. These are pretty low-tech, and notebook, pens, and paper feature heavily . . .

Into Practice

Each chapter has a range of exercises and activities to experiment with; some are paper-based, some will need other actors or a studio-type space. Some activities do follow on (it's hard to start without knowing the text you are working on, if it's an existing play), but they aren't intended to be linear or wholly sequential, and not every activity will be applicable to every project or process. Neither will every activity or exercise *click* for you on every occasion, so we highly encourage playing around with these, and considering what other activities might enable you to discover the detail and information you need each time.

Filling in the Gaps

When the chapter has a thematic focus that outlines text-based practice, we have also aimed to provide more free-form activities that are more about investigating elements of a process which go further than substantiating or detailing choices within the staged scenic action. Some of these may also generate ideas or performance material in their own right, which could also be useful within a devising process of practice research or to underpin a personal writing project – although this is not the primary objective for them.

Into Reflection

In parallel with active research investigation, we have found that it's vital for actors (and other creatives) to be reflective in their practice; to be mindful of how their skills are evolving, questioning of what works or doesn't in practice, and capable of appraising what is needed. This section offers prompts and suggestions to assist with generating reflection activities and approaches that keep a distinction between doing an exercise and then considering it – rather than judging the work while it's happening. Chapters 1 and 2 are focused on evolving reflective practice as an act of research pretty much throughout!

Handy Hints and Pitfalls

At some points we have identified some useful shortcuts to use or potholes to avoid. Many of the latter we have fallen into on occasion, and hope they help you avoid some bruising on your side . . .

Further Reading

These are some resources we have found insightful in various ways across our work and in writing this book. They are in no way intended to be required reading, and not all are *acting* books.

Acting as Research – The Manifesto!

The activity of research for an actor, in any or all of its forms, is intrinsic to creative practice. It's part of your professional skillset and fuels your imaginative development throughout your career. Knowing how to discover nuance in practice, respond imaginatively, and express with creative insight are the common aspirations of every actor we have worked with, however early on in their training or late in their career they may be. The choices that we make in evolving and preparing a performance that reveals these are the lifeblood of *acting*. Evolving and refining what choices, why, when, and how are just as much acts of research as they are of acting, however eclectic, lateral, or diverse the process may be to investigate, evidence, and connect these.

We have had a great time developing this book. As much as anything else, just bringing together all the different approaches and exercises we have used in practice, from the straightforward to the more leftfield, has reinforced our central starting points: the research an actor does is central to the practice of acting and can encompass using almost any source or practice if it's critically engaged with, and the specific skills of researching FOR practice as an actor should be developed and recognised on their own terms. Actor's research is creative, demanding, precise, practical, often slightly random, and, a lot of the time, fun!

We hope this book assists you towards recognising and developing your own skills and capacities with research as an actor and gives you some insightful discoveries in the process. May your investigations prove fruitful!

However, as any gardener will tell you, preparation of the ground is always a key element of this growing process. To start this off – before we get to the research activities – have a think about how you would like to organise the information derived from your work. We have suggested here useful ways of recording and collating your findings.

Starting to Build Personal Research Practice and Resources

- Get yourself a notebook. This artefact will pop up regularly throughout this book. Something journal-style is useful but big and solid enough to use practically and carry around. This is different from any notebooks you might produce within a rehearsal process (e.g. actor's notebooks). You may find you go through several!

- You can also use a note-taking app if preferred (Notability for iOS devices can be great, but it's not free).

- Try to avoid just using the notes function on your phone or creating lots of single documents on your laptop. This tends to keep thoughts separate and means we might miss patterns and connections which are useful. Decide how and where you will consolidate these in a central location.

- If you do find that computer-based activity suits you better for note taking/reflecting, set up a file/folder system where you can keep these organised. Think carefully about document titles so you can map the journey of your thinking (e.g. using dates might be helpful, or being specific about content) particularly if there's some key information you think you'll want to pick up later.

- ARCHIVE research done for previous projects. It's amazing how often you'll want to find something you looked at three years ago.

- Set up PROPER back-ups for your work with cloud-based storage or external drives, etc. Don't just rely on emailing material to yourself.

- Investigate speech-to-text apps for your phone; these can be really useful if something pops into your mind when you aren't in a situation to get out the notebook, but also consider how you are going to remember to join these ideas in with your overall documentation and reflective practice.

- Arrange your online filing; that is, how you organise material you encounter. Look at favourites/bookmarks folders, or investigate digital collations like Evernote [https://evernote.com/]. This app allows you to put together weblinks, documents, uploads, etc, and it also has voice action record and allows weblink collation through your phone. There are several other digital portfolio options out there – as well as options like Pinterest. Find a method/platform that suits you.

- Stock up on pencils, pens, and highlighters – get a good range of different colours. Find a pen that you can write with easily. This might sound ridiculous but if the ink flows freely it's much easier to jot stuff down rather than wrestling with a half-dried-up Biro.

- If you have reading-based visual stress/dyslexia related and have a colour filter/paper that assists with reading, invest in coloured overlays to carry with you. You may find that theatre lighting gels offer a broader range of colour options than standard sets.

Guy Stanley

1

THE ACTOR'S RESEARCH MINDSET – CREATIVE CRITICAL THINKING

Defining the Challenges and the Objectives

Within any creative research process – whether we are rehearsing an existing text or evolving a devised one – we continually go through a critical thinking process. We consider what *works*, what doesn't, what *tells the story*, what *creates a moment*, what *serves the text*, what reads as *truthful*, what *feels awkward*. Sometimes these areas can be relatively objectively clear to an external eye, sometimes they are filtered through a complex lens of subjective sensation and aesthetic judgements, and most of the time it's a bit of both. But ALL of the time it's an example of critical thinking in action, and critical thinking which uses a research mindset in order to solve the problems we encounter; we have to investigate, shape, and test out practical ideas as solutions to make that tricky bit of dialogue *work* and integrate within the *whole*.

As actors, we can often disregard much of our potential insight for critical thinking because we prefer the majority of this thought process to operate unconsciously, because it speaks to the perception that acting *should feel natural*, intuitive, *instinctive*, and unselfconscious. Our personal *frame of reference* is what informs what we feel to be *natural* and judge to be *truthful*, and shapes what and how we *imagine*; and most of the time we access this frame of reference *unconsciously*. While sometimes our instinctive and intuitive solutions are red hot, often they are just as worthy of scrutiny and critical appraisal as choices which emerge from painstaking analysis and conscious investigation. We need to be able to use and interrogate both our **unconscious** and **conscious** thinking in our research activity, and bring together discoveries from **both** in our practical choices.

One challenge we often find is the desire to place conscious thinking (including rationalism, logic, determinism, etc) into a false binary against unconscious

DOI: 10.4324/9781003226130-2

(intuition, instinct), and to find the unconscious more *artistic* or *creative*. We give notes to actors about *overthinking*, being *stuck in their heads*, being too *intellectual*. This sets up unhelpful blocks quite a lot of the time for actors – especially in terms of their research and preparation – and also can prioritise equally unhelpful ideas that confirm normative ideas about *neurotypical* thinking and processes intended to take an actor towards research for practice. Central to evolving your actor's research skillset is to consider *how* **you** think, and to be able to shift your **own** gears cognitively; making your research activity relevant and particular within the context of the role you're preparing to play, and not getting stuck in fixed mindsets or set methodologies. We have included some suggested further reading at the end of this chapter for those who are interested in thinking more about their thinking.[1]

Research skills for creative practice need to be highly flexible and adaptable: to meet a huge range of possible texts and characters, which might ask very different questions of us within our research and rehearsal processes; it's going to be different preparing to play *Hamlet* than *I May Destroy You*. We need to extract ideas and information from a constantly shifting range of possible sources to do so: starting with the written word of texts and other references, but also including imagery, sound/audio, film, observation of others' actions and behaviours, our own physical and sensory experiences, even spaces, furniture, or clothing. How do we *read* these things? What are we looking for? How do we capture it? And most importantly, how do we USE it in practice?

Much of the *data* we will need to infer or deduce (or make up!), sometimes it will be based on non-linear patterns and connections, and sometimes this data will need to be forensically accurate and evidence-based. At times we need to operate in extreme close-up and probe the precise nuance of a single word, whilst also having the ability to pull back the mental camera and look at an establishing wide shot that gives us the *world of the play*.

As an actor, part of the research skillset is being able to frame and ask relevant questions, to use these to direct us towards effective methods, activities, and useful sources, which we can appraise and *read* to identify information about a character, a circumstance or context, an idea, or anything else that's needed.

The acting process requires our research to be *iterative*; we don't finish researching and start acting, we need to take our own personal research discoveries into rehearsal, let the rehearsal discoveries reshape and develop our own ideas and understanding, repeat, refine and update our research, and integrate *feedback* from various sources and repeat this continually until the first night – and even beyond it!

So, the key skills we need to develop in our actor's research mindset:

- Be able to research actively in range of potential investigative modes.
- Vary and adapt your focus and activity according to specific questions/ processes.

- Recognise and evaluate personal factors in conscious and unconscious cognition.
- Appraise a range of sources and resources for selecting relevant detail.
- Build your cumulative understanding from feedback and iteration.

Prep and Tools for the Job

- Your notebook or journal (see introduction), blank paper, and/or a flexible notetaking app that allows you to note stuff down quickly and easily
- Your pencils, pens, and highlighters – a good range of different colours
- Access to a wide range of potential sources – images, poems/free verse, short stories, podcasts, music, journalism. Most things are easily accessible online obviously, but sometimes it can be useful to work from hard copies.
- Museums and art galleries' websites (and in real life) can be great sources of images or objects and allow you to go global in terms of material.
- Websites like *poemhunter.com*, *littleinfinite.com*, *poetryfoundation.org*, and *poets.org* have a huge range of verse: traditional, contemporary, some spoken, some visual. These are only a few – many others exist.
- Any overlays you use routinely for e.g. visual stress when working with written text
- Space and time – plan out when and where you are going to consciously explore exercises and activities. Avoid multitasking, or getting stuck in wormholes where you lose hours in a general slosh of staring at something. Less time with complete focus is always better!

Into Practice – Exercises and Activities

Appraising Your Research Habits

Some of you might be familiar with the idea of *learning styles*. It's been quite a common theme in Western education for some years – the idea essentially being that different people have different strengths in getting information/learning in different ways – often broken down into the VARK model (**V**isual, **A**ural, **R**eading/writing, **K**inaesthetic). It's important to realise that this is quite a contested area in terms of the science (evidence doesn't consistently back it up) and also the number of styles varies across different scientists. What is useful to recognise in this context is that humans have to be able to get information in ALL of the ways discussed (and they do, all the time), varying according to what is being done or learned. The idea of *styles* sometimes speaks more to our tastes and preferences, our habits, and often what requires least effort, and less to our actual capacity to engage creatively with the different modes.

If you have a specific learning difficulty this may very well offer different challenges to the suggestion that engagement is rooted in *style* or preference, and so in no way is this an attempt to diminish or dismiss that. The capacity to acquire or appraise information across a range of different modes and sources is central to the creative research of an actor, and in many cases the processes of doing so may mesh better with neurodiverse cognition; for example the capacity to see lateral connection and interpret information through *networks* rather than linear progression. We note this here in order to encourage the recognition of different methods and processes for engaging with sources as research, and to highlight that valuable information for the actor can and often needs to be acquired through non-typical critical appraisal of more than just textual sources, and is individual rather than standardised in respect of methodologies.

For our purposes we have found the following seven modes of acquiring or processing *information* to be useful starting points:

- Visual/spatial mode – images/looking/seeing
- Aural/audio mode – sounds/listening/hearing
- Physical/tactile mode – activity/moving/doing
- Verbal/reading mode – reading/articulating
- Logical/analytical mode – connecting/reasoning
- Social/collaborative mode – interacting/discussing
- Self/reflexive mode – reflecting/imagining

Your research as an actor is likely to require you to engage with all of these at some point – and sometimes more than one simultaneously. So, it's worth knowing that your capacity to work in these modes is something that can be developed and grown, whatever you might have been told in the past (you're not *good* with *words*) or whatever you *prefer*. Whatever adaptations or substitutions you may need to consider in order to work with your own needs and those of others in research and rehearsal are to be encouraged; there's never just one right way to see, read, or think, and differing approaches can often generate the most fertile ideas.

Exercise: Mapping Modes

Transfer the list of the seven modes to your notebook as headings with space below for notes, or jot them down on large piece of paper.

- Identify any modes you have an immediate strong positive or negative response to; e.g. you feel that you *prefer* or are *not good at* working in that way. Which activities would you avoid if possible? Why?
- Think about something you have done recently – it doesn't need to be acting-related, or a specific act of research – it might be anything you have had to engage with from cooking to planning a journey when you had to get information of some kind together in order to *do it*. Many activities may require constituent activities across more than one mode, so under each

mode try to identify what ways you had to get information and the medium you chose.

- Note down how it felt to do this: easy/hard, fun/boring, worthwhile/point-less, successful outcome/failure, clarifying/confusing, inspiring/frustrating, reassuring/disconcerting, time consuming/quick, enjoyable/uncomfortable, overwhelming/unchallenging.
- Be as detailed as possible and use your own vocabulary. It's quite usual to have complex reactions; something fun and easy might be pointless, something hard might be worthwhile and time consuming. There's no right or wrong reaction – you are simply mapping what your experience is.
- How quickly do examples of activities come to mind? E.g. you can identify lots of things you have done when you had to use visual/seeing modes to get the information, or really hard to think of something when you had to work with just audio/aural.

Looking at your notes, do you seem to have marked preferences or avoidances in how you tend to want to engage? If so, where might that come from? Have you used similar words more than once? What patterns can you observe in your engagements?

Exercise: Exploring Modes of Engagement

If you have marked preferences or ways of engaging that you tend to avoid, then these are good flags to pay attention to. Ease and facility with engaging in activities tends to come with active practice of them, and so if you find that, say, reading or joining ideas with logic is hard work, then get in the habit of practicing these more than the modes you already enjoy.

These are some activities we have found useful in expanding engagement in different modes – by no means comprehensive or instructions; play around with your own ideas:

- Sit quietly in a space and note down all the sounds you can hear in the background.
- Listen to a comedy podcast and take accurate notes of factual info.
- Read a serious factual newspaper article and free write an inner/character monologue for someone mentioned in it (or the journalist).
- Connect elements of a movement routine to a short piece of music (doesn't need to be dance, might be making breakfast . . .).
- Take an image and turn it into a factual description (think police evidence statement).
- Read a poem – really study the meaning of the words and then read it expressively aloud.
- Discuss why film x was good with a flat mate and connect the reasons why you think so.

- Pick a random Google image, study it, and do 15 minutes free writing in response to it.

Almost anything goes here, as long as it asks you to engage in a way that is not your habitual preference – be creative. It is important to view these as not leading to any specific outcome; you don't need to get something *right* or *good*, the objective is simply to engage in this mode.

For this reason, keep the time you allocate to the activity defined and set; in general we have found 15–30 minutes max is best. Make the end point the time you have allocated, not reaching an outcome of any sort.

Once you have reached the end of your allocated time, take 5 minutes to jot down in your journal HOW it felt to do this in this way. Was it easy or hard for you? What distracted you or interfered with your thinking or doing of it? What thoughts surprised you in doing it? Aim to recognise by reflecting, on different occasions you do this, how you can begin to shift and have agency over your engagement.

Mix up engaging with different modes AND what the obvious *engagement* with the source could be; practice both getting facts from a written documentary source AND responding and investigating what you find through imagined inner monologue, or physical activity.

HANDY HINT

It can also be useful to mix up the medium as well as the source; e.g. hard copies of images/text-based sources as well as digital versions. It can often be easier on the eyes to limit screen time, and often we can jot stuff down more readily in a pencil note on e.g. a poem on the page as compared to typing.

Exercise: Quick Fire Creative Mode/Response Activities

Several suggestions in the previous list are moving towards evolving creative responses to stimuli. As well as thinking about the mode of your engagement, these kinds of activities can also be considered in respect of developing your skill at detailing your response; what can you actually *get* from a source stimulus? It may be useful to use the mapping diagrams in the appendix as a way of starting to detail how you look at potential sources/stimuli (see exercise later in this chapter).

Playing around with a range of sources and modes of engaging with them can be a good way to keep your thinking agile and creative, and avoiding getting stuck in fixed interpretations and preferred responses. This can be done routinely on your own; set yourself a fixed time for the practice session (30 minutes can be a good max time to work with) and define your focus for a response.

• Start with a short-form source stimulus of any kind (keep these bite-sized and specific, not *War and Peace* . . .) and set yourself the task of engaging with it in a specific mode – particularly one perhaps that you wouldn't automatically choose – and frame a creative response to it. This can be anything, but let's say a piece of music which you listen to and then challenge yourself to write a free verse response to within 30 minutes max (it's often useful to use instrumental rather than song form, since lyrics often give us constraints or obvious interpretations it can be hard to shift beyond).

• When you have completed this activity, take 15 minutes to reflect on the activity: note down (journal/notebook) how you felt doing it (look back at the previous mapping exercise)? What aspects of the stimulus *provoked* your response (what did you see/hear/feel/read)? How specific can you be? Again the maps in the appendix may help focus your reflection into identifying specific details which sparked something. Try to avoid judging the value or achievement here; it doesn't matter whether you think the response is *good*, this is about the process of thinking not product.

• Leave the task for a period of time – say, a day – and then go back to the same source, but now define a different response to the stimulus and consciously shift the mode of engagement (the piece of music now informs a visual image; you might draw/paint this, or create a *mood board* type composite), or movement sequence/activity, or a narrative/story, or a relationship scenario, or a factual summary of what instruments you can hear and how the piece of music is structured.

• Then reflect as you did at the first step. What differences can you observe in respect of different insights or details you noticed this time? How did these connect to *how* and *what* came out in response?

• It's important that you aren't working to a specific outcome. The point of this exercise is not the creative product (a perfected dance routine!), it's about building your capacity to engage creatively with the mode in process, and to allow conscious and specific attention to different details and evolve what you are responding to and how.

• Again, leave the task, and repeat on another day and investigate a different mode. How many different responses can you play with? It can be useful to judge how long to stick with one particular source; in general within this kind of practice exercise after four or five engagements you'll probably be sick of it, whatever mode or creative response you are exploring!

• Once you have exhausted this source stimulus, look back over all your responses. What shifts and changes can you observe? What did you *find* in terms of specific details or ideas? What differences are there between the modes?

• It's completely fine to find something boring or uncomfortable, but the next time you revisit the task, vary HOW you are engaging with it and see if you can shift beyond this.

Experimenting with quick-fire activities will help you evolve a range of tactics to appraise potential sources, and the reflective aspects of mapping what seems to provoke specific responses is useful in respect of starting to forge connections between source engagement and the ideas which emerge in response, as you're actively looking for insight here, and expressing these in a creative form. Why do you *find* that, what *factual/literal* details stand out, what *imaginative/lateral* jumps are suggested?

Some of these activities may also form useful elements within a devising process, or as approaches to writing longer-form material. They don't have to be quick-fire, and if you are writing something more substantial they can often be useful ways of tackling blocks or obstacles you might encounter in script writing.

Understanding the Critical Eye

Alongside the need to vary and prioritise our thinking for research is also the need to be able to shift our focus not just in terms of modes of engagement, but also in respect of what *level of attention* we give the activity.

If you think about watching a film, the makers select a range of different *shots* to communicate their *information*; these are likely to range from wide, open establishing shots right down to tight, extreme close-ups. But we don't expect to get the same information from all of these. If we need to connect closely with the subtle detail of an actor's emotional response, the coherent shot is something close up; if we need to get a sense of the stakes arising from an external circumstance we may need a wider shot with more than just the actor included in it.

And the same is true of our research focus. Sometimes we need to go tight in on detail, sometimes we need to work with material that informs the holistic bigger picture. The range of focuses – the different *critical eyes* we need to use – also vary in how much effort and attention they require of us. Working close up can be knackering, and it's not humanly possible to work in that level of intensity all of the time; if we try to do so, we're likely to find that our research activity doesn't move us forward, and actually ends up giving us more obstacles and blocks. We're more likely to spend longer *researching* to less effect in practice. Often there's a lot of insight to be gained from allowing our attention and focus to loosen, and for responses to sit behind close-up critique and seep into unconscious thinking. But this is not the same thing as just mindlessly scrolling through web articles without really taking anything in.

Think about ways in which you might engage with different levels of attention, e.g. listening to audio while doing something else, suddenly pondering why that Instagram image connected with you while scrolling, finding that a five-minute sequence in a film stays with you even though you were only half watching. Our focus and attention come in and out, often not consciously – something external catches it.

An actor needs to be able to direct and manage their focus on different things/ activities in different critical eyes, rather than getting distracted, or bogged down over focused processing before doing something.

Exercise: Revisit Quick-Fire Creative Mode/Response Activities

Go back to the exercise in the previous section. Now do more of these where you also work with a conscious awareness of the level of focus and attention that the material and the activity require or suggest. It is important to manage the time here. If you are working in a highly concentrated and analytical <u>focused</u> way, keep the time to max 30 minutes; you may wish to allow longer if you are exploring a looser engagement.

- Pay attention to the physical experience here as well: What changes if you are listening/talking through a free writing response while walking, noting things down while standing up, or are outside?
- Try to identify what affects your focus and concentration. It's amazing how often being hungry or dehydrated or trying to do something for too long are the obstacles, rather than the activity itself or our liking or ability to operate in that way.
- Consider the context in which you are trying to complete the activity: Are you physically comfortable, knackered, or stressed? Or so relaxed you are half asleep?
- Are there distractions in the environment (noise, people, your phone, clutter?)
- Is there sufficient light/heat?

Experiment with consciously altering the focus in which you work; pay attention to how you manage this. Most of us tend to allow certain kinds of engagement to become habitual, diffuse, or unhelpful; TV/music on in the background while reading, random mindless scrolling online, getting stuck reading the same thing over and over again and it not *going in.*

Whenever you shift the focus of your engagement, allow yourself to recognise and note down anything new that comes to you in doing so; and make sure you are also attentive to the more leftfield ideas and thoughts that pop in even if they seem unrelated.

After doing any of these shortform activities, reflect on how easy was it to adapt and sustain appropriate focus and attention and what affected this. What new or different ideas struck you in the process of doing the activity? Did one level of attention seem more inspiring or informative than another? Can you recognise when particular kinds of engagement, stimuli, or information you are after need a different kind of focus, or activity? Which kinds of source stimuli seem to offer you greater amounts of insight or discovery?

Taking it Further

Consider the work you do in rehearsal or class. Can you identify moments when you were working under an unhelpful focus in practice? Perhaps you step back into broad focus and get distracted when the exercise is asking you to focus actively; or get caught watching yourself (or the director) and focus intensely on potential judgement rather than the activity itself.

A substantial amount of actors' research is conducted and tested in practical activities, which means we need to be sensitive to how we focus on these while *doing*. Too much intense judgemental focus on the self – when we sit outside ourselves and become self-conscious – is unhelpful; but we do need to be able to retain detailed awareness of what we discovered specifically from the activity, and be able to identify sensations, impulses, and thoughts which emerge from doing it. We need to be able to adapt our focus and attention.

Think about ways that you can bring your focus and attention under your agency and control. These might include physical and mental *warmups*, mindfulness visualisations as well as environmental changes and good self-care such as sleep, food, and taking proper breaks.

HANDY HINT

Always define the time you will spend reflecting on your work and consciously shift into an evaluative focus to do this (30 mins max can be useful, certainly in one sitting). This helps with moving out from under the self-critical mindset in practice, and if we delineate the activity, we can avoid endless, anxious rumination on how things *went*.

Researching for Truth

As actors, a lot of the time our research is intended to get us information – evidence – that supports our making of *truthful* choices. We process this idea via both unconscious and conscious cognition; when we encounter anything we respond according to our own intuitive sense of the world and other people and what we have actively learned from our human experiences. Usually, we trust readily that we know what we feel (and vice versa), so we prioritise conscious research and investigate the areas that we don't know in order to build an accurate understanding that evidences our expressive choices. So far, so sensible.

But even when we are actively and intentionally trying to discover new information, we tend to prefer and pay more attention to what we can *identify with, what makes sense* unconsciously and without cognitive effort, because it feels more intuitively *right* or truthful. This can be very flawed because anything that *confirms* our individual sense of truth, self, and reality will be automatically more believable to us than something which challenges this – even if that challenge is central to the character's perspective or experience within the play. Our unconscious brain makes leaps and assumptions which often sit on implicit biases, even when we think we are actively investigating for truthful and objective facts. Now while this obviously becomes seriously problematic around pertinent questions of, say, racism or homophobia in society, it's also problematic for the actor when exploring emotional or real *lived experiences* of characters.

Here are some key points to consider when considering research for truthful details:

- What *feels* true to our experience is not necessarily true and we tend to judge that unconsciously – something will make sense and feel authentic when we can map our own emotional response onto what we engage with.
- We find it easier to notice and pick up on even objective factual information which chimes and connects with what we have personally experienced.
- Our judgement of what we find accurate or relevant will be based more certainly and confidently when the info confirms what we already think/ know/feel or *want* to think/feel.
- The availability of memories of our personal experience (recent, or multiple examples) affects our instinctive trust in them as sources of *truth*.
- Shifting our thinking to consciously process something beyond our intuition or subjective perspective can be effortful and uncomfortable which can mean we reject the activity with specious logic (*that doesn't work for me, it feels wrong, I don't get it, my character wouldn't say that*).
- We cannot and shouldn't eradicate our unconscious cognition, impulses, and intuition but we need to explore active ways of developing these so we build our unconscious reservoirs.
- We need to be able to apply conscious discovery away from the subjective memory, then let it all slosh around further in the unconscious and receive/ respond to what emerges in establishing truth in performance.

Take for example, in the film *Love Actually*, the scene midway through in which Emma Thompson's character unwraps a present and the object (a CD) reveals to her that her husband is having an affair, and she retreats to her bedroom to cry on her own rather than spoil the family moment.

For many people this might be a good example of something that reads truthfully (whether we like it or not as a scene). The action reflects recognised *typical* understandings, e.g. that English people avoid public emotion, that upper-class English people are indirect and avoid confrontation, that mothers try to protect their families from emotional discomfort, that women are good at intuition and making connections, that women cry/suffer in silence rather than express rage, that crying reveals deep emotion, etc. Obviously we are also looking at highly skilled acting choices as well, from an actor whom we already deem to be authentic in that casting, and the soundtrack music is consciously emotive.

But part of how we judge the emotional truth of the scene also emerges from those generalised assumptions. Truisms may generally be true, and consensus positions that many people recognise are often important in shaping performance; but it's important to be able to critically appraise how far our judgement of truth and our selection of *relevant* information and details in our research are processed through simply confirming subjective perspectives or general or stereotypical opinions and cliches.

Exercise: Probing Personal Response

Identify a scene in a film in which the character's re/action struck you as particularly truthful and affecting. Watch it with a close-up focus – you may wish to do this a couple of times to get your eye in – and jot down in as much detail as possible WHY. What creates that recognition of truth in you?

Think about:

Direct/personal experience	Authenticity of casting/ voice	Generalised ideas/types/behaviours
Multiple similar examples	Emotive language/ content	Acting choices and connection
Framing and presentation	Narrative context/ stakes	Easy-to-find personal parallel/ identification
Visible/raw emotion	Evidence	Popular/critical consensus or *rightness*

You can apply this exercise to most sources – from *true life* testimonials to fiction – and it can be a good way of being able to shift your critical mindset; considering the potential details which form, imply, or communicate truth in source material, rather than working solely from your subjective emotional response to it.

It can also be useful to find and engage with oppositional and conflicting sources; often it's in the friction between our subjective sense of emotional truth and other perspectives in which we can find what is most interesting to play and explore in performance.

You are not aiming to eradicate your own truth or perspective – it's vital to your artistry – and rather than aiming for neutral objectivity, which is pretty much impossible, you are aiming to be able to recognise your subjective self in travelling towards inhabiting another perspective. This is more fully detailed in Chapter 2.

HANDY HINT

Watching performance is watching research in action! Critical appraisal, unpicking beyond what you loved/disliked, means you are continually sharpening and building your understanding of what you are researching for.

Selecting and Appraising Research Sources Beyond the Play

If as actors we carry our own assumptions and intuitive implicit biases, but also our own *truths*, then the same is completely true of any other human being in most situations.

Creators of sources (in any form or medium) may consciously present a specific account in order to achieve certain objectives, or their personal experience may mean they unconsciously view and respond to events in a specific way. This can affect the reliability or the usefulness of information contained within the sources, and can affect the kind of information you *read* it for and for what *purpose* you want that information.

As an actor, or for any creative purpose, almost anything can be a source (see the quick-fire creative modes/responses exercises earlier in this chapter):

Published Journalism	Fiction	Artwork /Image	Diary /Letters	Published Speeches
Data /Reports	Podcast	A Blog /Vlog	Critique /Review	Personal Testimony
Website	Text Book	Drama	Marketing Material	Audio /Music
Practical Activity /Studio Practice		People Watching	Documentary /Interview	

We could spend decades researching some subjects, and never hope to come up with a comprehensive position. So, the key way to select and appraise sources is to consider (again) what questions you need to answer. If you need factual information about a specific event or idea ('What is post-traumatic stress disorder?') then an image may not be the best starting point; if you want insight into a personal emotional experience then you might find a textbook or a medical manual less useful.

As actors, sometimes we need accurate data, sometimes we need imaginative colour; sometimes we need to work through our intuition, or sometimes actively challenge it; and we may need also to map out literal information, while also considering the lateral. We can *read* multiple sources, in multiple ways for multiple purposes (we're using *read* to apply to any engagement with any source, not just verbal ones).

Exercise: Selecting and Appraising Sources of Information

Give yourself something specific to investigate; this can be done with a text if you have a scene under work, or as a hypothetical scenario. Aim to shape something that is defined, and give yourself a question(s) to frame what you're looking for sources for, such as 'What are the symptoms of *PTSD*?', 'What does *jealousy* feel like?', 'What were the restrictions of the *Jim Crow laws* on African Americans in Georgia?', 'What happened in the *Second Battle of Fallujah*?, or 'What did *Cheapside* look like in the sixteenth century?'.

Obviously most of us now leap straight to the internet as a method of identifying sources, and there will be some selection of sources via this or any other means made on practical criteria around accessibility/availability, the speed with which you need to get your information, and nature of what you're after. There's an astonishing amount of information available, but it's not always reliable or useful for the actor or anyone else!

Working with your question, identify which sources seem like the most useful starting points and then consider these in respect of how far you can appraise the following.

Evaluating the reliability of sources:

- Date of research, location, and publication – connection to the actual given circumstances
- Proximity/primacy/first-hand knowledge – immediacy, actual experience
- Creator's biography and context – potential biases
- Intention and purpose – what the objective/purpose is in creating the source: fact, opinion, art
- Audience – who it's intended to be for, private/public
- Type of source and format – Has the info been tested by anyone else? Is it authoritative/fact checked? (Does this matter for your specific question?)

Evaluating the usefulness of sources:

- What **questions** you need it to illuminate, support, or provide *evidence/ideas* for in practice
- What you can infer or deduce from the source – what you can *read*, what is explicit or implicit

- What the content/scope of the source is – Is it enough to answer the questions, or do you need *more/other perspectives*?
- How you might practically use or translate the info – Can it offer *insight for the actor in practice*?

Look for oppositional material, and seek out a range of sources; be able to challenge the general perception of both the kind of source and its content/ideas and your intuitive sense of what something is 'like'.

You may not always need to scrutinise all these factors – sometimes something utterly fictitious and biased can unlock a brilliant lateral insight in creative practice – but by keeping them available to us we stay engaged with interrogating our assumptions, and then it's easier to stay active in our research practice.

Exercise: Active Analysis of Sources

Once you have identified some potentially useful sources, you'll need to actively interrogate these to pull out the details which are useful in practice. It's easy to spend a lot of time just passively scrolling/reading/viewing a huge amount of material, and while that might seep into our unconscious fruitfully, often we need to make sure we use our time carefully and make our research count for practice. While that more general engagement is never pointless, there is also a need to actively analyse and focus on probing for specific details.

Active analysis of sources for research:

- Use coloured pens/highlighters when you are *reading* – and separate what you are looking for when you read. It might be useful to print out written material, so then the highlights can go directly onto the source, but this can also be achieved with highlight tools on a digital source (i.e. copy and paste webpages into a document).
- If you prefer or you're working with a non-verbal/non-documentary source – i.e. video, images, music, etc, write the headings listed later in the following bullet point on a notebook page/app, and just jot down notes or thoughts under these as you read, watch, listen, or look at your source (see following exercise).
- Use different colours for grouping ideas and thoughts according to the following:

 Fact/object/practical info
 Emotional/inner experience
 Physical activity/action
 Visual/aural/sensory ideas

- Experiment with *reading* for information and ideas which specifically connect to DIFFERENT lines of enquiry, e.g. character, ideas, mood, situations, events – your text work (see chapter 3) will also suggest key questions you will want to explore.

- Multiple engagements with a source and in different modes and sources should all be considered (see earlier exercises).
- You can readily practice the skill of doing this in isolation, but as with the previous exercise make sure you give yourself a question(s) to frame what you're *reading* for.
- Not every source will give you loads of information under every grouping, but practice seeing beyond the literal and obvious, looking for the subtext and connotations/associations, and allow imaginative speculation as well as direct connection as you *read*. The *evidence* you are looking for needs to feed your imagination sometimes, not stand up in a court case! It's also useful to note down ideas which arrive in your head seemingly unconnected to what you are looking at.
- You may find that mind maps/spider methods are an effective way of noting ideas; often a phrase or a thought might sit under more than one heading, and it's often easier to capture this visually. For instance, colour usage in an image might connect to the idea of emotional/inner thoughts AND visual ideas. This practice is detailed more fully in the next section.

Reading for Facts/Practical Info

Look for tangible details – objects, facts, non-negotiables. If you are researching depression, for example, look for the symptoms, the medications/treatments, side effects, the processes of being referred for treatment, the time frames for this, the rules which govern counselling, etc. The world and the idea need to be concrete and brought to a human experience, particularly if your subject matter is drawn from a specific lived reality. How far do you need to test these out? Is the source reliable for this data?

Reading for Emotional/Inner Experience

Look for imagery, adjectives, adverbs – vocabulary from which you can <u>deduce</u> emotional experience, as well as literal attempts to describe an emotion ('I felt numb and sad'). Think about how sounds/visual aspects suggest emotional *feelings* or concepts: harmonious or disturbing imagery, tonality, melody, discord. The more this can be sensory, the better, in being able to turn that into character/action – and also the more useful it can be to find sensations which might be useful to explore if you want to work physically, such as weight, tempo, and heat/intensity. Some details may end up being contradictory, which might be great in terms of thinking about subtext/inners/outers; or they might end up being jettisoned.

Reading for Physical Activity/Events

Look for things that happen through suggestions for specific moments and events, physical action, impulse/drives, tension, tempo, rhythm and pulse, activity, gestures, or physical habits that might reveal internal conflicts. Emotion and inner experience are often filtered/read through action rather than a discussion about what someone is feeling. Situations need to be plausible, possible, grounded, and sequential, even if they are abstract or absurd. Consider the physical impacts of events on people psychologically, and the reverse.

Reading for Visual/Aural/Sensory Ideas

Look for any sensory detail that might inform the visualisation of the world such as environmental sounds, or thematic ones like music/effects, particular details of the world that might translate into visualising and inhabiting the character in given circumstances. Look for aesthetic qualities, spatial relationships, weight, textures, smells, temperature, light, clothing, furniture, props/objects.

Reading **Other** Sources

As was introduced in the modes/responses exercises earlier in this chapter, we also may need to be precise about how and why sources have informed ideas or understanding and how we might establish connections with the text and these ideas drawn from those other sources, which may not always be verbal/textual. This is particularly the case if the research ideas are imaginative and to be shared with others in the room, rather than just being part of your personal work creating your character's inner life, or a straightforward factual piece of information. Examples of this might be how the composition of an image assists with creating a physical stage *picture* for an ensemble; the objects which may also be used to create a soundscape; or the music which connects to the tempo of a physical sequence.

Aim to note down specific details that you observe, finding connections and parallels across modes of engagement that inform what you are trying to do in practice as an actor with your text.

For example, let's take a painting as a potential source image:

- If it's a figurative representation *of* something/where/one, what is literally depicted (landscape, clothing, space, furniture, etc), and what *characteristics* might be inferred from *how* they are represented?
- If it's abstract, how do the forms and shapes suggest ideas? These might prompt emotions (positive or negative), concepts (harmony, conflict), or spatial qualities.

- What sounds does the image suggest – ambient atmosphere, or perhaps clashes of colour suggest discord or conflict?
- How is the image presented? Are we close up or distant, focusing clearly on external appearance of action, things, or events, or seeing the suggestion of an internal experience or attitude towards these?
- What pace or energy of movement is suggested? Perhaps a hectic blaze of vivid colours suggesting speed of action?
- How do the compositional elements suggest ideas or emotion even if they are not representational? Perhaps a jagged abstraction suggests/connects to a character's inner panic, or colours and dark shadows connote a mood of sadness, or a threatening object (or a beloved one).
- There might be literal objects represented which smell or make noise, or carry symbolic associations such as a clock which might connect to ideas of time.
- We might see figurative disconnected figures in an image or a space suggesting a relationship of silence and stillness.

It's important to realise that in this area, there is not a fixed critical research methodology you must master (either for texts or for sources of ideas). There is not a set way of reading or using an image for example, no universal *right* response or *correct* meaning to acquire. You will often find that you *see* different things at different times, and different people will see different things again. The same is true of any other source.

Creative Critical Analysis (Please See Appendix)

We have found a mapping approach the most useful route into this kind of critical thinking because it can help identify specifics from a source, but also flex and expand around different kinds of sources. The critical maps included in the appendix may offer starting points, but these are not intended as prescriptions or instructions (See maps in the appendix).

We suggest using the maps to appraise your own initial response to the source. Try to unpick your intuitive *feeling* about it; we all have tastes and preferences, but if a piece of music/song really jars, aim to comprehend *what* it is that jars. Similarly, if something really chimes and connects to you, like a poem that says everything you felt in a situation, or an image that encapsulates your idea of peace, try to identify what specific elements are there within the whole that underpin your response to the source, the associations you make, the connections that strike you. Bring your response under the *conscious* thinking of analysis, rather than the more *unconscious* sense of likes and dislikes.

Be sensitive to friction, contradiction, and subversion. Many of the prompts within the maps will take you towards recognising contradictions between what is expressed in the source and what is our own *normative* understanding of the sensory external world of our experiences or assumptions about others.

For example, we might *expect* a photograph of the seaside to reflect the colours we *expect* to be present (yellowish sand, blue-grey sea and sky); an image which subverts or contradicts this expectation will often draw attention because it is not normative, and so we will spend more time pondering potential meanings or significance.

Keep considering how the different specific details you observe may synthesise in order to grow potential insights and *meanings* to explore in your practice. It is often in the friction between expectation and expression that we find more interesting and fertile ideas. Creative insight often comes from finding unlikely intersections, altering expected perceptions, and looking at many things from new angles in research.

For example, it might be observed that in general people move around according to an individual tempo and purpose, not tending to repeat actions on a beat, using the whole body most of the time, and so a group of people moving in unison, moving specific limbs very deliberately in repetitive patterns on a steady rhythm will automatically draw our attention as being significant because it diverges from perceptions of *normal* movement patterns. There is, however, a world of difference in potential *meaning* when that description could apply to both a ballet and a goosestep-marching army.

Exercise: Detailing Source Appraisal

Working in the same way as you did in the previous exercises, take a source, give yourself a specific time to work in, and focus your attention on your response to it. This can be done as a standalone exercise, or when you have a specific character/text that you are investigating.

- Take a couple of minutes of to look at the image, read through any verbal/textual form, listen to audio form, sit in a space, handle an object, observe movement (in real life or on video). Do this steadily, but just do it once.
- When you have done this in your notebook, or preferred form, jot down your immediate thoughts as response in the middle of the page. Do not edit this, make it as free flow and uncensored as possible. Big writers may find it easier to use a sheet of A3 paper for this!
- Then, using the relevant map in the appendix, note on the page the headings from the map around the edges, with space around these for notes.
- Looking at your initial response, consider the prompts on the map. What can you identify from these prompts that connects to *why* it made you respond

in that way? What specific details in the source provoked specific thoughts? What *evidence* underpins your thinking? (If you are working with a specific character/text, what specific details can you observe in the source which connect to these?)

- You are likely to want to look/listen/read/watch again and potentially go over small sections several times.

- Once you are happy that you have considered everything you can, take a few minutes to really consolidate your thoughts into clear practical notes that you could use in studio practice as an actor. These might include suggestions for character qualities or characteristics, clear sensory imagery for an inner monologue or soundscape, new ideas for actions or tactics to try, or physical details that might connect with techniques such as Laban efforts, tempo, or tension states, or with creating stylised physical sequences or transitions within the text.

Whenever you finish a *read* of a source for a specific character/text, come back later (after rehearsal) and consider how effectively you can give yourself these notes and ideas: Did they move you forward in rehearsal? Could you *play* them? Did they *work*? Are you identifying *useful* ideas in your research and appraisal?

If you are doing this as a standalone exercise, then see where the ideas take you as you translate them into a creative critical response (as per the earlier exercise in this chapter). This response can also then operate as a source, perhaps for devising or creative generation purposes.

HANDY HINT

If you are practicing your critical *reading* of sources, try to make sure you are encountering materials for which you don't already have fixed associations, e.g. not the *set text* poets and poems you studied in school, or the music, or history sources. If we have an idea about the significance of something, this will often mean we find what think we are *supposed* to find.

Testing in Practice, Feedback, Iteration

As we have mentioned previously, any acts of critical engagement with almost anything can be purposed as research for the actor, and developing a capacity both to investigate imaginatively and extract specific detail from any stimulus source material is valuable under any circumstances.

Primarily though, we will be testing our research ideas in embodied practice (as well as obtaining information *from* practice) which has to connect with the expressive choices made to serve performance. Our research information may need to be invisible, coded, and implicit, even if some outcomes are in visible performance choices. Consequently, we need to establish a careful blend of feedback inputs in order to refine and substantiate our coherent performance as character. External feedback may need to be part of this (we'll work with a director who asks us to adapt to serve a vision of a whole play), but we also need to sustain internal mechanisms which allow us to constructively appraise our own research in doing and feeling.

However diverse and imaginative our solo research investigations have been, however strong and interrogated our intuitive ideas are, the testing and refining of these ideas occurs through interaction, through listening and responding to other actors' offers in rehearsal (who will also have done similar and equivalent research activities). This must be integrated with the cohering vision of the director (and other creative team members) and *presented* through a repeated series of actions that need to balance spontaneity and meticulous preparation. It is fundamentally iterative, each session, note, or activity revealing information that then needs to be plugged back into the next repetition of a scene. While there is a linear progression towards performance as outcome, this is achieved through routine iterations in rehearsal.

While as individual actors we do need to *own* our expressive choices, these cannot stand alone; they must intersect directly with those of others, both as a feedback input and in respect of shared responsibility for the outcomes. It can be useful to pay attention to your thinking here, and ensure that you can approach repetitive activity, collaborative conclusions, and iterative discovery as intrinsic to your judgement of your work, rather than having an internal feedback process which recognises repetition as a personal failure to progress towards a self-authored outcome that is *right* first time.

We need to be able to present – to offer – precisely detailed research in rehearsal, that we may have spent some time investing in, researching in various ways and that we have built a strong personal intuitive connection with, and at any given moment be prepared to throw any or all aspects away. Perhaps our ideas and offers don't connect collaboratively within the whole, or we get a note that something isn't working in action. This can be challenging because it feels as if we have done something *wrong*, however much we intellectually know that that's not the case! Part of the challenge is that the external feedback almost can't help but feel personal; it's our whole self (body, voice, and mind) that is under scrutiny, not just a separate *piece of work* we can hand in and detach from to a certain extent. We can lose faith in choices, get stuck in the evaluative eye and much of the time retreat into fixed patterns (stuck in a rut), lose any sense of connecting one moment to the next (fall apart), or look for additional external feedback inputs to validate decisions because we now assume our creative judgement is *rubbish* (lose confidence).

What we essentially experience is a panic retreat into a fixed mindset, rather than a growth mindset. A fixed mindset (in this context) believes that there is a *right* interpretation, that the *correct* choices both exist and emerge from specific activity/*innate* judgement, that *challenge* to this is destructive, any feedback/*change* suggestion is negative, other people doing *well* is threatening, repeating activity is a failure, and the outcome of our activity is determined. We might not feel all of the preceding responses, but even in part they are cognitive patterns that may compromise our practice.

We have to be able to operate in a growth mindset, which allows evolution towards understanding of embodied character rather than evaluating against fixed models and externally derived standards, giving up when external feedback finds us wanting against these. You may find that your mindset provides quite fixed boundaries within which you operate; further thoughts about navigating these boundaries will be explored in Chapter 2.

HANDY HINT

It can be useful to remember that the entire point of rehearsal is to get things *wrong* so that we can start to identify what tiny discoveries come together in order to shape what works for this particular performance project.

Exercise: Appraising Personal Practice

Over the course of a rehearsal process, a scene study class or in investigating many of the activities we suggest later in this book, we'll encourage you to view your doing as an act of research. But this means we need to manage our focus and attention (as per the earlier exercise) to make sure when we are *doing* we aren't also trying to plan, appraise, or critique what we are doing while we are doing it.

- Before engaging in practice/exercise, work out what kinds of prep are going to take you to the right level of focused readiness to engage with it (might be a physical warmup, three minutes of centred breathing, or a music track).
- If the activity/material under exploration is emotionally affecting, intense, intimate, or highly physical, a planned and appropriate warmup and cool-down with **partners** should be agreed upon **prior** to starting the exercise.

- Commit to and complete the exercise/rehearsal activity.
- Step away from the exercise and consciously return to a centred awareness of yourself as you in the room.

As soon as you can after doing the work, try to jot down in your notebook any observations you can make in respect of the following:

- What was new about the activity? What new insights did you gain?
- What was different or what changed in doing it?
- What were the physical sensations of doing it? How did your focus sustain?
- What new or surprising emotions or impulses came to you? Can you identify what provoked them?
- What new questions, understandings, or ideas have been stimulated by doing it? What might be useful to do next?
- What unhelpful fixed judgements of yourself or the work come to mind? ('The activity was *pointless*', 'I was *rubbish*', etc)
- Can you identify what has provoked these? Intrusive evaluative eye, inner critic, or external feedback?

If you are working with a partner or others in the exercise, it's also going to be useful to exchange observations with them. Aim to keep these discussions based on observations of how their interactions affected your reaction, and to recognise the impact of your choices on their experience and action. Avoid judging their choices/actions and recognise that the next stage may also require you to shift and change yours!

Similarly, you may also have received notes from your director or the teacher you are working with. Note these down as well. How far does your appraisal of the activity match what the external perception of it was? How far can the discoveries from this activity be detailed, really consolidated in your work, and used to inform the next activity, or rehearsal? How far can you appraise your practice and yourself as a source of insight without falling into fixed value judgements? This will be further considered in Chapter 2.

Into Reflection

All of the exercises detailed in this chapter should lead you to viewing critical reflection and research activity as giving you multiple options, not looking for one right answer. Many of the exercises will feel similar, but some ways of engaging may sit better with you than others; sometimes simply by engaging with something with different questions or starting points can help shift our initial perspective. Aim to explore and reflect on how you can take yourself to any source and find a way into appraising it that generates creative and practical responses.

The rehearsal process, similarly, may need you to bring multiple options rather than answers, to reject your own personal babies of instinctive interpretation/response, and to ground and connect the specific aspects of your research that underpin your creative choices as an actor. This may very well feel fragmented or muddying at first. However, the fragmentation, friction, and contradiction will often allow you to shift outside your assumptions in solo research and in rehearsal. Recognising the friction, uncomfortable and challenging though it may be, is the practical manifestation of shifting from your remembered episodic constructed self, into your live, responsive, experiencing self.

Your long-term aim is to cement a personal research process that gives you a range of critical and creative engagements, and which can apply research-informed thinking to a range of sources and activities for many purposes. Can you shape useful questions to ask, find and respond to relevant material/sources, shift your engagement mode, interrogate your own assumptions/ intuition, manage your focus, and identify details that work in practice? Aim to jot down in your notebook the key activities that enable you to be an active researcher.

In your reflective practice, alongside continuing to engage in acts of critical reading of sources, it can be useful to reconnect this activity with some of the ideas explored earlier in this chapter. Every new act of research might expand your frame of reference and evolve your unconscious reservoir of imagination; each act of *reading* a different source or activity might ask you to engage in a different mode, refine your capacity to frame useful questions and adapt your focus according to the nature of the task. It's worth being active about recording and appraising what activities (and sources) were those which you felt gave you a *click*; none of the activities here are fixed and set methodologies, so aim to spend some time reflecting as to what ways you can use them (or rework them) to suit your own research needs.

Further Reading

- *Explaining Humans* by Camilla Pang
- *Mindset* by Carol Dweck
- *Thinking Fast and Slow* by Daniel Kahneman
- *Blink* by Malcom Gladwell
- *The Mind's Eye* by Ian Robertson
- *On Connection* by Kae Tempest
- *Better Living through Criticism* by A.O. Scott

Note

1   How our *thinking* works – cognition – is a subject of endless fascination for scientists as well as artists; and many ideas around this have integrated into common understanding, such as the idea of a left and a right brain, system 1 and 2 thinking, etc, as well as attempts to classify behaviours into cognitive habits such as the Myers-Briggs Type Indicator, etc.

Guy Stanley

2

SELF-EVALUATION AS RESEARCH – STARTING WITH THE SELF

Defining the Challenges and the Objectives

An actor offers their *self* (body, voice, and mind) in service of telling somebody else's story; the actor-self is both the artist (the interpreter) AND the canvas (the medium of expression), but our canvas doesn't start blank and empty. If you think about the craft of shaping performance, our actor self is also usually the paintbrush (tool) and the pigment (range of expressive options) and so we need to know HOW to use the self in these multiple and different ways. Many great acting practitioners (Uta Hagen, Stanislavski, et al.) start their process of character research with the question WHO AM I?, establishing and exploring the information that the actor will use to evolve their performance.

It's fundamental as an actor to consider your self, your identity, your practice, and your frames of reference, as a potential act of research, a focused investigation of what is imaginatively shaping your creative choices. If it's useful to ask what makes a character tick and why, then it's useful to know what makes you do the same.

As actors, we all start with a personal intuitive response to material – be that reading a play text through or engaging with stimulus material for devising work – we grasp the sense of a character from what they say and why they might say that from the events of any narrative, and we translate this into ideas about *how* we might say a line or physically respond to another character. We are relatively sophisticated about this; often we *infer*, read in, and deduce just as much information from what isn't said and what lies underneath the words of any dialogue. We connect this with our personal sense of what other human beings or relationships are *like*, what new or other experiences *feel* like to us, and how we imagine we would feel or react *if* we *were* in that particular situation. This is hugely valuable

DOI: 10.4324/9781003226130-3

as an actor; we make a personal connection as our *self* with the *other* character and we *feel* as though we *instinctively* can begin to journey towards *embodying* their action in performance.

But we, as humans, don't always see other people or the world as they are (in a play or in real life), we see them AS WE ARE. Our personal *frame of reference* (Jacqui and Aaron Schiff), our micro-perspective, our *window on the world* bring together all our individual personal experiences to enable us to make sense of the wider world and life beyond our own. This frame of reference informs what we feel to be instinctual, truthful responses, sometimes implicit, sometimes explicit – '*Grief* feels like *x* because I felt like *x*' – and it's a comfort because it allows us a sense of agency and causality over our life experience. Our frame of reference is what fills our unconscious reservoir; we imagine beyond this, but we start imagining *what if* from what we know and feel.

Whether we consciously recognise it or not, our frame of reference often means we make assumptions, judgements, and choices which aren't based in empathy but in projection. What we see or feel to be instinctive and *natural* often needs some research and critical thinking (see Chapter 1), to make sure we are appraising our instinct and intuition in respect of the character's impulse, not just surfing on our own tendencies.

The self is our most vital research resource as an actor; it's the wellspring for our insight, our empathy, our intuition, and our imagination, and our voices and bodies provide us with sensations, impulses, and the capacity for expression. However, the self is also the source of our fears, our habits, our tastes, our boundaries, and our biases, and these can block and interfere with our ability to connect, to explore, and to operate outside our own comfort zones and certainties.

Uncertainty can be an unsettling position to exist in. It can make us anxious, hesitant, and avoidant; yet within a creative process being able to sit in this state is vital. Without uncertainty, questions, and experiments, no new drama could ever be conceived, let alone rehearsed and performed. At the start of a rehearsal process, while we may have a general idea of outcomes (this play will open on this night in this space with these actors), beyond that everything is uncertain initially – what it will look like, how these actors will interact, what the audience will feel, whether it will *work*, what it is *about*, how we will *tell the story*. Rehearsal is a process of exploring the possibilities of the uncertainty in pursuit of the art we are engaged in making, and finding new boundaries specific to the world and the character. John Keats (poet) defined this state as *negative capability*, the artist's creative mindset in which they are '*capable of being in uncertainties, Mysteries, doubts, without any irritable reaching after fact and reason*'. The actor must be able to trust the creative potential of not knowing, not getting it *right first time* and working beyond familiar and habitual methods to achieve unexpected outcomes.

Sometimes our habits and boundaries are really useful; we work diligently, plan to reach outcomes, put the effort in, respect others, resist over emoting and falling apart, take responsibility for ourselves, make *sensible* choices. Sometimes though we can use our own habitual boundaries to hold us back; we resist committing ourselves to actions, we find it hard to find synergy with others because their *habits* don't mesh with ours, we evade emotions we're not comfortable having, we sidestep physicalities that we would feel reluctant to embody in our own lives, or we stick with a familiar process rather than trying something different. If your human self is a vital research resource for your actor self, it's phenomenally useful to be able to evaluate when and how that self is providing valuable information to use, and when you may need to look beyond for insight and ideas from other sources and activities.

So, if we consider the self as a research source, and engaging with ourselves as a research activity, we are aiming at the following objectives:

- Identifying and appraising our own *window on the world* and how that shapes our *instinctual and intuitive* responses
- Recognising and using our multiple potential selves and roles
- Investigating the self as an imaginative source for emotional and creative expression, and shaping practice to develop and expand this further
- Identifying and evaluating our habits and comfort zones, and building our capacity to work appropriately and effectively beyond these
- Defining and respecting our own personal boundaries and vulnerabilities, while recognising when these inhibit rather than protect, and allowing challenge and change

Prep and Tools for the Job – Building Personal Research Resources

- Notebook, pens, and highlighters
- Larger sheets of paper, such as A3
- An open, non-judgemental mind and honesty

Into Practice – Exercises and Activities

Opening Your Window on the World

Jacqui and Aaron Schiff, in their research in the 1970s, shaped the idea of the frame of reference model (see Figure 2.1) which outlines the thinking that we don't see the *world as it is*, but *as we are*, and the different aspects of ourselves and our experiences that create our frame of reference, the *window* from which we see the world. Our version is based on but slightly different from the original

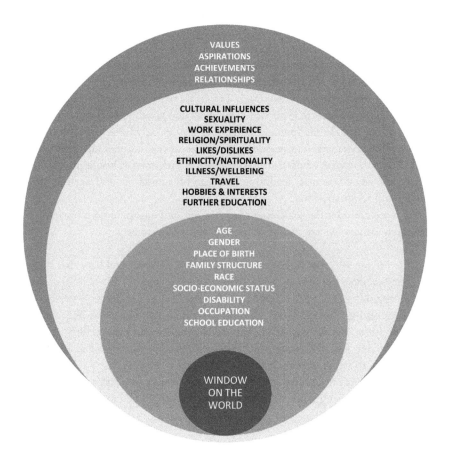

FIGURE 2.1 Mapping your window on the world

model. A great many aspects of what we think we know and believe to be true or real are fundamentally connected to our own truth, lived experience and our point of view, and not necessarily accurate, common to everyone/anyone else, or absolute.

This does not mean that we lie to ourselves, or distort things, consciously or unconsciously, but more that our *remembering self* builds our memories, recollections, and sensations into a narrative form that makes sense to us as we experience in the present. Think about childhood memories; it's quite common for different family members to have very different recollections of shared experiences. Even when we are *experiencing* ourselves in action in the present, we always do so from the context of our frame.

Exercise: Creating Your Window

On your sheet of paper, write out the frame of reference criteria as headings, leaving as much space as possible around each heading. Taking your time (you may want to come back to this several times to really build your picture), place who *you* are under each heading, being concise, factual, and specific about the information and experiences rather than emotional, qualifying, or value-judging. No one else needs to read or interpret this, so you can use your own shorthand.

Some headings may take more information than others since key information might have changed; you might have moved house, had different sexual experiences, changed hobbies and interests, built new relationships with different kinds of people, etc. Think about ALL the experiences you have had that have formed you, but aim to identify the significant things to you, even if to someone else they might seem less important. These do not need to be chronological, and in fact it can be better if they're not, since this takes us away from thinking about the self as a predestined, causal, single narrative.

- What do you think have been the strongest influences on your own self/ character?
- How do you think your experiences have shaped your emotions, behaviours, and actions?
- How do you think your experiences have shaped your desires, fears, or ambitions?

It's useful to use a visual marker (highlights, boxes, etc) to indicate significance and also to capture how details under one heading might intersect with another. Try to capture the detail of the connection between experience/event/fact and its influence/significance to you. Think about intensity of experience, longevity of experience, repeating patterns/events, life-changing moments, the scope of the impact on you (this might be insignificant to anyone else – the loss of a teddy for twenty minutes to a four-year-old can be devastating), how experience shaped a big decision or ambition, or anything else that has given these experiences significance to you.

Allow yourself time to engage, disengage, and return to this exercise; we don't tend to have all of this information readily available in memory, and so some thoughts may float up later when you aren't focusing in close-up. Try to make sure that you are concentrating on identifying the specifics, patterns, and connections, rather than just swimming in emotional memory of recollected pain or joy. You are not trying to get something *right* here, you may very well be uncertain and your perspective is likely to change as you do this.

PITFALL

If you have had traumatic lived experiences that you are still working through, do not focus on these within the exercises unless you are in a situation where you have expert therapeutic support for the activity, and are confident that you are ready to contemplate them in some detail.

Exercise: Considering Characteristics

With your window as complete as possible, available for reference, put the headings down around the edge of a new piece of paper.

- Reviewing what your notes are under each heading in terms of facts and significance, aim to locate adjectives/other qualifiers for each that reflect how *you feel about/see* your experience of that criterion of your frame of reference.
- Highlight/visually mark the headings that you have stronger feelings about and/or had strong significance.
- Try to avoid simple *goods* and *bads*. Work for an honest reflection of what your information suggests, but don't overthink or try to force positives or negatives because you feel you *should* feel something. There may be contradictions reflecting changes across time – that's fine. This is just for your eyes, not anyone else's.

For example, consider socio-economic background. Would you feel this to have been comfortable, stable, chaotic, limiting, unpredictable, exposed, settled, changeable, secure, privileged, constricting, struggling, extreme, lucky, or something else?

Then, again with a visual shift (change pen colour, put in bullet points, etc), note down

- what you *feel* to be *your characteristics*
- what you feel to be *your* personality traits and
- what you feel to be your defining *qualities* at this point in time – positives and negatives as you perceive them.

Again, take your time with this and be conscious of the thought process here. Consider how you identify these, and be honest; sometimes we'll note down what we *want* to be true, what we feel we *should* be, or what we have been told we are *like*. Aim to recognise which characteristics seem complicated to define honestly and why that might be.

If possible try to make connections between experiences and what you perceive to be your characteristics. This won't always be explicit or obviously related; and sometimes we might have quite oppositional reactions.

- What information seems most important to consider in order to *identify* what your characteristics are?
- Can you *see* your characteristics manifesting in your own emotions, behaviours, and actions? Or infer potential characteristics from your actions, behaviours, and responses?
- Can you *connect* your characteristics to your experiences detailed in the frame of reference? (Even if they seem contradictory in some way, they still emerged in response to it.)
- To what extent do your characteristics seem to be just because of *who you are?*
- What might you *wish* you could *change* about your character?
- Which characteristics do want to reject in yourself? Which are hardest to recognise and acknowledge?
- Which characteristics might be more what you *want* to be?

On your sheet or in your notebook/journal, note down any insight you have about how your sense of self emerges from the context of your frame of reference, and how different kinds of experiences and your own actions and behaviours reflect, evidence, and inform these ideas.

Again it can be useful to make this visual; draw lines between notes, add additional boxes for other information that comes to mind. Recognise potential conflicting ideas, e.g. you might be selfish *sometimes* but unselfish at others, so you are really looking at opening the shifting possibilities in you, rather than trying to come to fixed and finite list.

Don't get stuck in one way of finding coherence for your sense of self, a fixed idea of your characteristics, or set narratives of how your experiences have shaped you. We aren't fixed and static, we change and we respond to each new discovery in different ways; our moods might affect what we see positively or negatively and our most recent memories and experiences will often mean certain characteristics seem more important than others, or come to mind more readily.

By breaking down the idea of self into these connected parts, it can be easier to start viewing the self as a multifaceted and mutable concept. From this we can appraise the most useful parts of the *self*, in reference to each specific character we are researching, and what aspects of them we will need to investigate further. The character's own frame of reference is a key element of character research (see Chapter 4).

In focusing on our own frame of reference we're essentially evaluating the relationship between given/previous circumstances and characteristics and action, which can afford us sound insight into how to make these connections in acting practice. It can be a useful exercise to revisit because it may give us different insights and ideas about the self each time we do it. Allow these sheets to stay as live documents and keep them safe and private; you may wish to revisit, or find that additional insights come to you later.

HANDY HINT

If you want a warmup for thinking about your characteristics, a fun way to start can be to play around with some of the million personality quizzes available online, or use prompts from profiles on dating sites. Don't, however, rely on these to provide you with the list for the exercise; make sure any characteristics or traits you identify and use in this exercise are in vocabulary and words that you use and really understand, and which come from your thinking as per the exercise. Recognise when you answer as you *want* to be, rather than as you actually *are*!

Exercise: The Self as a Source of the Other

If we consider that our experiences and characteristics are not set and fixed, that we might act and quite possibly have acted in different ways, in different contexts, then we can actively break away from a fixed and rigid sense of self and explore what else *might* be *truthful* or a different way of seeing the *possible* aspects of ourselves.

For example, consider the experience of the loss of a beloved grandmother as an eight-year-old child. Initially perhaps one might see that experience as being something which could make a person loss-averse with people and so they desperately seek closeness and intimacy for security; but within that same experience of loss might also be the reverse, i.e. they withhold and avoid forming close relationships because there is a possible risk of further/future loss.

Both could be *truthful* while suggesting quite different characteristics, actions, and objectives connected to the previous circumstances.

If you look back at your notes from the previous exercise, give yourself a new sheet or page for each potential *self* you could create from the whole frame, and jot down thoughts in response to the following:

• Can you group experiences from the full frame, that would give a different pattern of characteristics or possible self? For example, you look at school, work, family structure, religion, and socio-economic status, and group characteristics and behaviours that are *steady, responsible, reliable, cautious, rule-following*; but relationships, hobbies, sexuality grouped might suggest *daring, extrovert, brave, rebellious, passionate*.

- Could you also find other *opposite* or *contradictory* characteristics that you might also *be*?
- Can you identify different characteristics with these groupings depending on different contexts/circumstances, or over time? For instance, you went from chatty as a child in the family, to uncommunicative as a teen in the family.
- Can you identify characteristics or behaviours in response to an experience that could be different from someone else's perspective? Perhaps you think you were confident and outgoing, but your cousin thought you were loud and bossy.
- Can you recall the physical sensation of those experiences?

Be *counterintuitive* and try to find *friction* with your original notes, thoughts, and assumptions, because in the conflict or the contradiction is often where the new ideas are usually to be found. Much of the time, the start of a journey from the self to a truthful embodiment of character can be rooted in simply identifying those aspects of the character (positive or negative) which already exist in our sense of self and our frame of reference, seeing elements in our experiences which could ground and inform different or contradictory characteristics and actions, or recognising qualities in our experiences which could *substitute* for the experience of the character since they offer a parallel or equivalent impact and sensation.

This use of contradiction or oppositional thinking can also be extended to shake up our intuition imaginatively. When you read a play and start thinking about the character, it's pretty usual for a sense of the through line of their emotional identity/journey within the play to establish itself. *Juliet* is passionately in love, so it's easy to get focused on generalised assumptions of what that experience is or does. Try thinking about the character with a specific antithetical identity (she is furiously angry at the world) or detailing the journey with somebody else's perspective (to Lady Capulet, she's a selfish, spoiled brat of a teen). The more you can shift yourself out of relying on intuitively remembered assumptions and consider the character as active and contested, the greater your chances of finding expressive choices that are connected and alive in the *moment* of performance and avoiding getting stuck in remembered shapes.

Practice exploring *characters* or ideas and emotions from different perspectives, especially if those perspectives challenge some of your strongly held personal beliefs. You may have to research for a character you think is repellent or awful – can you view their actions and opinions from their frame of reference? Can you find empathy rather than judgement, or recognise fears or experiences that inform behaviours that aren't yours?

The Self, the Situation, and the Role

We all have different *selves* which function quite coherently alongside each other in day-to-day life, *selves* who might behave quite differently depending on who we're with, where we are, what *role* we are supposed to fulfil in any situation. We adapt the self physically (not slouching in a job interview, flirting), vocally (we have a *calling in sick* voice, or we talk *baby talk* to children and animals), and mentally (we can switch on types of thinking, *motivate* ourselves to do something dull but necessary, say the *right thing*). High-stakes situations, traumatic events, or panic can mean we act *out of character*.

We often find we have an *internal* sense of self that might be different from our *external* or perceived *identity*; we might *edit* or present the inner self in certain ways to try to make other people identify and respond to how *we wish to be perceived*; we might shape what we do and say to fit our idea of *what something is* or *how we should be*, or other people's ideas and expectations of what our selves are or should be. We carry remembered images of how certain activities or roles look or sound and adapt what we do according to those images, even if they are flawed or unhelpful in pursuit of what we want. And we don't always process any of these responses consciously or intentionally.

We all have different selves: the vulnerable self, the dominant self, the instinctive self, the decisive self, the trusting self, and the unresolved self,[1] and usually a sexual self, a professional self, and many more. Much of the time it is different contexts that enable us to inhabit different selves, vocally, mentally, and physically.

Exercise: Identifying Selves

In your notebook, jot down how many *selves* you are conscious of inhabiting at various times – you don't have to use the suggestions above. Pay attention to vocal, physical, and mental details. Then jot down the contexts in which that self tends to appear: locations, situations, whom you are with, what activities you do, what you are wearing, etc.

- What physical sensations do you associate with being there? How relaxed are you?
- What affects your physicality or energy?
- How confident do you feel?
- What vocabulary do you use?
- What vocal changes are you conscious of making?
- What behaviours are appropriate?
- How much do you feel like *you*? (Do you feel as if you're putting on a role, or as if you don't need to think about it consciously because it seems so natural and easy?)
- What parts of your wider/other selves do you feel you have to withhold from that self? What characteristics of your self come to the forefront of what you aim to BE in this role or context? Why?

Take some time to visualise those selves, flesh out the details you have noted down and imagine yourself wholly inhabiting that self in different contexts from those you initially identified. What does your trusting, vulnerable self look and feel like in the workplace? How fully can you visualise yourself in that context? What would you need to adapt?

It's also worth paying attention to and reflecting on when and why we feel the need to edit the self (in any context) or change it to fill the shape of an outer persona or role to meet our or others' expectations. It's often an act of self-protection or projection we do unconsciously, but it can mean we put a judgement edit between impulse and action, which might impede sustaining an open channel in a scene, and really listening and responding in the moment. But it's very human, and often characters will do the same, so it can be useful to really identify in your own life that sense that there is sometimes an inner and an outer self, which may be different or in conflict.

It's worth reflecting on the fact that one dominant outer persona can be that of defining ourselves as actors; to inhabit a fictional *persona* (for example, we're all wild bohemians, careless of convention, or perhaps charismatic, intense, devoted to our art). Our desire to be perceived as *creative, talented, playful, spontaneous,* or anything else again may mean we avoid making offers on impulse, or connecting as ourselves, for fear of somebody judging our self as not credible or worthy as an actor. In your reflective practice, keep an eye out for when blocks you encounter may proceed from inserting something unhelpful between impulse and action, and consider why you feel provoked to do so in different contexts.

Keep identifying and visualising the possibility of various selves, because it keeps available to us, imaginatively, the idea that we aren't just one homogenous self. We all carry aspects within us which can take us towards different characters but still use embodied aspects of ourselves to connect to these, simply by recognising the different characteristics and adaptive behaviours we already employ.

Researching Emotional Self

Various philosophers and psychologists, from Aristotle to the present day, have attempted to articulate what emotions are, and have developed the idea that they can be grouped in to basic or primary emotions such as anger, happiness, sadness, and fear, and secondary or complementary emotions like love, optimism, awe, and shame, which may emerge from blends of the primary ones (think about how colours can be blended to create an infinite variety of shades and hues). The primary emotions are not culturally specific; the secondary ones can be complex, varied, and nuanced, and shaped through social and cultural norms.

We are all constantly in a shifting state of feeling and response to our lived experience and these responses can be driven by sensory (physical, chemical, and environmental) fluctuations as well as our frame of reference (personal memories, relationships, intuition, and intellect). We are all utterly individual in how we respond, and often it can be hard to identify or pinpoint why and what we feel in any given moment.

The development of emotional intelligence is what allows us to navigate our own emotional experience and engage and empathise with the emotional experiences of others. This skill can be learned through research, process, and preparation – and acceptance and reflection.

Our capacity to connect to and process our emotions, self-soothe, and respond to others' emotional needs is a core human attribute for survival. In the context of being an actor it's vital artistically as well as practically, because this shapes our ability to explore complex emotions we may not have directly experienced ourselves, in response to experiences we may have no frame of reference for and our ability to express truthfully for those characters who have. It's the actor's job to engage directly and truthfully with those emotions, perhaps difficult, painful, traumatic ones, but to be emotionally resilient ourselves so we can let others' pain and fear (also joy and passion) speak through us.

But it's not the actor's job to damage themselves in the process. Acting is a performance of the imagination under artistic control, not the recollection or pursuit of personal trauma or an act of iconoclastic self-destruction. There are often anecdotal stories of actors who engaged in extreme research or rehearsal practices in order to 'get' somewhere emotionally, in which the personal repercussions were longstanding and destructive. That's not art or craft. The mental scars are not indications of great performance – but neither is avoiding the emotions, shutting down, or justifying blocking them.

We may want to see or indeed to be actors who can *really go there emotionally* and artistically, but we don't feel safe as an audience watching if we're not confident that they can come back. Terminology like *it needs to cost you something* may give us a sense of dramatic stakes, but some costs are frankly too high, and purchase nothing that actually serves the performance.

Exercise: Exploring Emotional Characteristics and Habits

We all have emotional habits and tastes but may limit ourselves as actors/ characters because we prioritise those emotions we prefer. We can avoid certain emotions because of societal or cultural expectations or feel the need to transmute them into other emotions we feel more comfortable feeling or expressing.

On a sheet of paper, write down one of the basic emotions in the centre (numbers of these vary, but a good working line-up for this are the eight proposed by Plutchik: *joy, sadness, trust, disgust, fear, anger, surprise,* and *anticipation.* But you can use any you identify).

As swiftly as possible, and without editing or judging your response, note down on the page all the words or ideas that you associate with that primary emotion. Allow these to emerge from memory, situations, images, sensation, seeing others experiencing it, anything that pops into your head when you think about the emotion.

Once you have got these down, review and start to group these thoughts (and any additional ideas that arrive in the process) under the following questions with as much specific detail as possible:

- What *provokes* that emotion in you? Are there different situations?
- What does that emotion feel like as a *sensation* when you have it? What do you *do*?
- How does it physically *manifest*? What does that emotion look like when you *observe* it in others?
- What *impacts* does expressing the emotion have (either on you personally or on others)?

You are quite likely to find that several of your answers include additional emotions (e.g. someone's anger may impact on you as fear), and that these may be contradictory (your joy may make you sad or guilty that others aren't so joyful). You may also find that the answers aren't clear, it can be hard to define or pinpoint the emotional detail, or that you can't really remember *feeling* it. Allow complexities and uncertainties to be present and note them down. Repeat the exercise several times with different emotions.

Looking across your sheets, you are likely to find there are some emotions that you can identify and explore more than others. The ones which seem elusive are likely to be those which you may have evolved a negative perspective on (you got told off for losing your temper, or hated upsetting someone) and so you may also try to avoid them as an actor, or stay in broad outlines rather than find personal detail. Anatomising the emotion in terms of these questions can help us move away from our own emotional habits and give us a way into thinking about emotion as action/response, rather than personal instinct, and allow us to build emotional connection in respect of triggers, impacts, and affecting others, rather than trying to inhabit an isolated emotional state.

Exercise: Expanding Emotional Research

Identifying and processing our emotions can often be helped by looking for ways to express, externalise, or reframe emotion, especially if mentally ruminating or constantly reflecting on analysing yourself leads you into anxiety-based thinking.

Think about *reading* but also creating or writing poetry/stories, songs/music, painting/drawing, etc. Much artistic or creative impulse is emotional, and engaging with art in any media is often a way into identifying emotion. Engage as many of your senses as possible: sounds, images, touch, taste, and smell, as well as exploring the possibilities and connotations/associations with verbal expression. Vary exploring the points of engagement; sometimes it can be useful to consider the idea in abstract, sometimes to find a character (not you) in a context which provokes a specific response.

Allow yourself time to consider emotions you find difficult or unfamiliar – particularly if something is triggering recollection – and think about developing activities that allow you to engage safely and creatively with reconciling these, exploring and imagining beyond just your recollected experience. What is grief? If you have experienced it, probe, *read*, and view to see how your recollection chimes or connects with others, actively connect and compare your experience from your window on the world with that of others. Even if you have not experienced it, explore other's experiences, listen to recollections, pay attention to physical sensory details, images, sounds – what does it feel like, what does it look like, what provokes it? Research to build an imaginary bank of ideas from beyond your own window and open it wider.

Emotion in Motion

It's often useful to consider physical routes into expression of emotion in order to both identify and process our own moods and emotions, but also as an exploration beyond these. These include but are not limited to dance, yoga, kick boxing, meditation/breathing, going for a run, or finding a connection between music/sound and how that suggests physical impulses and activity, observing others' physicality in action, exploring the physical activities, gestures, and postures that might accompany an emotional experience (or be defences from experiencing it), and whether these might be literal or abstract. Our physicality is intimately connected with our psychology; they cannot be separated.

There's a reason we find the word motion in emotion. There's always movement and change, we have emotions physically as well as mentally, they change our voices, our postures, our engagements with the material world; they escalate and build, and dissipate in energy and intensity. The more you can explore the sensation and movement in emotions, the easier it is to move away from sitting in an emotional psychological *state* as an actor, and to explore identification with emotions which builds from but isn't wholly reliant on your own emotional habits and tastes.

Our emotional habits can be blocks or fixed patterns which need to be removed to create an open channel to your emotional centre and to your connection with your instincts and impulses. Keep an eye out for potential blocking or fixing habits you might have:

- Discomfort with expressing anger/aggression/rage
- Fear of having character intention/attraction misinterpreted as real
- Valuing dramatic emotional intensity as truth/catharsis, feeling more *real* at extremes, not nuance
- Fear of loss of control/discomfort/pain in response to personal identification with content (triggered memory)
- Avoidance of personally connecting with *nasty, wrong* or conflict-reliant emotions
- Denial of any emotion that reveals vulnerability, or feels *inappropriate* or *self-indulgent*

Experiencing emotion is fundamental; it's healthy to react emotionally to stimuli and if we experience something sad, we should be upset or even profoundly moved. It is not automatically a problem, it is often entirely appropriate.

Exercise: Personal Journaling

Some of you may have encountered personal journaling as an activity that contributes to your wellbeing, within a therapeutic journey or simply as a habit that allows you to engage in conversation with different aspects of yourself.

As an actor it can be particularly useful because so much of the work explores the navigation of complex emotions, and these in and of themselves can impact our own emotional selves, particularly when we may be trying to connect personally to pain and even trauma.

Consider routinely reflecting on your emotional experiences in life as well as in your work – what you feel, what has provoked it, what it feels like, – record it, and consider.

- What affects your moods and emotions most strongly? (Include physical effects as well, such as hormones, hunger, and exhaustion.)
- Do you tend to shy away from owning some of them, deflect strong emotion into something flippant or trivial, or find it hard to articulate or specify your own emotions?
- Which emotions do you actively enjoy exploring?
- What personal emotional instincts and expressive impulses do you trust confidently?
- How open are you when engaging with emotions?
- Which do you feel reluctant to engage with, or recoil or retreat from in fear? Why?

Remember the tiniest details of human specificity can be what you need as an actor, so your day-to-day subtle shifts and nuances may be just as fertile to process and celebrate; not everything is about agony and ecstasy.

HANDY HINT

If a scene/moment isn't working – you can't find the impulse or connect to the action – step away from the text dialogue, pull out the focus, and try anatomising the emotional action as per the exercise. Explore what connections you can find between your own emotional profile and the character's, and pinpoint the leaps of imagination needed and the personal blocks which may be stopping these.

HANDY HINT

There is a conundrum affecting all actors that can be defined as Diderot's paradox. Simplistically, he observed that one of the problems with evaluating acting is that there was a discrepancy between what an actor feels as a person, and what an actor communicates as a performer. In performance, the emotional experience as an individual might not actually communicate the truth of the emotion as the character needs to convey it. You aren't necessarily trying to *feel* the emotion, you are working primarily to communicate the controlled *expression* of it as a character.

PITFALL

Anytime we are using an emotion in these exercises (and in rehearsal) it is as an idea to explore, and one that can be anatomised and reconstructed in dramatic action. It is NOT an exercise in *emotion memory*, hysterical overidentification or staying trapped in personal trauma. These approaches do not make you more emotionally available or authentically *raw* as an actor; they remove your skill and agency from the active communication of emotion in action.

Considering Habits of Confidence and Comfort Zones

Our self-confidence tends to be constructed on a complex base of self-awareness, experience, habits, and preferences, and we're confident when we're looking through our own window on the world. Often we have quite marked comfort zones emerging from our confidence map, and when we are asked to explore work in other areas, we can experience a collapse of confidence and so we might tend to avoid (often unconsciously) having to shift out of our comfort zones or sidestep working in modes in which we don't feel we can confidently operate (see Chapter 1).

However, it is important to realise that where you are most/least confident can affect how you connect to your work as an actor and help you understand why you may find some things difficult, whether you are very confident in one area and so find it hard to move out of it, or whether you don't have confidence in yourself in one area. Too much or too little confidence can both make life difficult for you!

If you are finding something difficult to be open to, or if you find yourself wanting to block or dismiss an aspect of the character's action or your practice generally because it seems pointless to you, make sure you think carefully about how the work sits within your confidence map. Confidence isn't one single attribute, we can be more and less confident across different areas, which we might view as a map of distinct, but at times intersecting aspects:

Areas of confidence

Social/Interpersonal	Intellectual	Intuitive/Instinctual
Creative	Practical	Moral/Personal
	Physical	

Exercise: The Confidence Map

Jot these areas down on a sheet of paper, with space around each for notes. Using colours, circle/highlight any of these areas in which you feel *confident* – the idea/ related activities don't cause you anxiety, you trust your judgements and decisions in these areas, and the areas reflect things you feel you are *good at* or value in yourself as a strength.

Then do the same for those areas in which you feel *unconfident*. You may very well end up with some areas which are hard to appraise; or feel they could be either, depending on context; or which overlap. That's fine!

Then, starting with the areas that seemed clearest to you, consider what you thought about in order to come to that decision, or why it was difficult or uncertain. How did you *evaluate* your confidence? What did you consider as *evidence*? Note these thoughts down under the headings. It may be helpful to think about the following, but there may be other criteria that shape your evaluation:

External approval	Repeated practice	Control of activity/ risk	Enjoyment of process
Ease and facility	Excellence	*Right/Wrong* judgements	Expected outcomes
Comparison to others	Consistent achievement	*Rational* purpose	Visible measurement

Looking at your notes, consider whether you have marked habits in how you evaluate; and this might also apply to other aspects of the self, and your work, as well as your confidence. Are you tending to use ease or enjoyment as your main criteria, or perhaps you need to see clear outcomes and achievement? Do you need external inputs to decide, such as validation, approval, *good marks*, or measurement?

For example, if you are very confident intellectually and unconfident physically, you may find that you evaluate on the basis of rational purpose and achievement, that you have a struggle really finding a confident connection to some physical practice since it may be less specific and *rational*, and you may be told you are 'in your head' too much. You may overthink the work, and resist working on intuition, instinct, or physical impulses.

If you are someone who is firmly in control of personal emotions, and you don't like being out of control in terms of your life, being asked for *vulnerability* in an improvisation or a scene might be very challenging. You may find yourself self-editing impulse or finding justifications as to why your character 'wouldn't do that' when 'that' is a highly emotional/physical reaction that you find uncomfortable and risky, and do not enjoy.

None of these examples are set predictions. We are all very individual and complex, and don't always follow predictable patterns. However, it can be useful when you are encountering blocks and struggles in your rehearsal practice to appraise how the issue sits on your confidence map (i.e. are you being asked to work in a way that you don't automatically have confidence in? You feel stupid, and it's Shakespeare) and how you are thinking about the difficulty (you are judging yourself or what is being asked against unhelpful criteria; you need ease and enjoyment, and all this text analysis is HARD). It is also worth connecting your thinking here to the modes of engagement outlined in Chapter 1. What connections can you observe between your blocks, confidence, and evaluative judgement?

As with modes of engagement, we are all capable of operating creatively outside our confidence and comfort zones, and we can train ourselves to evaluate more helpfully and less judgementally. It can be useful to realise that we all act intellectually, practically, instinctively, and creatively all the time as humans, even if we don't consciously process that; we learn to like new things, to allow the random and unexpected to be a joyful discovery, to take informed risks. We already know we CAN do this, we just have to remember HOW.

Recognise when you have a strong need to evaluate against quite fixed criteria, which may not be useful when looking at the nature of the activity. Recognising when there's friction and what aspects of the self and the work this friction exists between can be a useful first step to unblocking.

Confidence in any area can be developed, so it's worth spending some time thinking about active ways that you can practice and explore the areas in which you feel less confident, (you may need to be counterintuitive here and work against your immediate tastes). Think about oblique and incremental approaches in terms of building your confidence (and solving any problems). Attacking head on will often mean you reinforce lack of confidence rather than improving it, e.g. grimly forcing yourself to do something that you don't yet have the capacity to integrate and build from. Recognise that this will take time, practice, and trial and error!

Be active about noting and consolidating progress you make; i.e. consider when you clear a block, how you managed it, and how you can sustain it. Take some time to consider how contexts, situations, and relationships can affect our confidence and capacity to work outside comfort zones; what enables you to free up and be open to exploring beyond habits?

Breaking Boundaries and Navigating Uncertainties

Please note we are using *boundary* here in respect of defining the mental and physical frameworks in which we operate habitually and comfortably. Rehearsal exercises which cross boundaries of harassment, invasive physical interaction, bullying, or emotional exploitation are not questions of you *lacking* confidence or *bravery* or being too stuck in your habits and comfort zones; they are **inappropriate, unacceptable, and often, reportable incidents**.

Breaking through our personal boundaries as an actor can often feel uncomfortable and even risky; it can be exposing, and make us feel vulnerable, fearful, or unsure. It's an acute state of *lack of confidence*. We can feel as if everything we know has been taken away from us, there are no certainties left to us, or (perhaps more typically) that we are a bit of an idiot, and what on earth were we thinking trying that . . .

Yet, when we DO cross some boundaries, when we find new discoveries, take risks, do something we hardly dared to believe we could or connect with that magic *click* of new insight or inspiration, it's exhilarating. Often we can barely remember after what stopped us from taking the leap in the first place, and because we have done it once, there is a growing *confidence* in trying again.

As actors, we are always operating at boundaries, the line we need to find between ourselves and a character, the line between the truthful immediacy we need to convey and what is still a performance that can be repeated eight shows a week, or the line between embodied action and fictional narrative.

We are always responsible not just for managing our own boundaries appropriately, but also for respecting and working with those of others. The trust in ensemble relationships is vital and has to be mutually evolved and inclusive; one person's catharsis may be another's overwhelm. Even if you as an actor feel confident and open to any kind of exploration, you can't do this in a vacuum, and so the following may also assist in the development of an empathetic understanding of the boundaries of others.

The *negative capability* of an uncertain and evolving rehearsal situation can give us an unsettlingly boundary-free context to navigate; we get caught up in feeling *pressured* to *be bold, get it right*, and even though we tell ourselves there are *no right answers*, we all tend to want to move as quickly as possible through the uncertainty of having few boundaries and many potential outcomes, towards something more defined. We need to avoid *becoming fixed*, or *set*, focusing only on outcomes or *endgaming*; but also we need to make *choices*. We often find we lurch between *getting stuck* and feeling as if all the work has fallen into fragments and we can't connect anything, or feeling overwhelmed and exposed.

When we butt up against our boundaries, even if we are doing so unconsciously, most of us tend to fall into avoidant behaviours in order to escape uncertainty or working in uncomfortable *unconfidence* —what we might call working out of our *comfort zone*.

Exercise: Recognising Boundaries

Think about your rehearsal or studio practice, and identify several experiences in which you have felt uncertain, unconfident, or uncomfortable (the boundary-crossing alerts!).

Try to note down as many factual specifics of the experiences as you can:

- What kind of exercise or activity was it?
- What did text say?
- What was the emotional content or action?
- What was the difficulty?
- What had you anticipated it being like?
- How did it actually make you feel?
- What did you actually do while working on it in practice?

Try to avoid value-judging yourself (*I was rubbish*) but it may be useful to consider the director's notes or feedback if they were part of the experience.

With the details of these in your mind, think about what your own habits are when you are faced with a boundary-crossing experience in a context; these might include getting feedback or notes, being asked to do something you didn't anticipate, being asked to do something that you cannot see the point of. What makes you uncertain is very specific to you, so do not worry if you feel it might be ridiculous to someone else. The point is to try to identify what your boundaries are, and how you navigate crossing them.

PITFALL

We stress again that this navigation of your boundaries is in your agency and your evolving artistry; and your management of this is entirely yours. Each actor has their own boundaries, many of which do not need to be crossed for the sake of it. What IS useful is to be able to build your judgement authentically of when these may impede your work and development and should be tackled AND when it is imperative to respect them for your own safety and wellbeing.

Responses and Tactics You May Recognise

Nervous/anxious physical symptoms – rushes of blood to the face, pounding in the ears, stress headaches, sweaty palms, nausea/ 'butterflies', stuttering and tripping over words, swallowing a lot, shoulder (and other) tension, hiding behind hair, fiddling (with jewellery, the chair, etc), mind blank

Self-defensive tactics – finding that you end up 'feeling ill' before something that you are unconfident about, telling yourself that you aren't in the right mood for or feeling up to whatever it is on that day, making excuses for yourself, saying *I WAS doing x*

Self-deprecation – running yourself down, telling everyone you're 'bad' at this, exaggerating your lack of knowledge or competence, dismissing effort you have put in in case it's *wrong*

Emotional explosion – bursting into tears, losing your temper, hysterical laughter, running out of the room, stopping activity dead in its tracks

Procrastination/Avoidance – finding every activity under the sun a higher priority than what you know you should be doing because it's easier than feeling as if you can't or don't know how

Justification/Dismissal – finding lots of very rational or personal reasons why what you have been asked to do is unreasonable, irrelevant, or impossible; stonewalling with 'I don't get it'

Self-sabotage – consciously or unconsciously not committing fully to the activity or the prep for it, so when it doesn't go well you can blame that, rather than the fact you weren't sure you could do it

Denial/Refusal – ignoring instructions/notes and just doing it *your way*; not hearing; obstruction or resistance

Over-questioning – continuing to ask questions and ask for clarification or explanation so you don't have to start trying to do something; checking a lot even though you always get the same answer

Hiding – trying to make yourself disappear in a session; avoiding saying or doing anything so there isn't the opportunity for you to get it wrong

Self-censorship – not letting yourself go with the ideas, impulses, or thoughts that you have in case they might be wrong; always being tentative and half-hearted, even when you're pretty sure you have a strong instinct

Overthinking – acute anxiety, trying to work out every possible outcome that you might experience in advance of doing something, trying to consider every option or possibility in order to establish the right one, using thinking/making sure/going into detail as a reason why you aren't doing something well

Focus pulling – making people laugh, upstaging, or being mocking or disrespectful of the work or the emotional content, so no one ever sees you actually trying it with conviction, because you think you are likely to *fail* at it

Hyperawareness of external factors – constant comparisons to what others are doing, panic that you can't find a grip on something yourself, copying what they are doing, 'checking in' with a director

Catastrophising – giving up completely because a small area isn't working, 'chucking the baby out with the bathwater' when you hit a block, giving up too quickly when it doesn't come easily or swiftly

Do you recognise any habitual tactics you apply or find as regular obstacles when you are asked to explore beyond your boundaries? It may be useful to consider that we can often apply different tactics to different situations; we might act very differently when avoiding a physical task than a text analysis one, we might *hide* from improv, but feel okay in pure abstract movement because there's nothing to *get wrong*. Make a note in your journal of any habitual tactics you observe and the context and the kind of practice in which they tend to present.

It will also be useful to detail out your experience of positive habits/contexts you can identify in yourself in the same way, in reference to the confidence mapping exercise and the factual specifics listed here; simply change the 'What was the *difficulty?*' question to, 'What was the *achievement?*'

Exercise: Unpicking and Tackling Habits

We all have certain specific ways of defending ourselves against the unpredictable, cruel, and judgemental world. Habits that protect us from feeling exposed or vulnerable, or uncertain and fearing failure. These habits may also give us confidence or reassurance but they can also be obstacles – fears – that hold us in patterns that actually stop us from exploring creatively; we may *fail* by avoiding *failure*. What has always worked before may no longer be sufficient. Different characters or projects will ask us to work in uncertain, new, and unfamiliar approaches.

Looking at your notes from the previous exercise, and allowing additional and new insights in as they arrive, consider the following and jot down your thoughts in your notebook. It might be useful to take each habit/context separately.

- Can you identify what fears may be underneath your habitual action/ response?
- What are you avoiding feeling or experiencing (perhaps failure, embarrassment, shame, judgement, getting it wrong, being overwhelmed, looking stupid, pain, loss of control, being vulnerable)?
- What is the inner voice saying to you in this context? What is your *self-talk?*
- Where might this fear or obstacle come from? What has influenced your thinking about it? (Think about your frame of reference notes.)
- How do you explain this fear or obstacle to yourself?
- Why do you allow this fear to be an obstacle?
- How does this fear/obstacle affect how you engage with the character or text (perhaps avoiding emotional/complex content, getting stuck in set interpretation that keeps you close to you, playing your own habits and tactics rather than theirs)?

Try to pinpoint what it is you are avoiding, and why you have this fear. This may not be easy to identify immediately or explicitly obvious; and so you may wish to allow additional reflection and revisit this later on.

It's also important to do this in a documented form, rather than just through thinking about it. This encourages you to quite literally get the negative thoughts and problems *out of your head*, and means you can see progress and changes as you look back at your notes.

Once you have mapped out your thinking as far as is possible here, take each habit/context and reframe it in respect of the following prompts. It's important to do this immediately after trying to detail the fear/obstacle because this will encourage you to move into an active state of moving through the struggle, rather than getting stuck in the problem.[2]

- How does it/would it feel if this fear or obstacle was removed? What is the positive objective you want to reach?
- Visualise and detail the mental and physical sensations of what it would look and feel like to not have those fears in this context. Write these as *I* statements in the present tense: *I volunteer to go first in improv, I get up relaxed physically and feel excited anticipation about playfully exploring the exercise . . .* Use these as your self-talk, and give your attention to this rather than the snarky inner critic.
- Looking at those habits/contexts in which you don't have this fear/obstacle, pinpoint and note down the physical sensations of this experience, the mental state, the freedom, and the confidence, and use these to flesh out the visualisation.
- What immediately obvious practical actions might assist you towards your positive objective? It's always useful to consider simple things like arriving on time, having time to prepare appropriately, not being hungry or knackered etc.
- Where you can see clear fears affecting you, how reasonable these fears are in this context? Start to detail out what a less *fearful* assessment of the context would be as objectively and rationally as possible. Again, use *I* statements. Give yourself agency over solving this.
- If you can identify where your learned habits have come from your own experience, unpick how your inner voice keeps you stuck. Most of the time it's not based in actual *evidence* that affects this context. Challenge this thinking, by testing out different approaches in practice that supersede unhelpful learned patterns.
- Break the fear down into smaller components when you can; especially when the context might include more than one boundary-crossing alert. It's easier to think about tactics that tackle these specifically, than trying to find the one miracle that solves everything at once. Physical effects might need different strategies from mental freezes.
- Include physical actions and prep as well as mental, whatever the fear/habit. If you know that five minutes of mindfulness meditation reconnects and centres you before something you are anxious about, plan to integrate this in your prep.
- Map out an incremental and staged strategy; e.g. challenge yourself to *get up first* to something, the target being simply to get up first, not to do it

brilliantly. Once you have reassured yourself that the world hasn't ended, add in another element for the next session, *get up first* and *stay on vocal support in the exercise*, and then add another and so on. This can also be time specific; commit to five minutes of working in uncertainty, then ten minutes.

- It can also be useful in some situations to engage a scene partner or fellow actor in activities. For instance, if you are working with difficult content or at a pitch of intensity, agree on mutual tap-out points, or a *traffic light* system for stepping back while staying in charge of your connection to the work.

After you have worked through this series of prompts, make sure you have evolved a plan that you can put into practice as soon as possible; there won't ever be a *perfect* time for this, so don't make that another obstacle! As soon as is feasible after any session in which you have been actively working to tackle a fear/obstacle, jot down in the journal your immediate thoughts and discoveries. Really make sure you are identifying positives, however small or insignificant they may be to others. Forgive yourself if you don't quite hit your target; and reflect on what the obstacles were in respect of that, and then consider perhaps different strategy for next time. Breaking through our boundaries or changing our habits is rarely a one-stop exercise; it takes time and self-care in the process.

HANDY HINT

It's worth also considering that characters may also have defensive boundaries and habitual strategies that you can explore with this in mind when thinking about actions or tactics (see Chapter 5).

Into Reflection

Obviously much of this chapter has focused on specifically reflective exercises; but the line between considering the self as an act of reflection and the self as a source for investigation as an actor is pretty blurry. You may find it's worth taking some time to evolve a coherent reflective practice for yourself specifically: personal journaling (vlogs/audio or written) may not suit everyone, and practice-based journals might be project-specific or over a period of time.

Our assumptions, our intuitive biases, our unconscious cognition emerge from our own personal frame of reference, our emotional self, and our confidence, habits, and fears, which are constantly evolving. Probe and consider how these really affect your responses and your creative choices – what new information you allow to affect your frame of reference, whether you dismiss ideas and information that you, consciously or otherwise, don't *want* to explore, and when you fixate on those which already suit your framework and get stuck in one way of thinking that reflects your subjective biases, not your investigated discoveries.

How might you take yourself beyond your own defaults? How might you start to adapt your thinking to a growth mindset? Consider how you think about and value challenge, setbacks, effort, and feedback.

We have tended to find that if you are evolving this practice in the context of a formal training course, it can be useful to make a distinction between the work you engage with directly for yourself, and any reflective tasks you are expected to submit for assessment. Sometimes the most substantial insights and discoveries are intensely personal.

Further Reading

- *The Mind's Eye* by Ian Robertson
- *Who Am I?: Psychological Exercises to Develop Self-Understanding* by The School of Life
- *Daring Greatly: How the Courage to Be Vulnerable Transforms the Way We Live, Love, Parent, and Lead* by Brené Brown
- *Facing the Fear* by Bella Merlin
- *The Power of Accepting Yourself* by Michael Cohen
- *How to Be Comfortable with Being Uncomfortable* by Ben Aldrige
- *Overcoming Anxiety* by Helen Kennerly
- *Creating a Character* by Moni Yakim
- *Grit: The Power of Passion and Perseverance* by Angela Duckworth
- *How To Stay Sane* by Philippa Perry

Notes

1 Moni Yakim proposes several practical exercises in terms of how to pinpoint types of selves within yourself, but also how to use the knowledge of the different selves when approaching different characters with different characteristics.
2 Many of these ideas are based (very generally) in the kind of principles which underpin CBT (cognitive behavioural therapy). This is a relatively widespread practice in therapy, but the *Overcoming* series of books offer a really applicable self led route through into tackling some of these habits and fears with more specific engagements.

Guy Stanley

3
INTERROGATING THE TEXT – CLOSE-READING THE PLAY

Defining the Challenges and the Objectives

On the page, the writer(s) provide dialogue, sequenced action, and sometimes additional information (*stage directions*) – selected to communicate their vision and intention. However, this is NOT the PLAY. The play is the realisation of embodied interpretation of these aspects. The research activity of *interrogating* the text is what gets us from the page to the stage.

Because many of us encounter drama in a literary academic context, which often encourages specific types of critical enquiry – *the text is about theme x* – we can tend to feel like any *good* research activity is that which supports a coherent literary interpretation. It is crucial to start from the text, so that any creative decisions you make will not stray from the playwright's intention and vision and also underpin any specific directorial interpretation, but not to focus entirely on the conceptual centre or the holistic impact (that's the research of the director, arguably!).

An actor has to understand why their character is in the play and how that character serves the storytelling and journey of the audience. How does this character drive the story forward? How important is your character to the play? Why is your character in the play? Understanding the character's role from this perspective will direct you on the right path in terms of making appropriate performance choices. For example, if your character's raison d'être is to make the protagonist look unfairly treated and get the audience on their side, it is not useful from the point of the story to make choices that prevent that from happening.

For the actor, the research priority is mostly about the particular and the personal, fused in a character, which might not obviously serve the coherent overview or bigger-picture themes. Good performance *usually* emerges when the

DOI: 10.4324/9781003226130-4

small details (of the character in the *world*) are meticulously realised in practical embodiment of the text and when all these details integrate to evolve the whole piece coherently. As discussed in Chapter 1, we need to be able to shift our critical eyes, focusing in tightly on details to get the specifics, but also able to read to ensure we can see how these connect and cohere within the whole.

In order for the actor to identify these specific potential details and elements, it is important to start with the first piece of research that you need – read the text. We need to prioritise and we usually need to start small, from the specifics of the non-negotiables provided by the writer. Hence, the information we can gain from the text is incredibly valuable and will form the basis for any further research we may need to do – either in practice by working the action of a scene, or in investigation to discover additional information – but it also details what we are working to as *givens*. Analysing the text is the starting point for identifying and selecting the *evidence* that supports our practice and the additional *questions* that inform our research.

It can be useful to think of the character research as three main areas:

- Personal: habits, posture, tensions, energy, needs, wants, characteristics
- Interpersonal: relationships, proximity, status, tactics
- Locational: space, setting, time, objects/furniture, given circumstances, the world

These elements are all integral to the actor's research into the character, and they are all highly dependent on each other and at times undistinguishable from each other. However, in Chapters 4 through 6 we have attempted to split up the character research into those three sections, making it easier to navigate one section at a time in order to use the initial text research and transforming it into action and performance choices.

Often research and rehearsal periods are short, and so we need a reliable and flexible research process to use that time effectively, getting to grips with the relevant detail to inform acting choices for character rather than spending hours on areas of general interest or bigger-picture overviews which serve knowledge rather than practice. It's not unusual to need to do a first read quickly and be able to identify useful information that enables us to make swift choices for an audition scenario, or a cold read of script when we may not have the luxury to explore at our leisure.

When characters talk, use words, or are described or referred to in a certain way within the words of the text on the page, there is usually a reason for that; if nothing else, they are the words that the writer has selected for you. Being precise in the analysis of these allows us to identify ways to embody those aspects in terms of the practical work on characteristics, actions/tactics, needs, etc. We may make quite swift judgements about what people are like from how they talk as well as their ability to adjust to a particular situation. In a script, the majority of information we get is from looking at the dialogue between characters in a specific given circumstance. For example, a character who uses long words fluently and accurately, in long well-constructed sentences, will usually 'read' as being intelligent.

However, we also need the words of the text to give us ideas about that which is NOT said. What is the potential subtext? Why those words; what prompts them to be spoken? What are they thinking when they say or don't say something? What are the gaps that need filling to shape a through line in the performance, that we don't have on the page?

Our job as actors is to build a living, breathing person from the text we are presented with. To be able to do that there are numerous factors we need to grasp to form an understanding of the situation as a whole, but also to create a past, present, and future for the character. The character's past will play an important part because we are often affected by upbringing and past experiences, and our personality is shaped through a combination of both hereditary (nature) and environmental (nurture) factors. Those factors will combine with our current circumstances and create a present for the character. The future will be involved to the extent that our hopes, aspirations, and wants – as well as our fears and anticipated consequences – will affect our behaviour in the present.

Not all texts give us the same amount of information; more classic texts often give us considerable detail, more contemporary texts may be intentionally ambiguous or fluid. Not every text intended for performance starts with conventionally arranged scenes and characters. Some information will be solidly available to us with a close reading of the words of the text, some information can be inferred or deduced from clues which are present but not explicit in the words, and some information will come from personal imaginative speculation. But ALL this information must emerge from and return to the text we are focusing on.

So, the key objectives and skills in engaging with the text as research:

- Develop *active read* skills that connect us swiftly with obtaining information for practice.
- Recognise the given facts of the text *and* the questions we still need to research.
- Be able to focus tightly on potential nuances and details of all of the words.
- Identify potential details and ideas to fill gaps by deducing or inferring from our reading.
- Select information that affects practical embodiment.
- Connecting specific details, given or inferred, with the through lines and the text as a whole.

Prep and Tools for the Job

- A notebook – if you are looking at this chapter for a specific play we suggest cracking open a new one, so all your work can get concentrated into one central point. It can also be fine to work on sheets of paper and then collate in a folder.

- Pens and highlighters
- Your script! It's also worth getting several photocopies of your scenes, so you can use them as working documents for text research, without scribbling all over your main rehearsal script.
- Access to a dictionary, and depending on the specific text it might be useful to have different kinds – for example, *Shakespeare's Words: A Glossary and Language Companion*; for this and more poetic texts, *Brewer's Dictionary of Phrase and Fable*.

Into Practice – Exercises and Activities

First Read and Analysis

As you are reading plays – and this can be done even if they are not plays you know you are preparing for rehearsal – it's useful to read through a couple of times just to get a sense of the shape, pace, and story of it. Even if you know what part you will be working on, try to keep a neutral engagement with all the characters and scenes (even if you're not in them).

If the text isn't conventionally structured or expressed, the same approach applies. What is the organising principle for the words? What seems to be the shape or the idea explored?

If particular questions or confusions arise, note them down briefly, but keep the focus initially on reading for sense and familiarity; the following exercises for close analysis of the text are usually easier when you have a sense of the whole.

HANDY HINT

Organise your time so you can focus intently in short bursts. Break down and focus on one scene at a time, or one aspect of an exercise at a time and avoid trying to do it all in one sitting. You are likely to find that you miss details and possibilities if you concentrate too hard for too long – it'll all get blurry.

Exercise: Mapping Scenic Action

What actually happens in the scene (or the play)? Whatever work you do personally, and whatever your character's point of view, both have to correspond with the objective view here. The scene is created by the visible/audible actions within it regardless of their impact on individual characters, and the whole play is constructed from the events of the constituent scenes (even if *your character* isn't in them!).

Scenic action varies immensely across texts and the details often need to be unpicked; there's a lot of plays in which the action on a first read is simply *they talk about x*. It will be useful to look at stage directions as well as dialogue here. Read through your scene(s) and think about looking for the following in the order in which they occur in the scene; on your page, think about keeping these two lines of enquiry separate but sequentially connected, i.e. a revelation in dialogue might lead to a fist fight. Treat each scene/act independently.

- Plotted activity/action – a physical fight, an embrace, exits and entrances, *Othello kills Desdemona*
- Dramatic discoveries – new information, revelation, decision, *X declares love for Y, W confesses to something, Macduff was from his mother's womb untimely ripp'd*

These are things which definitely happen and so must affect your choices – otherwise you aren't doing the play; these are the WHATS and WHENS of your performance. Aim to clarify in detail the *spine* of the scene, connecting the individual vertebrae of events that form it. This exercise is to establish details which aren't up for negotiation, because they are aspects which all characters in the scene encounter albeit with varied stakes, impacts, and reactions. The potential impact of the scenic actions on the specific characters is a matter for further research – the HOWS and WHYS of how they behave subsequently. It is also worth noting that the action and spine of the scene will most likely be further explored in terms of units/beats of action within the rehearsal process itself.

You are also likely to identify additional WHATS for you to consider if, for example, you have a series of scenes spread across a period of time and need to identify what might have happened between each episode. These will get fully detailed as we consider previous and given circumstances.

Exercise: Breaking Down the Given Textual Character

You will need to read the script several times in order to start to form a deeper understanding of who the characters are. Actor's reading for research is different from how you read a novel, when you might let the story wash over you and get lost in images and impressions; you are engaging with the script for a research purpose and need to look at the underpinning detail, not the overall effect. A good way to start pinpointing your individual character, and shifting into a close-up focus, is to read the script answering these four questions ONLY from what is given on the page – avoid value or qualitative judgements on the notes:

> *What do I do in the play?* Write down all actions or activities your character does throughout the script. This can include both tactics and physical actions such as *manipulate, boast, makes dinner, puts the children to bed*; however, tactics can be changed depending on how you play the character, so

unless it is clear in the text, stick to what the character is obviously doing. Make sure you also include stage directions when applicable. This will give you a start in mapping your character's journey.

What do I say about myself? Make a note of everything that your character utters about themselves: statements, claims, and acknowledgements of yourself, your characteristics or your actions, any relationship data (I'm a *mother, wife, child,* etc). Make sure you also include stage directions when applicable. This will allow you to begin to build a picture of how you view yourself or how you wish others to view you.

What do I say about others? Make a note of everything that your character utters about those characters around you, include seen or unseen characters. Again, these appear as statements, claims, acknowledgements, and views on character(s) or actions. Make sure you also include stage directions when applicable. This will allow you to start to discover your relationships with others and relationships others have around you.

What do others say about me? Make a note of everything that is said about your character including by the writer as to age, identity, etc, other characters' views on you, comments, statements, claims, and views on your characteristics or actions. Make sure you also include stage directions when applicable. This will allow you to start to understand how you are viewed by others which will help you build your characteristics and tactics.

It is often necessary to read the script several times with these questions in mind to fully get the best use out of them, because we often miss things the first time around. In breaking down the text in this way, make sure you use the words that are given in the text; don't interpret or redefine them, or at this point start filling in any gaps you perceive.

Note other ideas that come into your mind while you are focusing on these factual elements – further questions, images, points of personal recognition, any thoughts on interpretation, or inferences that you can deduce from implicit or unspoken elements. Keep these notes separate from the information obtained from the questions. What you have as a result of this is still the writer's words, but now reorganised in such a way that you can begin to build your research further towards answering questions in practice. These are the notes that you will use when going into deeper character research, as outlined in Chapter 4.

PITFALL

When thinking and noting make sure you can clearly separate *evidence* from the text and the ideas and thoughts which come from your own *speculation* or *inference*. All are vital, but what comes from the text explicitly is generally non-negotiable. Ideas from inference and speculation need to stay open and flexible and not get fixed in your mind so you can't move from your first interpretation.

Exercise: Identifying Previous and Given Circumstances and Context

Given circumstances will encompass everything that provides information to set the scene, characters, and relationship in a context, including mapping where the scene sits in time and in space, what has happened prior to the scene, and the world situation and history, if mentioned. The chapter on given circumstances will explore these aspects in more detail; however, it is important to start from what we can get from the script.

Reading through the text again, and referring to your notes from the previous exercise, identify the information given in the text including stage directions under the following:

- The *dramatic present*: *When* is the *now*? Include any clues (or data) as to where the scene occurs in time, such as year, season, month, date, time of day, and temporal qualifiers/adjectives (late, early, unseasonal, Christmas, *medieval*).
- The *time axis*: Where does the scene sit in comparison to the previous? Later or earlier (flashback)? What MUST have happened before the start of the play/scene or between each scene? What do we know WILL happen after? How long are the times between scenes?
- The *dramatic space*: *Where* is the scene *now*? Look for the country, the city, the building/outside space, the room. What furniture and objects are identified as being present? What/who can we see and hear in the scene? Whose space is it? What doors/entrances and windows? Include place names and spatial qualifiers/adjectives (*home*, cosy, stark, cold, bright).
- The *space axis*: Where have we been/come from? What surrounds the dramatic space? What is going on outside it? Where are we going? What connects the various spaces?

Again, keep your focus tightly on just the information that is provided by the writer's words and text, which will again vary immensely as to how much detail is given. On a separate page, note down anything that you can't obtain from the text, any logical assumptions, questions, or decisions that will need to be investigated further in the next stages of research. These investigations will be further explored in Chapter 6.

Exercise: Unpicking Vocabulary and Language

Any words chosen by the writer carry an actual meaning of the word by definition (a book is a book), but the association is not always literal and absolute. Under any circumstances the first activity has to be to properly look up the actual meaning of any words used, especially when you feel you have a general idea, but not a precise one. Beyond definitions, the kinds of words used also create additional layers of meaning and associations between words and ideas; the words construct our knowledge and recognition of the topics/ideas referred to, time period, supposed intelligence of character, stakes, social status of character, relationships between characters, etc. Words can be an identifier for social groups (age, sex, ethnicity, cliques, workplaces, etc) and locations (formal work, intimate family), as well as loaded with emotional significance.

There can also be effects (often comic) created by word play – puns, spoonerisms, misquotations, double entendres, malapropisms, dysphemism/euphemism, clichés, nonsense words, irony, exaggeration/understatement, wrong word usage, etc.

Moreover, scripts may contain words, expressions, or language structures unfamiliar to you, or that you don't use yourself. The character might speak lines in a different international language, which means you would have to research how that sounds and what that means. Whether the unfamiliarity is because it is a classical or stylised text, or because it uses a slang/accent/jargon vocabulary or sentence construction that we do not immediately have a frame of reference for, you still need to be able to understand the words, the usage, and the origin to fully inhabit the character, make connected performance choices, and communicate those to an audience.

Reading through the text/scenes again, and referring to your notes from the previous exercises, identify the information given in the text (including stage directions) considering the following questions. It can be useful to work with a *clean* photocopy of the scene here, and to mark this up with your trusty highlighters.

- Are there consistent patterns or repetitions of words? Or types of words?
- Do the words form images or metaphors? Are they used figuratively? What images are used?
- Are the words concrete, practical, and/or literal (or abstract or conceptual?)
- How do the punctuation and the grammar frame the sentence structure?
- What kinds of words/language are used as identifiers? These may be formal/ informal (status), dialect/slang/jargon (social group), pet names/titles (intimacy), complex/simple (education/intelligence).
- Where do the words come from? Are they coherent or historical? Quotations or references?
- Are there jokes and attempts at humour?
- How does the vocabulary choice relate to given circumstances?
- Can you identify any habits the characters have in how they use words? For example, single-word responses, avoiding *nasty* things with euphemisms, swearing a lot?
- Does the vocabulary reflect any identifiers such as words written for an accent or dialect?
- How do the literal meanings of the words connect to the character and/or action?
- What extra layers of meaning or significance could be found in the vocabulary choices? For example, X constantly talks about food/sex.
- Is the dialogue clear in respect of reflecting character identity and relationship between speakers – or is it ambiguous? Is it single characters or a chorus/ ensemble?

- Does the conversation as written suggest any specific vocal habits for characters, e.g. accent, stammer, ums and ahs?
- Does the text follow normative conversational patterns appropriate to the content, or is there a mismatch between the structure and the content?
- Is the dialogue following or subverting 'normal' speech? If so, whose 'normal' speech'?

Try to keep your attention closely on the detail on the page; much of the time (particularly in realistic texts) words are quite functional and they don't all reward profound scrutiny. Characters are likely to vary – sometimes being quite literal, sometimes more figurative depending on what they are talking about, and to whom – and so if there aren't any clear patterns this doesn't mean you are doing it wrong! This is NOT an exercise in literary criticism, so you don't need to appraise the *quality* of the language choices. However, it is useful to be able to attend to the specific nuances the vocabulary choices could imply. These skills – using extremely focused attention and being able to identify details – will take time to develop.

We usually choose our words carefully for conscious effect, but they are also capable of revealing our thinking and intention subconsciously; for example, we may have more words for and refer more to things that engage us or things we know, we may repeat ourselves, or we might avoid certain words in certain contexts. Complex emotion might mean we use more words, or less literal ones in the process of trying express something nontangible or unclear. Sometimes we can also apply reductive normative thinking and assumptions to how we connect to words, so be attentive to how words can also suggest and create stereotypical readings of who uses which words.

Allow yourself to recognise the difference between what something *means* literally, and what it might *mean* in this context, what you might infer or deduce from the choice of words. Stay alert to how your own intuitive self makes unconscious decisions about details. By tracking the potential nuances and shifts in the words used and their connotations, you can start to ground your interpretation of what MIGHT be going on inside the characters, their potential thoughts, characteristics, and objectives, and growing these from specific details, not just a general sense of the scene, or your own subjective response to language or emotion.

PITFALL

Watch out for falling into habits of literary interpretation, or mistaking attention to detail for being too *academic*; get your eye really focused on the specifics that *ping* in your brain, and capture them in your notes. You don't need to provide a cogent literary reason for this; recognise *what* comes out of your reading, even if *why* is less easy to pin down.

Dramatic texts are, for the most part, written in a dialogue form – words to be spoken in interaction with others' speech acts. The conventions of realism expect the dialogue to replicate the patterns of characterised interpersonal conversation, but obviously there are also many texts which explore different patterns (cross-cut monologues, physical dialogues, direct address to the audience, chorus work, etc). Even within a conventional *realistic* scene the words that are said also carry subtext, what is not said; we can see the characters' potential thoughts emerging through patterns of speaking by how the words are organised and structured, and how we might speak them and to whom. The character talking the most may not be the person driving the conversation, and a pointed silence might have more impact than a lengthy speech.

Textual clues and rules which govern the language are often explained by the playwright in the beginning of the play, where they will present what the different punctuation marks and text-indicators mean. Some will use '. . .' to demonstrate that the character did not finish the sentence or trailed off; however, others use '—' to specifically illustrate the character being cut off, whereas at times you will see a "/" to mark where characters overlap each other in their speech. Lines might be written in capital letters, which could mean it is an exclamation or shouted line. These are specific textual clues that need to be noted and can come in many different forms.

You are likely to find that some questions arise that can't be answered from this work; note these down. These are the priorities for the next stages of research:- how long is that pause, why does x ignore that question, why is y talking so much, why does z respond with that offer?

We carry a broadly normative idea of what speech and conversation sound like in various contexts. In replicating conversation dramatically we are riding a fine line between actual conversation and theatrical conversation. An audience is *reading* a theatrical conversation from a distance, when normally as humans we are *reading* a conversation from participation in it or at close proximity. The actor has to be able to represent conversation with a different level of clarity so it can be perceived externally; because of this the structure of the textual conversation is more important in underpinning the *meaning* or finding the intention of the characters speech in action with others. Chapter 5 will explore conversation analysis as a fundamental basis for relationship exploration.

Taking Text Information Into Practice

Give yourself some time after reading and noting the text in this way to review and consolidate your questions – the aspects you couldn't *answer* from the text analysis activities or potentially infer from considering subtext, patterns, and connections.

It's worth also considering what kind of research activity is going to be a useful next step. Questions about how a character speaks might be most usefully explored by listening to an audio recording of the accent, an online search might be useful to visualise the image of a specific location, but you are probably going to need other people in rehearsal to explore questions of interaction. Concentrate on identifying HOW you are most likely to get relevant information, not just WHAT that information might be; some questions will have to be interrogated through rehearsal practice, some may require locating factual data, some will be vital to answer quickly, and some may take time to clarify and explore.

It's quite usual to end up with a lot of scattergun information by engaging with the activities outlined so far, and to have a real mix of clear data, direct questions, and speculative ideas. There are a lot of pieces of LEGO on the floor, and so we need to start building these pieces together. You may find that some information you have noted down in the previous exercises doesn't immediately give you anything when grouped in the following areas, and that's fine. Start selecting the elements that you can see being useful for practical purposes.

Try to identify how your own frame of reference contributes to the information selection process, when you are needing to use your own intuitive *sense* to make implicit connections and decisions, as well as grouping explicit textual details. You are going to need both in rehearsal, but we need to keep the intuitive details open and adaptable, rather than getting fixed in what we *feel* we know.

Many of the areas listed below intersect, and may not always need to be done in the sequence they appear in. The terminology we have used is relatively common across rehearsal processes, particularly those emerging from the Stanislavskian tradition, and we have found they are useful areas in which to start joining information since they all underpin developing practical choices for performance. Substantiating this information in your practical choices is the purpose of research.

You are not *done* with the processing of the text and should expect to revisit and revise all these notes as you go through a rehearsal journey!

Finding Characteristics

Start collating your notes from the text and thoughts about what the *character is like* – their personality, their qualities, their traits, their values, and their habits. Refer to the *vocabulary used with the other characters*. What types of *words does the character use* to communicate? What do *others say about them?* What do they say? What does that say about them? Think about how physical activity, vocality, or physicality can also reveal characteristics; for example vocal hesitation might suggest nervousness of some kind, physically grabbing another character might suggest aggression. Don't ignore contradictions; often these can be useful clues as to different inners and outers or adaptations characters make depending on relationships and given circumstances. Similarly, keep a sense of any changes you observe in the scenic action, some traits grow in intensity, or start neutral and become positive or negative through a narrative. We can often identify multiple characteristics, but it's also important to bear in mind that they may not all always be needed all the time in practice.

If we have a sense of what someone is *like* and why, we can begin to build a more connected understanding of *how* they might act/behave and why. Characteristics can give us starting points for physical and vocal choices, as well as beginning to shape why and how a character operates. Note that Chapter 4 will further deepen the elements of characteristics research.

Defining Objectives

Who or where we are often shapes and informs what we want, even if in real life we don't consciously and constantly process it. Getting what we *like*, want, or need motivates us to action with intention, we do what makes sense to us fulfil that goal (which might be sensible or not . . .); and the same then is true of characters. To start to understand and choose an objective, you will need to understand the super objective of the character – what ultimately is driving them? What do they want or need? Every character starts the play at one point and is in a different point at the end of it; this may mean they have moved towards their goal, or that it has been frustrated or diverted (see obstacles). This objective can be tangible or emotional – 'I want to be king', or, 'I want forgiveness' – but essentially the objective is what allows us to construct a coherent through line for the character, the journey, which allows the audience to see a believable *living* person in the experience of the action.

Objectives can change within the scene/play, depending on what new information a character receives or what they discover. New information can range between a change in the circumstances, a change in the relationship or knowledge about someone else, or indeed something the character discovers about themselves (look back at the *spine of the scenic action*, the *time/space axis*). In Chapter 4 objectives will be investigated further.

Negotiating Obstacles

While it's a bit of a truism, navigating conflict is central to drama; we don't tend to invest in scenes in which nothing much happens or in which it all happens too easily. While obviously there can be epic external conflicts – good versus evil, man versus machine – a great deal of dramatic conflict exists in an intrapersonal basis (internal struggle) or an interpersonal basis (between people), with human-scale obstacles. For acting purposes, obstacles are defined as something that is either in the way of the character getting what they want or impeding their ability to achieve their goals. Obstacles can mostly be divided into two categories: *outer obstacles* and *inner obstacles*.

Outer obstacles are mostly straightforward to identify through the *scenic action*; however, they can be dependent on identifying the objective of the character first. Inner obstacles will be more dependent on the deeper character research that will be explored further in the following chapters. Both outer and inner obstacles will influence a character's tactics, which in turn will be influenced by the importance of the goal – the stakes – because the more urgent a situation gets the less the inner obstacles will influence the character. Both inner and outer obstacles will be delved into further in Chapter 4.

Considering Tactics

Tactics – or *actions* depending on the vocabulary used – are what the character does to achieve their goal in the scene, i.e. the active choices a character makes in striving for something, HOW they navigate the scenic action, the *readable* representation of thought and intention. The tactics we use can also be connected to who we are (physically and mentally) and what we want to achieve. A *nervous* character might use different tactics and actions from a confident one, and we use different tactics according to our relationships with other people with whom we interact.

Ideas for tactics usually are revealed by looking at the impacts on other people or events, so review the notes you made around what *other people say about the character*, and also the *words they use*, and how *they wield them in dialogue*. How does the character *affect others*? What different options and ideas emerge from looking at *what they do in the text*? How do they go about doing what they do? Again, allow contradictions to exist; in high stakes situations (not uncommon in drama) anyone might be capable of acting *out of character*. Tactics are rarely explicitly stated; the act of research is to use your investigation of character and relationship to substantiate and inform these choices in action, which is further detailed in Chapter 5.

Exploring Relationships

Typically, the text will identify the nature of a nominal relationship – like siblings, parent and child, romantic partners, or friends – from either the playwright's character information or stage directions. But this structural relationship is general, not specific; any relationship needs to be characterised according to the specific text. Look back at the notes; for example, if you have a mother and daughter, how do they *talk about* each other in what they say, what *words* do they use when *speaking to each other*, how do they *interact* in *conversation*? How physically intimate and close are they, is there a connected relationship, or are they in conflict, misunderstanding each other? When, if at all, do they shift and change through the *scenic action*? Relationship research will be delved into in a practical way in Chapter 5.

Previous and Given Circumstances

Ultimately your given circumstances are the context in which your choices are made. Everything that surrounds us in time and space affects what choices are available or appropriate to us in the dramatic present. Who we are has been shaped by our previous circumstances. And this is true of real life as much as on stage! (See Chapter 2.)

Looking back over the notes from all exercises, group together information that builds a picture of your character's *previous experiences* – this can start the idea of a *biography* that provides a coherent frame for how and why your character might act or behave in a certain way at certain points, how significant your characteristics are, and how this shapes what you want, as well as leaving gaps that you will need to fill and yet more questions to research further.

Looking at the *time and space information* from the *dramatic present*, you can start to organise details that might shape the potential *physical sensations* of the character, the energy and intention with which they experience the scenic action. Information gathered here will form the start of the research presented in Chapter 6.

Filling the Gaps

Depending on the kind of process you are involved in, this activity may come at a different point in the development; you may be unable to answer the following at the start of a devising process, or while working on a more fluid text, which doesn't automatically identify characters and scenes. In the context of your initial prep work on an existing text, from your research and your practice so far, you will have amassed a wealth of details, but in order to focus the next potential research steps it can be useful to review where you are:

- What *gaps* do I currently have in my notes?
- Where do I feel more information or inspiration is needed?
- Do I feel I need a verbal detail, visual reference, aural trigger, or something physical or embodied?
- Are my gaps personal to my character, or do they affect others?
- Are my gaps connected to my inner life, thoughts, and/or internal visualisation?
- Are my gaps to do with elements of stylised physical staging which will need to be manifested in the performance (i.e. not routine character interaction)?
- Are my gaps to do with transitions between moments within the scenic action?
- Are my gaps to do with really detailing the qualities of a specific moment?

Aim to come to a sense of the priorities you have, and how these need to connect to your practice. You may find even if the need is for an inner image, it might be easier to evolve that through word pictures initially, or music; there is no imperative for the source and the solution to be literally connected! It's useful to evolve a sound sense of what research work will need to be personal and independent to fill gaps, but also what work will need to be collaborative in conjunction with your fellow actors and creative team. Some research practice will need to be driven by more than your personal needs and process, and these are more fully explored in Chapter 7.

Into Reflection

Reading plays isn't just useful as preparation for rehearsal and can again be practiced to build your skills in reading swiftly and effectively. It is also worth making sure that you practice across different forms and styles of text. Explore expressionistic, poetic, classical, physical – screenplays as well as theatre – and not just conventionally constructed realism. How effective can you be at getting to grips with any text for dramatic exploration?

It can also be a useful exercise to do active analysis reads with single scenes in which you don't have lots of overview information. Think about getting sides at short notice for an audition; practicing will build your speed at identifying core information and core questions for your research, and focusing in on key details for a self-tape or an audition. In an audition scenario you are not expected to provide your definitive take on the scene, but you will need to play connected choices NOT questions. How quickly can you identify key aspects (however rough these are at this stage) and connect this with how you might *read/play* the scene? How many different ways can you do so? (You are playing different specifics, NOT trying to play *all* potential options in one choice.)

Take some time to reflect on the experience of doing this each time. How easy is it to engage with the exercises? Is your eye or mind drawn to certain kinds of information more than others? What do you tend to identify in the material as either evidence for your notes, or questions that arise?

How much do you rely on quick assumptions and speculation? Can you recognise and value your intuitive response, but also appraise this? Can you connect your personal response to precise details in the text, as well as being able to shift beyond your own frame of reference and consider other *readings* and potential interpretations? Are there certain kinds of situations, characters, or textual material that you find easier to *read* than others? Can you feel your acuity developing?

HANDY HINT

Breaking the exercises down and putting some time between looking at one scene and the next will often make you more sensitive to spotting nuances and contradictions, because you will have fresh eyes and won't carry your earlier notes and assumptions so vividly in your mind.

Further Reading

- *Tackling Text [and subtext]: A Step-by-Step Guide for Actors* by Barbara Houseman
- *Words into Action* by William Gaskill
- *Script Analysis* by James Thomas
- *The Scene Study Book: Roadmap to Success* by Bruce Miller
- *Directing Actors* by Judith Weston

Guy Stanley

4

INVESTIGATING FOR CHARACTER – SHIFTING FROM SELF

Defining the Challenges and the Objectives

Character research is an essential component of an actor's craft, because it helps define who the character is as distinct from ourselves. The character will likely have many differences from ourselves, so we are not able to just rely on our own intuition, knowledge, and experiences, but we will have to investigate where the differences, and indeed similarities, between us and the character lie. These differences will be found in such things as the character's instincts and impulses, their view of the world, their environment, cultural and social fashions, upbringing, relationships, challenges and needs, etc.

Similarly, in terms of physical attributes and vocal expressions, although the character will be created from your bodily constructs, your breath, and emotional centre, they can differ from you in their tensions, rhythm, pitch, and physical behaviour/mannerisms. Physical and vocal exploration allows the actor to develop ways to decide on the character's physicality and physical habits, vocality, and speech, building away from but still integral to the self.

Acting teacher Sanford Meisner likened actors to icebergs, meaning that what is visible above the surface is only a small part of who they really are. The rest – the exciting, the interesting, the true sense of self and all your experiences, failures, successes – is hidden away below the surface.[1] The same can be said about the characters we play; what is exposed in the script is like the tip of the iceberg, but to understand where the character comes from and the experiences that have led them to become who they are will have to be researched, explored, and developed by the actor in order to make the character a full and multidimensional being.[2]

To understand what we need to research about the character in a play, we need to ask how we understand other people in real life, which we do all the time

DOI: 10.4324/9781003226130-5

as part of our survival skillset as a social species. We gain an often unconscious understanding of somebody through their actions, what they say, their habitual responses and their wants, according to our own frame of reference. There are aspects we comprehend from such things as background, upbringing, class, location, present and previous circumstances, experiences, and aspirations. But as humans we need to understand people in order to negotiate them and to respond to them, rarely to try to inhabit or embody them. As actors we usually start with words on a page, not a whole human being to read in *real life*, and so our research will have to evolve one through a combination of conscious exploration, textual research, and intuitive imagination.

We cannot underestimate the importance of observation and practical activity as an actor's research skill. This pertains to the observation of ourselves doing as well as others. As actors we must become adept at observing, *reading*, and understanding the specific human being beyond intuition and our instinctual response to them – appraising the details of who people are, how they communicate, think, do, interact, respond, and feel, and being able to adapt ourselves to replicate these. This will also extend into inferring and deducing from physical and vocal behaviour: how someone moves and interacts physically with others and their surroundings, as well as how their body language and vocal expression changes depending on what the situation is or how someone is feeling and testing how we might recreate this in and from ourselves.

Often, we will read character's underlying *thinking*, emotion or intention from physicality and vocal expression, subtext as well as text. Characters, as well as people, may not always do or say what they think, or may respond in ways that seem not to correlate fully to the text and it may not always be explicit why. They may carry internal conflicts and hidden doubts, they try to play roles, or unconsciously try to manipulate others and events; and it is up to the actor to discover, by their research, where this may be the case. Researching a character allows us to explore all those potential angles, and to justify what shapes the character's choices, what *makes sense* to them, rather than judge them as ourselves, and then to make this manifest in performance.

As explored in the previous chapter, much important information can be extracted from the text; however, the wealth of this information can vary. Many writers add characteristics, background information, mannerisms and other information within the script, stage directions, or even in notes attached to the script, whilst other writers hold back on such information, in which case we have to rely on our intuition and imagination in practice, especially in regard to fictional characters.

Similarly, at times you might be playing a real person (dead or alive) in which case the research will prioritise accessing available factual information regarding the person via books, films, documentaries, internet searches, and testimonies; and it will be more important to accurately depict this character according to the existing information and with the help of factual research, rather than mostly rely on imagination.

The deeper the research goes, the more *human* the performances can get. Character research needs to become practical: taking the knowledge we have acquired through the analytical means and using this to further explore, refine, and embody those choices. It is what sets apart the generalised and the nuanced performance, and which often leads to surprising or unique character revelations.

So, the key objectives for and skills we need to develop in our character research:

- Be able to define and shape the specific character from textual information and imaginative activity.
- Develop the capacity to think, feel, and imagine as that character.
- Evolve how the character moves and is physically embodied by our body.
- Operate in action and circumstance as the character behaves.
- Communicate the given words/dialogue as the character speaks through our voice.

Prep and Tools for the Job

- Your notes from the textual research from Chapter 3
- Your notebook (it can be useful to have a new one in which to consolidate all your work on a character for a specific play/scene study)
- A working space with routine objects (your bedroom is fine)
- Pens and paper

Into Practice – Exercises and Activities

Defining and Shaping the Character – Facts and Questions

Typically, we use question models as a starting point for defining a character – particular questions designed to focus in on the important aspects of mapping character in action and help you find active performance choices.

Konstantin Stanislavski highlighted six framing questions[3] which have in contemporary times been given the name 'the actor's questions'. These questions have been extended to ten questions, most recently by Dee Cannon,[4] and are – in some form – integral to many actors' processes used today. They encourage the actor's investigation by bringing together what is established by the text – the facts (Chapter 3) – and fusing this with what you still need to discover in order to find the most appropriate performance choices. This would involve asking questions about time and place (given circumstances), what has happened before (previous circumstances), the character's wants and needs (objective), the importance and possible consequences of the situation (stakes), and who the character is (biography).

In reading the scene/play text, we are also usually likely to have amassed a wealth of details and potential facts, as well as specific questions, many emerging from our personal engagement, which may contribute to detailing the framing questions and give us specific lines of enquiry.

Exercise: Character Frame of Reference

As when looking at your *self*, it is useful to create a frame of reference for your character, and to revisit the *opening the window on the world* exercise as a structure for you to use as you build the information needed to understand what has informed your character's perspective at the point of the start of the play (not what happens during it). By focusing on each heading as a question, you can begin to organise the notes and information you have identified from your close reading of the text and investigate the questions you still have.

In order to detail your character's *window* you will need to start from the script, since any decisions should be made with the text as the first port of call, and then be boosted through the use of the deductive imagination as needed. The questions presented in the previous chapter, *What do I do in the play?*, *What do I say about myself?*, *What do I say about others?*, and *What do others say about me?*, should provide you with the basis of your investigation, supplemented with what you jotted down from your time and space axes, close read of words and how these might suggest individual vocal habits (catchphrases, habitual idiomatic phrases or words) or speech production (accent, clarity, nervous laughs, running out of breath, stutters/stammers).

Using the window on the world as the structure, questions can then be split into tiers:

* Tier 1 – background and foundational information:
  Questions in this tier are of a more factual nature, and will relate to socio-economic status of a character, their background, place of birth, hobbies, age, employment, gender, race, and schooling.
* Tier 2 – character traits, nurture, and directions:
  Questions in this tier will relate to the character's identity, sexuality, beliefs, disabilities, health, likes, dislikes, aspirations, and education. This tier asks that the actor infers more personal decisions about the thoughts and desires of the character, ideas that will be based in the script but elaborated on by the actor's imagination and ability to engage with the character's world view.
* Tier 3 – choices and summative paths, emotional connections:
  Questions in this tier will combine the objective information of the first tier with the subjective research in the second tier and explore how certain situations have affected your character, what makes them feel certain emotions, their relationships, and their values.

If needed you can find various other question-based models from various practitioners (online and in books); however, it is useful to form your own questions that can adapt across a range of texts and processes, take you to specific information in the text, and provide you with an effective method for establishing key information for exploration and evolution of character.

The information and criteria[5] in the window on the world are a starting point for you to build a character biography, but they are not fixed and static. You may need to return to the frame of reference and revise aspects, since details come into greater clarity or gain greater significance in rehearsal.

Exercise: Character Biography

In forming your *biography* (or *backstory*) you will have to develop your answer to the question of 'Who am I?' This question forms the foundation for the character research and is also the question that requires the most elaborate answer.

Your biography will emerge from the information you have mapped out in the previous exercise and the other notes you have made. However, in this exercise make sure you are engaging with the character as 'I', rather focusing on info, because it will help you start to take ownership of the character's experiences, actions, and feelings (not just facts), which will also help you justify and join up the character's behaviour.

It is useful to think of this exercise in a narrative form, connecting the biographical details from their perspective at the start of the play, thinking about cause and effect, and allowing your imagination to really flesh out and join up the facts and details from the text to answer the questions. How has what you have experienced affected you? What seems to be most significant to you? What seem to be the strongest influences on you? Are there any specific experiences referred to in the text you need to absorb or explain within your biography? Do you have any specific behaviours revealed in the text that you need to root in your window on the world?

You may find that not all of your notes from the text or the frame of reference are equally important. In this exercise it's useful to begin to select the information that is most relevant and creatively useful. You may also need to take some time to explore the connections (how x might affect y, why you would feel or do that) so you can really build the idea of your/character's *remembering self*.

As a narrative form, this could be written or spoken, but in either form really pay attention to the words your character uses in the play and how they speak; aim to explore your *voice* as the character.

Of course, as understood, there will be additional factors which inform and shape this biography; given circumstances (in what era and location a character lives) as well as the previous may have an impact, not just through their own experiences, but also due to social norms and cultural impacts. So, again, this biography is a fluid and live document, that you may wish to revisit and amend over the course of your practical work on the character.

Life-Changing Events

If characters react or behave in extreme ways or encounter extreme events, it can be hard to find a reality that can give you a truthful root – or see the clear path from experience to behaviour. In most cases abnormal behaviour is justified by the character because they have a strong and coherent but distorted experience of reality and psychology, for example in the case of revenge, murder, and insanity. Where and how does the distorted view influence the truth and reality?

However, there are some experiences that everyone can have that have strong effects on personality and behaviour. They are events that can change personalities in unexpected, irrational ways, and yet don't lose truth because of it; some of those events could encompass the following:

- Trauma – shock, post-traumatic stress, violence
- Bereavement – death of significant others
- Other rites of passage – sexuality, parenthood, pregnancy, leaving home, divorce
- Physical injury and illness
- Mental breakdown/Mental illness
- Midlife crisis/identity crisis
- Revelation of shocking secrets/profound taboo breaking

Any of these can cause a personality to demonstrate 'out-of-character' behaviour, and since they are highly dramatic events, can often be found in drama, and therefore are a useful way of profiling a character.

Exercise: Responding to the Big Stuff

It can be useful to research not just the documentary details of these events (funeral legal arrangements, symptoms of psychosis) but also a range of other methods in which people have to express or communicate their responses to these events. Think about writing a letter to someone to break news of your bereavement, your eyewitness account of a violent event for a police statement, or your confession to a past *crime*. Again, pay attention to the voice and language of the characters. It can also be worth thinking about this as activities, such as packing up your stuff to leave a relationship, being interviewed for *your side of the story*. Even if the significant events happen in your backstory and not within the events of the scene/play, it can be helpful to give yourself an embodied memory of the moments which surround these; this can help fill in gaps and give substance to characteristics and tactics you want to use within the scenes.

Exploring Characteristics

Just like us, characters are often complex with several conflicting forces. Many characteristics or traits will be identified within your notes on scenes as how your character behaves during the scene and what they say. Some also emerge from biographical and frame-of-reference ideas; we learn to *be* from what we experience and its impact on us. Other characteristics may come out from rehearsals with your partner or decisions made about inner and outer obstacles in a scene – we often display different characteristics depending on our relationships and the situation we find ourselves in.[6]

We can differentiate between inner and outer characteristics – some will of course cross over – and often the characteristics we want others to see are outer characteristics, and those inside us that influence our reactions and emotions are inner characteristics. These can often be complete opposites of each other and create an inner obstacle for the character in presenting themselves a certain way, for example someone who might be insecure as an inner characteristic could overcompensate and want to come across as very confident – hence the inner and outer being contradictory. The inner characteristic will work against the outer and create a difficulty and a hurdle to overcome for the character in presenting themselves to others as confident – in turn giving the actor a possible inner obstacle.

Characteristics become visible depending on factors such as the given circumstances: Am I in a rush or in a high-stakes situation? Am I in a place I like or do not like? Am I with someone I like or dislike? Am I trying to impress? Do I feel at home? No one has all their characteristics on display at all times, it depends on who they are speaking to, what they are trying to do and their relationship to the other characters, the stakes, and the urgency of the need.

The objective, relations, and given circumstances will hugely affect which character traits will be on display in your scene, and it is important to understand that and avoid demonstrating (or *acting*) a characteristic. We instead make active performance choices based on our character traits; that is, we use tactics and actions (verbs) rather than trying to *be* a characteristic (an adjective). Equally we observe a situation through the filter of our character traits and respond to how we read the situation in terms of our personality, and the traits we *read* from others. For example, if one of my traits were *jealous*, I would not 'play jealous'; instead of *inquiring* about my partner's night out, I might *probe, interrogate*, or *blame/accuse*, and this might also be affected and provoked by them revealing themselves *unreliable* because they *distract* us, *dismiss* concerns, or *avoid*.

It is important to note that we cannot fix these characteristics (and tactics), and especially not until we have rehearsed and worked in the space with the other actors. Our tactics will be wholly influenced by their tactics; hence it is not something we can decide by ourselves. More about this work, as well as how characteristics can influence our tactics, will be explored in Chapter 5 which focuses on relationships.

Exercise: Exploring Different Characteristics

Pick a couple of potential characteristics from your notes on the scene and explore the scene from the perspective of those two qualities and then switch which characteristics you decide to focus on. You will come to a more substantial sense of what characteristics are most connected to the action and dialogue of the scene and can begin to distil your list into the most useful options. Experiment and explore and do not censor what comes out of the situation. You will start to see when inner qualities are in direct conflict with each other and when they are in sync, making it easier to establish inner obstacles and rich character portrayals.

PITFALL

Don't judge your character! For example, it is not helpful to think of yourself as 'a bitch' or 'an idiot'. Others may see you as that in the play; however, you need to justify all your behaviour at the time. We might look back at our actions and think we acted stupidly, but at the time it made sense to us to do so.

PITFALL

Do not try to inhabit too many characteristics at once. It can confuse you and the audience and can result in you trying to demonstrate to the audience, rather than responding in the moment with your partner.

Thinking in Character

Sculpting the character from the frame of reference, biography, and the textual characteristics keeps us really connected to the previous circumstances and qualities and the potential *remembering self* of the character. However, this only offers one angle on the character's thinking, and we need to be able to take that research into action as the *experiencing self*. The more we can explore opportunities to think spontaneously as the character, in the moment, whether within the scene/play or in experiences which may exist in the gaps around it, the greater our ability to respond with immediacy and nuance.

HANDY HINT

Try to imagine the character in situations not presented in the script. This will allow you to find new characteristics and create depth of character.

Exercise: Character Diary

It can be useful to create a character diary entry. This can be as long or as short as you feel is useful for you at the time. It can be an entry concerning one specific day and event of the play, or it can stretch over a period in your character's life; it can also be helpful to try to work out how the character spends a typical day. It is important to understand what has happened when the play starts and even more important to know what is happening during the parts of the play when the character is not on stage, because this will inform your previous circumstances in each scene. How you decide what to base the diary entry on is up to you and what is happening in rehearsals.

It can be appropriate to flesh out, from your character's perspective, the aftermath of an incident that is either acted out in the text or indeed mentioned in the text – if your character has been affected by it. The same goes for relationships and meetings. Make sure you choose things that do have an impact on your character during the story, or historical events that are still having an impact on your character. Character diary is a good way to justify actions and words spoken by your characters and can also aid subtext and inner monologue. If suitable for the actor or the character this journaling could also be spoken and recorded.

Exercise: Hot Seating

Hot seating is a very useful exercise for identifying and closing any gaps in your character and circumstantial research. This exercise can be done with minimum two people. In the exercise you can sit facing your colleague(s), or you can all sit in a circle, depending on how many take part. One character at a time will be questioned by the other(s) and the rest will not need to be 'in character'. The person questioned will communicate as their character, allowing for more time to develop mannerisms, vocal choices, and character traits.

Make sure your colleague(s) asks questions that are both related to the play but also things that might not be mentioned but that you would need to know. You will have thought of some of these questions; however, if you have not, try to stay in character and continue either by not answering it or by coming up with an answer on the spot. Later you can go back and think about that information and add or adjust it in your biography.

Exercise: Changes of Self

This exercise is based on Uta Hagen's practice[7] and allows the actor to explore different versions of the character's self:

> You will have three different telephone conversations with three other characters with whom your character has very different relationships. You

can make or receive the calls, and the information imparted can be the same to all three or different. For example, you can receive some news and pass it on to others, you can give each of the characters the same piece of information, or you can have three completely different conversations – it is up to you. Make sure the calls are around two to three minutes each.

Do not script the conversations – only the scenario, objectives, obstacles, etc. you can say different things every time you practice this; it is more important that it is spontaneous to fully grasp the versions of the character's self. Make sure you focus on hearing the other person responding and find the impulse to respond.

This exercise is very good for establishing the different aspects of the character and to pinpoint at which moments particular characteristics are on display. As already expressed, no one is the same with every person in their life, and your character will display different qualities depending on who they are with. It is useful to use relationships with other characters in the play or at least characters that are mentioned or referred to within the script. Use your character research to pick out which characteristics and relationships to focus on in each call and make sure what you want to achieve in each conversation. You can decide which questions to answer for each conversation – bearing in mind that the most important changes will be in the relationship, needs, obstacles, and stakes.

The telephone exercise is possible to do as yourself as well to get a sense of how you interact with others and how you display your different versions of yourself. For the character this might be similar or different, but it will stem from the information in the text.

Thinking About Objectives and Stakes

There are numerous ways to *deliver* a line, and this will completely depend on the intention behind the line and the objective in the scene, and this may also be shaped by their super objective. Any intention or objective will stem from the text and the greater wants and aspirations of the character. It will influence how we interact with someone else, hence will be fully tried and tested when you start to interact with other actors in the space.

Where do they want to get to, or what do they want to achieve in life? How and in what way is that present in this scene, or different in the next? The super objective is not, of course, always on their mind in every scene, but it may be embedded in their smaller wants; it drives them from within, even when they are not thinking about it.

You rarely encounter a scene in which nothing matters to anyone or which have very low stakes for those interacting. Drama is based on conflict and the presumption that the action matters to those interacting within it, making the exchange interesting and dramatic. It is useful to keep this in mind if you yourself do not find the situation meaningful or significant; you will try to find where that meaning lies for your character.

Ask yourself why the character is having this conversation right now. Why can it not wait until tomorrow? Next week? Next year? Have they been pushed into the conversation and have to respond? Have they initiated the interaction? Have they waited until it's impossible to wait any longer? Why do they need this to happen right now?

It can be helpful to frame the scene objectives this way:

I need to . . . (immediate need/scenic objective)
In order that . . . (future need/super objective)

It is important to understand how your character would act under pressure; this is also why it is useful to understand how you yourself act under pressure. What is high-stakes to you might not be high-stakes to your character and vice versa. In your character research you need to explore what high stakes are for your character – what matters and what is urgent for them, what kind of situations would have great would be seen as a high-stakes situation for your character.

One way would be by asking yourself:

What would I do if I found myself in a similar situation to the character?

And if the response is different from your character's, then:

What would have to happen for me to react in the way that my character reacts?

These are questions that will bring you to life and connect the character's predicaments with your own experiences, emotions, impulses, and intellect.[8]

Exercise: Inner Monologue

As an exercise it can be valuable to write out what you are thinking between lines, what you are thinking during someone else's lines, and what you are actually thinking when you say your lines.

Similarly, you can write out your objectives in a scene and why they change, and equally what the main changing points are in the scene. You can write this out like a monologue making you understand the character's opinion on what is happening in the scene and why they do what they do.

You can do the same with the objectives throughout the play/film/story. It will help you see the full journey – the through line – and the struggle and achievements of your character. It may also help you see the super objective more clearly as well as the obstacles – both inner and outer.

To help you build this inner monologue it can be helpful to explore the answers to these questions:

- How strong is the character's need? (Even in a high-stakes situation there are levels of importance and force in the actual need.)
- How far is your character willing to go to get what they want? (Will they stop at nothing? Will they harm or kill to get what they want?)

From Outer to Inner Obstacles

Outer obstacles can range from something physical blocking your way, such as a locked door, or another person providing the hurdle which you have to overcome. Outer obstacles can also come as physical or psychological impediments – both temporary and chronic – such as pain, sensory/physical conditions, neurodiverse abilities, intoxications, etc.

Inner obstacles are either psychological barriers to going after what you want, or things that influence the effectiveness of reaching your goal. They are often based in fear of something and can stem from the biographical past experiences or characteristics of a character, such as 'fear of being rejected' and 'shyness', or from aspects such as expected conventions or societal constructs like 'politeness' and 'social manners'.

Inner obstacles are internal matters, experiences, values, characteristics, and views that keep us from or hamper our attempts to get our objective. As opposed to outer obstacles, – which can be more easily defined through the text what is externally in the way for the character, inner obstacles are more dependent on your character research and being able to *think* as the character does. It might be useful to refer to Chapter 2 and think about how the character's fears or uncertainties might provide an obstacle through recognising self-protective behaviours.

In terms of the practical exploration of inner obstacles, they will be explored further in the Chapter 5, since the inner obstacles are integral to the choice of tactic in a relationship. Similarly, inner obstacles will change in importance as the urgency of a scene is growing; i.e. we forget about being polite if someone is in danger. Our tactics might change from enquiring to demanding, from nudging to pushing, etc.

Working for Character Physical and Vocal Choices

The other way we understand and view people is through visible and audible characteristics such as physical tensions, mannerisms, conditions, movement, and vocal expression. This requires the actor to develop the physical language of the character and make choices as to how the 'inner' characteristics influence the 'outer' personality traits and vice versa. It is also important to understand that the physical life of a character doesn't mean constant or exaggerated movement or vocal expression, it is just as prevalent in stillness, silence, and breathing and how we are connected to the rest of the body as our character thinks and acts.

This means we are able to consider movement and voice quality as capable of expressing something other than conscious verbal material and practical info, and we tend to carry a strong (if unconscious) awareness of what *normal* qualities look and sound like, meaning that when we see or hear something that is different, we are quick to notice and consider what the potential *meaning* of that difference is, often judgementally. It also means that we can have a precise (if flawed) sense of movement and voice and how that creates our sense of the *truthfulness* of action on stage in respect of realism, and how we can use this form to communicate elements of character. It is important to be critical of how much this sense of *truthfulness* is reductive when based solely on concepts of *normal* qualities; as these can lead to generalised, stereotypical, and inaccurate observations, which aren't helpful to the actor.

Habitual mannerisms (nail biting, hair twiddling, throat clearing, humming, place holding ums and ahs) as well as tensions held in part of the body (tense shoulders, upright back, crossed arms) or pitch and volume expressions (whispering, high pitch, reedy unsupported tone) helps us understand and read a person's inner state (nervous, aggressive, defensive, scared). Any of these typical norms of movement and vocality can be explored to create a detailed realistic character for performance. They can also be separated from the norm since they can be exaggerated or isolated to make them significant and encourage reading different layers of meaning into them.

Exercise: Character Observation

One practical activity you can start with is by observing somebody on the street or on video and paying specific attention (close-up focus) to their physicality. We have an acute capacity to read the body as a source in day-to-day existence, but much of the time we don't consciously analyse the physical information. However, we do as a species tend to operate with a strongly *normative* appraisal as to what a body is, does, or ought to do and what this *means*. It can be useful to use the following prompts consciously in order to pinpoint specifics to detail your practice; but also to recognise where there is a strong sense of *normal* and *appropriate* in your thinking (which will be worthy of further objective interrogation).

- How we position our bodies
- Our closeness to and the space between us and other people (proxemics), and how this changes (mirroring, intimacy, flirting)
- Our facial expressions and physical changes, such as flushing or tears
- Our eyes especially and how our eyes move and focus, meet others' eyes, etc.
- How we touch ourselves and others

- How our bodies connect with other non-bodily things, such as pens, cigarettes, spectacles, clothing, and chairs
- Our breathing, and other less noticeable physical effects, like our heartbeat and perspiration
- Our gestures and habits (literal or symbolic)
- Ease, range, direction, speed, energy of movement (or lack thereof)

After the observation we can try to recreate it, finding similar tensions, similar walks, habits, and intentions. Try to work backwards and create a biography for this person based on what you see in them physically. It will open up your eyes as to how important physical qualities can be for character creation and storytelling.

Similarly, listening to podcasts can also be a great way to look at aural observation in the same way; how you can hear breath, pitch, and tone, or what deductions you can make from how they say words, pause, and breathe. What connections can you make between what they are saying and how they are saying it? Can you recreate the vocality? Does the vocality suggest characteristics? (This podcast is worth checking out: https://themoth.org/podcast).

Textual Influences on Embodiment

Every physical and vocal choice we make as the character will be rooted in the scenic action and dialogue of the text, and will also reflect your detailing of character's experiences, their given circumstances and their objectives. Review your notes- what ideas emerge connected to physical or vocal character? How might characteristics be seen through vocal or physical choices? Does your character have a particular physical or vocal habit that is exposed in specific situations or during certain emotional states?

Previous and given circumstances and professions will influence a character's physicality and movement; someone who has been working in the field 13 hours a day for 25 years in 1780 will move differently than one that has a 9–5 desk job in 2022, in the same way as someone who has run through the woods before entering a scene will move and sound differently than someone who has just had a long hot bath. Our physical tension will be different relaxing in our bedroom, compared to visiting the in-laws or strangers. You may also encounter text-based projects where there are challenges to nominative embodiment as written (for example, casting cross gendered identities) and so your reading of a text may require more nuanced understanding of potential details than the literal.

Garments and Objects

Much of our physicality can be explored, revealed, or deduced by introducing garments and objects into your research. Without needing the full costume, simply adding some pieces of clothing that aren't just yours can assist with shifting into a character's *skin*. Clothes reflect how we present our bodies, and so if you need to find something different in terms of characteristics the sensation of wearing something different can be a simple way of moving further from the self. Period characters may need to explore physicality while wearing restrictive items (corsets). Even different shoes, hairstyles, and clothing may affect our whole posture or make us (as the self) feel exposed, and so part of the research is to become accustomed to inhabiting these.

Similarly, we may need to negotiate specific personal objects, which might affect our activity. Think about the capacity of objects to reveal character, circumstance, and priorities – where is your phone, or your purse? How often do you need to check your watch? Do you know where your cigarettes are? How hot is that mug of tea you have been given?

In looking at the text you may be able to identify specific objects you will have to integrate and form a psycho-physical relationship with, which may be significant in scenic action. It's good research to identify and work with these from the beginning of a process, so you can embody the familiarity with them that the character has.

Considering Physicality, Physical Qualities, and Physical Sources

In the same way as with characteristics, we are not always carrying the same tensions or physical tempo. Tensions and tempo can be dependent on the circumstance, the stakes, and whom you are with. Urgency and stakes will influence the rhythm and pace of a character, and this will change and fluctuate depending on where in the story you portray the character. Exploring different physical tensions or tempos can help with specificity in respect of how your character is affected by the moment and the events in the text. It will also help you begin the journey of transformation and open other avenues of physicality from your own physical traits and points of reference. None of these ideas and approaches presume all bodies are homogeneous; either as an actor, or in respect of a character; every human body reveals and expresses its experience on its own terms.

Remember that even if you make character decisions in terms of physicality, those will fluctuate and change depending on the situation; however, it is useful to find your character's 'neutral', or default rhythm and tension state and compare how they differ from yours.

For example, some people are naturally *laid back* with a slower inner tempo, but that doesn't mean that when something is urgent they will not have a much faster inner rhythm. However, it could take more for them to get to that place, and it will be out of character when they do act like that. Equally, someone with a very high inner or outer tempo can still find moments of relaxation and rest, but it might dissipate more quickly than others. In the way that obstacles can be inner and outer, rhythm can be different inside and outside the character. Just as with inner and outer characteristics, inner and outer tempos can work against each other, but can create the essence of the inner conflict of the character.

Physicality in performance isn't just based on the specificity of a body in action, it can also rely on a more abstracted, stylised, or collective movement expression. Movement can be functional (we reach for the remote, or leave the room), but it can also be shaped to explore profound emotional, internal, or aesthetic ideas. In creating this aspect of performance language, our research needs to be precise because we have such an intrinsic capacity to interpret the body in day-to-day terms. That is, if we need it to say or mean something different, we have to be specific as to how that particular physical *body language* communicates in this context.

The movement/physical map in the appendix provides some prompts to consider when appraising movement or physical sources in this mode.

There are many ways to research and practically explore the character's physical qualities and their changes in physicality as they interact with others and different situations. Laban's physical efforts can be explored as both physical character traits as well as tactics. Lecoq's tension states can provide you with a variety of options and discoveries, as can animal work and Viewpoints training, while making sure that all choices are based in the character research already done and come from within and the circumstance. (Suggested reading is listed at the end of the chapter.)

Exercise: Experimenting With Aural and Visual Stimuli

Sometimes it can help to explore a range of pieces of music/sound that connects with the character's potential moods, inner or outer tempo, or emotional state in the scene. Work through the scene as a physical journey, which can be outer activities and actions, or a more abstract sequence of what the inner feels like as expressed physicality. Do this against a range of pieces which vary in tempo, dynamic, and tone. What changes when the tempo is fast and staccato, or slow and languid, or syncopated and fragmented? Aim to find the dynamic changes within the scene, and how that affects your character's effort, tempo, and rhythm. As with obstacles, it can also be useful to consider what the inner tempo is compared to the outer. You might be frantic, but desperate not to seem worried.

Images can also be helpful stimuli in realising your character. These images can be literal of what you think the character looks like, or if you are looking at a classical character, it could be useful to visualise a modern equivalent.

Locating abstract images may also give you ideas and starting points for your character's inner thinking and imagery which can nuance your vocality (particularly useful with Shakespeare), as well as those which suggest a movement quality.

It can also be useful to think about researching literal images of aspects of your biography, such as homes, family members, and locations, even if you don't encounter them directly in the text, to give your character a visual memory.

Physical and Psychological Conditions

Physical conditions can range from a headache to physiological disabilities and anything between, both temporary and chronic, whereas psychological conditions encompass such aspects as mental illness or neurodivergent tendencies. If a condition is explicitly written into the script, make sure you understand the reason for it in terms of storytelling and the impacts it has on the scenic action and relationships, as well as the character psychologically and physically. This is particularly vital if you are asked to explore anything of which you have no direct lived experience; respectful, comprehensive, and factual research is an absolute imperative. You may also wish to query the appropriateness of manifesting conditions of protected characteristics with those who have lived experience.

Conditions may be permanent or short-lived, and impact inner and outer obstacles as well physical embodiment, sensation, and action. For example, when a character experiences pain, you will need to determine the kind of pain from the script. Be specific in where the pain is and what sort of pain it is – there are many types of aches and levels of pain. It is important to use the self and the self's pain threshold in order to connect to the particulars of pain – this does not mean that you have to have felt the exact same pain because the imagination will provide the stimulus in the same way as you connect to a new given circumstance.

In researching physical and psychological conditions, answering questions like these can help you get your research started:

- What does it feel like?
- How does it change how you move?
- How does it change your outlook on life?
- Does it change your thinking?
- Which other senses get affected?

Intoxications

Intoxication is a character's altered state due to alcohol or drug intake. Accurate research into the history of the drug and the usage, side effects physically and mentally, witness accounts, documentaries, books, and films that explore the impacts and realities should be the starting point. However, equally important is to understand *the reasons* the character is intoxicated. Is someone addicted or a routine heavy drinker, or have they just gotten drunk for the first time? Did they drink because they have lost a job or to calm their nerves before a date? What relationship does the character have with the alcohol/drugs?

Further, different types of drugs will result in different manifestations,[9] and there are different levels of intoxication and physical response; these may accumulate or dissipate over the course of the scenic action. Understanding and applying these will help you avoid routines and generalisations that will only point to stereotypes. Instead, focus on what mannerisms or hidden character qualities become more outward during pain or intoxication. Intoxication may loosen the boundaries of the inner characteristics that are already there, as well as exaggerate the outer characteristics or affect movement and voice, such as walking unsteadily, blurred vision, and slurred speech.

Exercise: List the Symptoms

List descriptive terms and sensory side-effects of one particular condition, such as a hangover or a stomach flu. Such a list might contain sensations such as *headache, nausea, dehydration, tiredness*, etc. Make it easier to connect to each one by being specific and descriptive: for example, *throbbing headache that gets worse as soon as you move, nausea that keeps getting worse as you move or smell food, dehydration that makes your mouth dry and makes you want to drink water which then makes you feel sick, tiredness that makes it an effort to sit up straight or walk around*, etc. When you start to practically explore those conditions it is advisable to question which is the predominant symptom at any one time. Trying to engage with too many symptoms at once can make it general, and you also run the risk of playing the action of the impediment, rather than the objective of the scene.

Exercise: Exaggerate the Characteristics

Play the scene emphasising the inner characteristics that become more noticeable as the character becomes intoxicated/pain increases, and which outer might become more exaggerated. Switch which ones you are working with and the levels of each to explore the states that are more useful for the text and the scenic action.

Finding the Character's Speech

Physicality (tension, their centre, pain, etc) will affect our voices, as will given circumstances, obstacles, and scenic action which might cause us to shift vocal actions in order to play specific tactics, but we also need to be precise in establishing how the character speaks.

Review your notes from the text exercises. Are there any specific details you can identify in the text you will need to absorb?

These might include: Suggestion of accent? Ease or hesitancy around certain kinds of words? Habits of expression? Really specific, obscure, or hard to articulate vocabulary? Identifiers such as age-related terms? Do they use jargon, or drop foreign language idioms into conversation? Can you confidently pronounce the words?

Research activity here needs to really focus on being able to inhabit the words of the character; it can be useful to listen to accents and practice them consistently, not just in rehearsal; explore the tempo of their conversation, and the connections between this and their physical activity.

HANDY HINT

Online sources such as https://howjsay.com/ can be useful for working out accurate pronunciation, and www.dialectsarchive.com/ is great for researching accents and dialects.

Going Towards Doing in Character Activities

It is important that, if your character has a specific activity within the play, you practice this activity on your own, especially if it is something that the character does often, and in particular if this is something you yourself are not well versed at. This will include any type of daily physical activity such as sewing, cooking, polishing shoes, and smoking, which might be habitual.

This may also include specialist activities such as playing an instrument, handling weapons, fighting, riding, and dancing. It is important to understand how well practiced your character is at these activities, in order for you as an actor to know how far you have to travel to get to that proficiency. In instances of some of the more advanced skills like weapons handling, horse riding, and fighting, you are likely to need professional expert training.

It is useful to consider that a great many activities we do are not done consciously, and we *do* other things while engaged in these – they slip back in our focus. The activities given within the scene can also be displacement ones, through which we can deduce further a character's thinking: HOW they are doing them might comfort them or reveal inner frustration.

Exercise: Everyday Activities

It can be a valuable character exercise to practice doing everyday activities and chores as your character. Applying characteristics, inner monologue, and physical choices to activities such as washing, ironing, tidying, or shopping will give you several ways to explore both the differences and similarities between you and your character. It will also give you a way to apply physicality choices to a specific activity.

You can vary this by applying the emotional inner circumstance of a scene – or an event from the biography – and consider how that emotional impulse changes the *doing*, or the stakes (for example 'angry ironing'). This can help fill gaps in your biography and keep you connected to being active in the action, rather than staying in your head.

Exercise: Character Destination

For this exercise you will need to decide on a moment that would have some significance for your character, either mentioned in or related to the action of the text or the previous circumstances. It would have to be a moment when your character is alone and preparing for something of importance, before they leave the space to a specific destination. You would have to come up with three activities that your character will do in the space – something they have to achieve – before they can leave for their destination.

The activities will have to be related to each other and follow the same objective, for example if you are getting ready to meet someone of importance, your three activities might be to *get dressed*, *do your hair*, and *pack a bag* before leaving the house. Or you might be expecting visitors and making sure things are set up to host friends or loved ones by *laying the table*, *hoovering*, and *tidying* papers and items away, before leaving the room to let them in. You will also have to set up the space in a way you believe your character's space would be set up and fill in the rest with your imagination.

The questions you will have to ask yourself will be similar to the questions you ask for each scene. Start with the questions concerning who you are, time and location, objectives, obstacles, and stakes, and if useful extend by adding questions regarding your present state of mind:

*   What is my present state of mind?
*   How do I perceive myself in this moment?
*   What am I wearing?

This exercise is based on Uta Hagen's physical destination[10] exercise, which predominately works with the actor's self, but can be equally useful to explore as character research.

PITFALL

Don't try to engage with too much information, and/or try to demonstrate all of your research simultaneously. Think quality not quantity, specific action not general slosh!

Filling the Gaps

The following exercises can serve to provide additional ways to explore character possibilities. Although they are all useful in terms of textual research, they also provide a basis for research in non-text-based and devised work.

HANDY HINT

If it isn't broken, don't fix it. If something is working, you don't need add things for the sake of demonstrating research. If there is a lack of information, fill the gaps to play the scene – not for the sake of filling the gaps.

Six-Sense Metaphor Breakdown

Play around with distilling an emotion into six separate similes or simple images that connect with all the senses – your eyes, ears, sense of smell, taste, skin, and physical activity. Be visceral but no need to be literal; this may not translate into dialogue or action, but it goes some way to looking at the response from a sensational perspective, not a sentimental one. Aim to write these as quickly as possible. They don't need to correlate with each other; also, allow for contradictions.

For example:

Humiliation

I see hundreds of eyes looking at me as though my clothes just fell off.
I hear cold voices laughing like breaking glass and my heart is loud in my ears.
I feel hot in the face and cold in my gut.
I smell salty, burning, ashy tears in my nose.
I taste sick in the back of my mouth.
My skin feels so tight I have to work hard to breathe.
I want to run but also dissolve, so I am just pinned like a dead butterfly in a display case.

Oppositional Experiments

Take one element from your character breakdown and explore it with an oppositional frame. What shifts if abandonment becomes liberation, aggressive becomes joyous, violent becomes seductive – or if all the metaphors become specific concrete actions? It can often be useful to consider that the angry rant of a parent is actually them expressing care and concern (you missed your curfew time and they have been worried sick about where you were). It can be useful to explore playing against the obvious function of an idea/action/emotion/moment in terms of finding a precise delineation of inner/outer connections, but also sometimes clarifications can come from identifying what something is not.

Portrait Work

Find portraits that capture aspects of your character – composite or single, inner aspects/characteristics, or external/visual elements. Print them out and pin them up. Consider how the portraits suggest characteristics, qualities, relationships, etc, and then see how these might connect to physical embodiment, tempo rhythm, Laban efforts, etc. as this emerges when you are working on them. Create a visualisation of the character separate to yourself, and then it can be easier to take steps towards the embodiment of them.

Objects in Space (See Object Map in the Appendix)

Find the things that your characters interact with, whether symbolic, literal, connotative; these can be as simple as a comfy sofa, or as specific as a beloved childhood toy. Make the relationship as three-dimensional as possible as early as possible. Play around with the story of the object; sometimes within devising processes the object itself can be the stimulus of a character or event. Who would own/live/throw away an object like this? Or how many different things can an object be? A bamboo cane can be a fence or an umbrella with a change of grip by the actor.

Emotion in Motion

Pay attention to deconstructing the physical experience of an inner emotion/idea – it's not fixed, and it changes. Try to anatomise tension location, posture, breath, and the physical contact the body has with others and the environment. Then explode what these might be in terms of the size and scale of physical action; how big and violent is this grief? It can be useful to intersect this with image work or audio work as partial prompts and accompaniments. This can help with really exploring stakes and the inner impulses that underline moments/scenes.

Into Reflection

All of this character research can contribute to the difference between a nuanced performance of a human being, and a general slosh of a stereotype, but it can be time consuming. Spend some time identifying what exercises or activities really gave you a click of insight, or allowed you to forge a mind-body connection with the text, BUT be mindful that some activities are *slow burns*, and will evolve over time within your research practice, not in one hasty go at an exercise. Even the exercises that have not added insight for you this time may prove invaluable on another occasion.

Any work with the text and the idea of character ultimately has to feed into rehearsal practice, so it can be useful in your reflective work to really consider how effectively you are reading and identifying textual material that shapes your character research, which you can apply in practical rehearsal – or whether you are spending hours studying, and still finding that this labour isn't paying off in the studio.

While all of the areas detailed in this chapter are important, MOST will not be fully realised or investigated on their own. Research into characters' relationships and given circumstances are intimately connected with the researching of character itself. Any or all of these exercises and ways into exploring may provoke EVEN MORE questions which will be more fully investigated in the activities of the following chapters.

HANDY HINT

Be prepared to throw away something if it doesn't work. Nothing is set in stone and ultimately you are there to serve the play.

Further Reading

- *In-Depth Acting* by Dee Cannon
- *Creating a Character* by Moni Yakim
- *The Actor's Guide to Creating a Character* by William Esper
- *The Stanislavski Toolkit* by Bella Merlin
- *The Power of the Actor* by Ivana Chubbuck
- *A Challenge for the Actor* by Uta Hagen
- *The Moving Body: Teaching Creative Theatre* by Jacques Lecoq
- *The Viewpoints Book* by Anne Bogart and Tina Landau
- *Laban for Actors and Dancers* by Jean Newlove

Notes

1 Quote taken from book, Esper, W. (2008) *The Actor's Art and Craft*, Anchor Books, New York City, page 100.
2 Generally, it is assumed that the character or personality of a human being is created by a mixture of nature (instinctive or hereditary qualities in the individual) and nurture (how that individual is treated or responded to, or what they have experienced), with often an intersection in the biological and chemical makeup of the body and mind.
3 Stanislavski, K. (2016) *An Actor's Work*, Routledge, London & New York, page 87.
4 Cannon, D. (2012) *In-Depth Acting*, Bloomsbury, London, page 46.
5 More in-depth questions on character can be found in Abbot, John (2012) *The Acting Book*, Nick Hern, London, page 86; Cannon, D. (2012) *In-Depth Acting*, page 140.
6 In Dee Cannon's book *In-Depth Acting*, she lists a helpful collection of characteristics on page 139.
7 The changes of self exercise is referred to in book, Hagen, U. (1991) *Challenge for the Actor*, Scribner, New York, page 161.
8 More about this type of work can be explored through Stanislavski's exercises on 'as if' and 'the magic if' referenced in his book, Stanislavski, K. (1989) *An Actor Prepares*, Theatre Arts, New York, page 59.
9 Ivana Chubbuck's book (2004) *The Power of the Actor* describes behaviour associated with several different types of drugs, and also gives the actor ways in which to portray such intoxications as well as different impediments, paralysations, pregnancy, etc., Gotham Books, New York.
10 This exercise is the first of the Object Exercises as described in Hagen, U. (1973) *Respect for Acting*, Scribner, New York, page 91.

Guy Stanley

5

CHARACTER INTO RELATIONSHIP – INVESTIGATING INTERACTION

Defining the Challenges and the Objectives

However meticulous your research into your own character is, ultimately all of your detail and discovery has to be interrogated and manifested through collaboration with others; how your character intersects with others (and the audience) within the script in order to tell the story, as well as how you as an actor work with your peers to refine and distil choices and actions which serve the direction of the ensemble interpretation, not just one person's singular character study.

In absolute terms, you as the actor playing a character need a relationship with the space, the setting, the situation, the objects around you, and even the clothing you wear, and these relationships are more fully explored in the following chapter looking at given circumstances. This chapter concentrates on the investigation required for the evolution of interpersonal relationships between *characters* on stage, as well as those for which there is no connected dialogue, but a relationship that is only manifested through staging in a shared space, or a shifting relationship with the audience directly.

The key challenges for the actor researching relationships in preparation for performance lie in the fact that relationships (as much as character or personality) are never fixed or static; they are intuited or interpreted through oblique or non-verbal signifiers (subtext!), never tangible or really concrete, and while nominal information in the script is vital (mother/child, lawyer/defendant, boss/employee), the drama is usually in the cumulative changes through a script, or conflicts and contradictions that exists within these.

As the actor you will need to research all your character's relationships mentioned in the text, even if you are not physically interacting with those other characters, or even if they don't appear on stage. Your relationship/history/feeling

DOI: 10.4324/9781003226130-6

towards those mentioned in the dialogue will inform your performance choices. This can also include relationships that you believe have influenced your character's view on themes and points of conversation in the script, and that you believe have contributed to making your character who they are now; even a one-time meeting can have a significant effect on the character, depending on the stakes of the situation.

Some relationships might only be mentioned in the text briefly; you may then have to use your imagination to evoke an image or visualisation of the person in your mind. The amount of information needed will be determined how much information you need as an actor to be affected by the memory of that person – or the relationship itself – in order to detail your expressive choices in playing the scenes directly in the text.

Our real-life relationships are usually pretty complex and they affect our selves – and so also our characters – emotionally, mentally, physically, and vocally; we talk too much about someone important to us, we might gush about someone we feel guilty that we dislike; fear or attraction might make us physically defensive or restive, a casual put-down from someone important might crush us. We reveal this even if we are not directly talking about the relationship, because the clues are often in how we are talking or acting. We adjust our characteristics, our personality, and our communication, actions, and tactics according to the person with whom we are interacting (as well as what we want from them), and our judgement of the appropriateness of these depending on the relationship.

As cultural groups (nations, regions, social groups, families) we often identify ourselves through the ways we verbally interact, and these can often be highly specific, while at the same time not being explicit about how those groups work. For example, we are often subconsciously aware of the 'rules' which govern interactions, but they are often ambiguous and difficult to explain to someone else, because they evolve and are often subject to change.

Relationships only exist in the interaction with another person, and as an actor it's vital to experiment and explore the dynamics of a relationship with the other actor. As noted in the introduction to this book, some of these exercises tread a fine line between research and rehearsal; however, it is important to understand that a relationship cannot manifest on stage purely through intellectual understanding and research, for the research must be indelibly practical in its methodology. Moreover, the practical research elements add another dimension of activities ensuring that the information gathered is channelled both from and into practical choices, allowing the *doing* to be a source of research in itself.

From the information you have collected, you can start to bring together ideas to explore in rehearsal practice: how physically intimate and close they are, if it is a connected relationship or if there is a conflict or misunderstanding, as well as when (if at all) these shift and change. Whilst you may be investigating a relationship between characters, the manifestation of this is through yourselves; and so however disturbing or vulnerable the textual relationship might be, it is of vital importance that this isn't achieved as a result of the same dynamic being replicated by the actors' interpersonal relationships in the studio.

So, the key objectives for and skills we need to develop in our relationship research:

- Be able to read/interpret and detail specific relationships from textual information and relevant factual data.
- Shape imaginative activity to flesh out potential subtext, stylistic impacts, and gaps.
- Develop the capacity to act, adapt/respond, and affect others effectively as the *character* in the context of any given (or inferred) textual relationships.
- Explore how the character interacts with all the other characters encountered through the scenic action.
- Communicate the detail of the textual relationships through coherent and nuanced vocal and physical choices.
- Evolve truthful interpersonal relationships between characters on stage based in safe, professional, and appropriate interaction with fellow actors.

Prep and Tools for the Job

- Your play text, and potentially clean copies of scenes to highlight
- Your notes from the textual research from Chapter 3
- Your notebook, but also some free sheets of paper (large sheets A3 work well for big ideas)
- Sticky notes such as Post-it®
- Access to online sources
- A working space and access to other actors!
- Pens and highlighters
- Intimacy/combat guidance, and agreed working practice and methods for evolving these aspects if needed

Into Practice – Exercises and Activities

Mapping the Relationship Network

Exercise: The Relationship Map

Starting with the text, but also referring to notes from Chapter 3, take a clean sheet of paper (big is often helpful) and using your character as a central point in the middle of the sheet, map out their relationships with everyone else in the play/text. It's often very useful to play around with how this represents on the page, so you evolve something visual that represents the significance to your character (not just how big the roles are), with sufficient space on the page for notes accordingly. For example, you may want to place higher-status characters at the top of the page. We advise starting with pencil, or better, using sticky notes for each other character so you can shift things around with greater ease! It can also be useful to do this exercise for each scene, especially if your character interacts with multiple characters, across complex action within scenes.

Here are some key things to identify:

- *Named/identified relationships* – Write down if they are your character's parent, child, sibling, boss, rival, lover, old school friend, etc; but also potential changes here, like the lover who is rejected, the enemy who becomes an ally
- *Encounters* – Describe encounters with your character: multiple/single, incidental (limited impact on story/character) or important (fundamental to story/character), scenic action, or referred past.
- *Status* – Are they dominant, inferior, inspirational, or constricting to your character?
- *Impact* – On a quick read, is the relationship with each of these positive or negative? Cherished or endured? Comfortable or difficult?
- *Shifts and changes* – Does the relationship clearly evolve or change? Are there discoveries within one encounter or there are multiple encounters? Note anything specific which shifts this; e.g. a confession of desire, a withdrawal of trust, a game-changing discovery. What is different between the first and subsequent meetings on stage? What has occurred off stage?
- *References* – Who else does the character refer to? Even if they don't meet in the scenic action, are there any suggestions as to why they mention that person?

It's important to view this as a live document, so keep it pencil- and sticky-note-based; your rehearsal process is likely to reveal additional info which may change your first read notes. This is not an exercise to map the whole play or a family tree (unless you are the director), and so you can absolutely keep the focus on your character; this is about detailing your character's relationships and giving you potential offers to play in your scenes. You can absolutely expect your director to contribute and shape these according to the overall vision, but if you are playing the butler who serves drinks to the lord three times in the same way throughout the text, aim to give yourself something specific to each moment, even if the impact on the whole is unremarkable.

It's also very likely that this exercise will throw up more questions and gaps to fill (e.g. 'Why does she say that to her mother at that point?'); this then gives you really specific questions to explore practically in rehearsal with the other actor. This exercise is not intended to provide a rigid framework from which you cannot deviate, but to pull out clear and specific lines of enquiry which may substantiate or be rejected altogether as you discover something different in practice.

Exercise: Unpacking the Named/Identified Relationship

Typically, the text and your mapping exercise will identify a given relationship – like siblings, parent-child, romantic partners, friends, work colleagues, boss – from either the playwright's character information or stage directions. But this structural relationship is general, not specific; any relationship needs to be characterised according to the specific text.

While you might be working on a two-hander piece and only have one explicit given relationship to explore, it's likely even within this there will be other relationships to consider (other people *referred* to in the scene). In larger-cast texts, you are likely to find that characters have multiple given relationships; for example, Hamlet is a son to both a mother and a father, stepson to a stepfather, good friend to Horatio (less so to Rosencrantz and Guildenstern), enemy to Laertes, lover (or not) to Ophelia, and Prince to the soldiers, gravedigger, etc.

We tend to carry solid and workable preconceptions about given relationships: what *mothers/brothers/friends* do or which actions and characteristics suggest somebody is a *good* mother/brother/friend; but in the context of dramatic texts, as much as in real life, the detail and interest is usually found in the behaviours and actions which contradict the expectations of the given relationship.

Assuming you have some info here (see the following if you do not), and that you have already identified some characteristics through your explorations in Chapter 4, on a clean sheet jot down the givens on the top of the page. For example, you might have (for Gertrude in Hamlet)

Mother   Wife   Widow   Queen

Looking back at your notes from Chapters 3 and 4 (characteristics, frame of reference, etc.) underneath each of these headings, note down the scenes in which this given relationship is at the forefront, and then start to detail out which characteristics, elements of scenic action, and frame-of-reference information seem to be revealed accordingly. It can be helpful to subdivide these columns into two – identifying which revealed characteristics appear to mesh well with the nominal AND those which contradict or oppose it. These may be judgements against expectations; a *good* or a *proper* husband/wife/child.

These will not always be literal or explicit and we don't stop having one relationship when we are interacting with another; but characters' different *selves* (see Chapter 2) might be in conflict – and it's often from this that the juicy detail in respect of actions and tactics emerge. The contradictions but also the qualitative judgements are usually good indicators of where objectives and connections can be found; why and how they engage with others.

In more contemporary texts you may also find that there are specific professional/social-role relationships as well as emotional/familial ones to play with (it turns out being queen is not a typical job role . . .). We carry similar expectations around these; for example, we might expect a lawyer to operate and relate to people differently than an actor, and they are likely to carry different kinds of status in different situations. An affluent sister dealing with a brother who has got stuck within the criminal justice system, a working-class parent having to negotiate authority on the part of a disabled child, a psychologist who is the recipient of a confession that should be formally reported even if their client does not want that to happen. These do not supersede the emotional relationships, but they may offer useful insight into the stakes and obstacles that impact your character, and potential tactics they employ to navigate these.

Some given relationships between characters within a text will require more factual research than others: a police officer will be expected to follow certain rules around relationship interaction, and similarly, doctors, psychologists, teachers, etc; indeed, there are many roles in which there are external, professional standards governing behaviour with others. It is not unusual to find drama that looks at characters who *transgress* in some way – they break those rules; and so knowing when a conversation shifts from the prescribed relationships into potentially dangerous territory is going to be vital as an actor. Similarly, while most of us will have an emotionally embodied understanding of *friendship* as a relationship to evolve; it also might be the case that there are specific relationships that need to be explored from a more evidenced factual investigation of lived experience; caring for someone ill or living with disability, experiencing violence, coercion, or abuse at the hands of another, or the specific interactions that are required by a particular situation such as dealing with the legal profession, class- or status-related codes of interaction.

It can be useful to build a factual understanding of what the professional/social role might imply in respect of expectations, codes of practice, or personality traits associated with these, even if the character doesn't explicitly participate in the scenic action in this role/relationship.

Here are some useful sources of information:

- Careers websites: These often detail specific jobs in the format of role descriptions and routine expected activity of interacting with others.
- Professional organisations: These often outline expected practices, behaviours, and interactions, and what is expected from members in how they engage in that role.
- Good old-fashioned 'people watching': Almost any situation can provide incredibly useful data in respect of relationships, whether this is looking at couples interacting in restaurants, or spending an hour in the park watching parents and children and the different dynamics and engagements you can observe (we suggest you use the reading physicality/movement map from the appendix).
- Support networks/organisations: These will often include personal lived-experience testimony of those dealing with specific challenges and the navigation of unexpected relationships and situations. While much of this may be

freely available online, any actor researching should NEVER enter into a live group online forum/chat platform without being explicit about their objectives in doing so, and ensuring that participants are comfortable with that.

Again, identifying the potential contradictions or conflicts with the expectations are the things to focus on; what about the relationship gets them to act *out of character*?

PITFALL

There is often a currency in the use of qualitative relationship terms – co-dependent, controlling, passive aggressive, *toxic* – which can feel truthful as an emotional starting point, but often lead to painting a relationship with rather broad and unchanging choices. It's valuable to use the givens to establish what our and the audience's expectations are, but to recognise early on that we will be most interested in the conflicts and contradictions, not the manifestation of stereotype.

Exercise: Unpacking Realistic Conversations

A dramatic text that is stylistically realistic/naturalistic fundamentally looks at revealing relationship info through conversational dialogue. Even when we explicitly engage with talking about a relationship as a topic of conversation, whatever our culture, we reveal relationships more indirectly through what we communicate, to whom, and how.

Using your notes from Chapter 3, keeping the idea that you have a mother and daughter: *How* do they speak *about* each other? What *words* do they use in talking about each other, but also *to* each other? How do they interact in conversation? Does that change through the scenic action?

From a textual perspective (i.e. what we might see written on the page) the following can be useful to look for as indications of how a character might *reveal* aspects of a relationship through what they are talking about, how, when, and to whom. It can be useful to work again from clean copies of the scenes and use highlighters to pick out different elements of the dialogue.

- Fluency/Ease – rants or hesitancy, pauses, place holders like 'er' or 'um', suggestions of speed, rhythm, and pace
- What's the volume or intensity of the conversation?
- Direct/Indirect – blunt or covert objectives and tactics, explicit manipulation, or seeming non sequiturs

- Salutations – names/titles/nicknames
- Grammar and sentence organisation – formality and clarity, typical structures; for example, jokes: When is it relaxed and when does it feel contrived? Does it feel spontaneous/impulse-driven, or as though the character is just following an expected script with constrained conviction?
- Vocabulary used – jargon, slang, dialect, complex/intellectual, practical/literal, swearing, *role*-based words (Doctor/Patient, Manager/Employee), taboos/crudity. What does the dialogue suggest about the relationships between the characters?
- Connotations and references – referring to previous shared experiences, patterns of word use, intimate shorthand words/idioms, cultural references
- Taking/responding to offers – answering or changing the subject, blocking, dismissing, ignoring. What provokes or triggers the next response, what are they reacting to? What do the characters *hear* – which might be different from what is *said*?
- Who is driving the conversation (topic, direction, subtext)?
- Sentence length and complexity – concision or circumlocution (brief and to the point or going round the houses, quick-fire or longer speeches?)
- Audience – Who is listening on stage/in the room (intentionally or by accident), who is paying attention, who the speech is aimed at? Who is responding? Are characters actually talking to each other?
- Clear segues and connections – *Naturalistic* conversation tends to be cumulative and purposefully joined, with participants listening and responding to each other, with identifiable and connected thoughts, and a discernible through line.
- Content and associated emotional stakes – Do characters seem to communicate in an *appropriate* way to express something (e.g. breaking bad/happy news, confessing secrets)? What is the apparent importance of the information? Is it new/exciting or repeated/old?
- Status, etiquette, and convention – conversation reflects *appropriate* manners, politeness, social expectations, deference/respect according to the nominals
- Acceptance/status in the group/relationships – older people using 'young' expressions, or vice versa, over-familiarity/over-sharing

It's important to realise here that many of the previous criteria, even if they are present, do not always lead to fixed and specific interpretations. We might respond randomly to a conversational offer because we are excited, nervous, irritated, or preoccupied; we might be blunt and direct with sensitive information because we are furious with someone, or profoundly uncertain about how best to deliver it, and so talk around a subject or make haphazard segues; sometimes innocent statements make us *see red* because it's the two-hundredth time we have heard it. You are likely to find that unpicking a scene in this way gives you a range of different lines of enquiry and no fixed answers; BUT it will allow you to identify the specifics of the text that will underpin the range of options that you try out in rehearsal – the *how and why do I say/do that* element of your process.

Exercise: Tackling Non-Conversational Dialogue

It's not uncommon to be working with texts in which nominal relationship information is non-existent, or the structure of the text isn't replicating conversational dialogue.

If you are working with a text in which you have limited or obscured information around character, identity, and situation, without conversational or prosaic dialogue to analyse, the text analysis work suggested through this and other chapters will still give you potential characteristics/ideas to research in this way, and to find potential intention and action in practice – although the questions may need to change or be augmented.

Vocabulary used will always be useful in order to identify emotions and characteristics, even if these are not immediately connected to an individual character identity in a specific situation. It can be useful to look at the text more technically, more perhaps as poetry or music, and find the underlying patterns which might suggest how the actors could be interacting.

Working with a clean copy of the text, use the highlighters to pick out the following:

- Indicators of change of speaker (i.e. writer uses dashes to indicate changes of speaker not character *name*)
- Topic or thought changes – new information or ideas, whether responses to something or arriving apparently randomly
- Trigger words –words which *seed* the introduction of new ideas/topics, have an impact on the subsequent text in the scene or that refer to earlier one (this can help with establishing potential through lines)
- Verbs/adverbs –words that underpin actions/doing/movement, and will help in finding tactics to investigate in practice
- Repetition and patterns – of words, phrases, ideas, or structures
- Structural changes – shifts between sentence length, punctuation use, spatial layout on the page
- Suggestions of dynamic, stress and tempo – i.e. capitals, italics, pauses
- Imagery – vivid, visceral, or sensuous images, and references these include (this can be useful to explore stakes)

This will usually generate quite a lot of haphazard notes and ideas rather than immediate coherent interpretations; however, it gives you clear ways to start to experiment in practice with the text. For example, you can work with scene partners and focus on stressing all of the verbs/adverbs and see how that begins to suggest what the potential action could be; or hitting all the points which trigger change of thought or dynamic to start sculpting a through line.

Exploring Actions and Tactics

Ideas for tactics are usually revealed by looking at the impacts on other people, or events, so review the notes you made in Chapter 3, because the tactics you choose for your character will be completely influenced by all the other research you have done up to this point, including work on the character's inner being. Choices are what make a character unique and what defines not just their relationships to the other characters, but also to themselves – the inner obstacles will have an effect on how your character goes about getting something they want.

The same is true for characteristics, as mentioned in Chapter 4; we do not necessarily *play* a characteristic, but we let the different characteristics influence our tactics and responses in the scenes.

Table 5.1 shows how you can use your investigations into characteristics and inner obstacles in determining a tactic or an action. The first section on the left illustrates how a characteristic might highlight certain tactics or limit the scope of tactics for this particular interrogation. The second section on the right presents how the same characteristics – coupled with an inner obstacle – could change the tactics further. It demonstrates how the foundational research may alter how you present a characteristic through doing, rather than 'showing'.

The tactics will have to be flexible (not fixed) until you come into the space with the other character, because that is where the relationships start to flourish, and you will explore the tactics fully – taking into account *what they are doing to you* in equal measure as to *what you are trying to do to them*. But you can have an idea based on how the scene plays out regarding what your character does to achieve their need.

By investigating the textual clues, you can start to form an understanding of how the line might be spoken and additionally what intention might be behind

TABLE 5.1 Connecting characteristics, obstacles, and tactics

Characteristic	Possible tactics	Characteristic	Inner obstacle	Possible tactics
Jealous	Attack Interrogate Blame	Jealous	Fear of losing partner	Probe Question Flirt
Aggressive	Threaten Push Lash out	Aggressive	Social etiquette	Challenge Patronize Mock
Childlike	Pester Razz up Exaggerate	Childlike	To be taken seriously	Provoke Excite Press
Realistic	Waken Warn Lecture	Realistic	Fear of upsetting people	Rationalise Manipulate Evade

the line. One can also discover tactics and intentions by process of elimination and deciphering what the line is *not* saying; sometimes narrowing down the choices can help you get on the right track.

Exercise: Stressing the Different Words

Mike Alfreds[1] uses an exercise in which you say the line repeatedly, stressing a different word each time. This gives you a remit in which to experiment and explore, but also to discover new possibilities and meaning in the text, which evolve from practical interaction, not just intellectual analysis.

Example:

> **Don't** look at me like that.
> Don't **look** at me like that.
> Don't look **at** me like that.
> Don't look at **me** like that.
> Don't look at me **like** that.
> Don't look at me like **that**.

Each way of saying the line presents a new subtext and tactic, and by relating it to the rest of the scene and the relationship on the whole, it will become clear which options are workable.

Although the tactics will be adjusted once you start interacting with a scene partner, this exercise can be good for keeping an open mind, not setting decisions in stone and understanding the different tactics that can come out of each way of saying the line. It could also be useful for lines and sentences in which you struggle to connect with the meaning or intention behind it, or when you are working with material that is opaque in terms of style or form and has no prescribed or suggested interactions on the page.

Basic Actions

Another good way of finding the character's actions/tactics might be to start by exploring a limited number of actions. Through his work with acting coach Kim Stanley, David Krasner pinpoints six basic actions[2]:

- to beg/plead with
- to accuse
- to celebrate
- to seduce
- to destroy
- to dominate

These are so-called 'umbrella actions', in that they are big actions that could encompass many smaller tactics and actions depending on how they are played. There are many ways to play a tactic or action, but these big actions have an even fuller scope of variations and could help you identify which tactic is the right one. All the six actions need another person to whom to direct the action. They are also often emotionally charged and bold, and when played sincerely will leave the actor vulnerable, infer meaning/intention, and add to relationship dynamic. The actions can also be played without words, as simply physical actions.

By using only six to start with, we can also eliminate the intellectual ways we try to establish our tactics/actions and find variety in a more practical and engaged way. One way of starting to find new tactics, from the six basic actions, is to play around with the variety of tactics within one basic action. At this point do not try to name them, but simply adjust the *way* that you use one of the actions. How can you accuse a different way? Try levels of intensity, volume, and physical expressivity.

For example, an accusation can be made differently in that it might be direct, a sudden attack, or a casual comment. Rudolf Laban evolved the idea of the action *efforts*, which recognised the different potential qualities of physical action; these can be useful to explore as a modifier of these actions. We might then consider the basic action *to accuse* with drives behind it, which might change the physicality of the playing of the action or the verb we select to specify that. We have worked an example through in Table 5.2; please note this is not meant to be a fixed analysis. You might find different connections between actions and efforts, and also identify different verbs.

You will see that there are many ways to play one of the actions. There might come a point at which a new word for what you are doing pops into your head – you can now start to jot those down – or you find you need more named tactics to do what you really want to do. This is fine, that is the intention of starting with a few: to find a need to use more, instead of being overwhelmed by the amount you could have used to start with.

TABLE 5.2 Connecting actions/tactics with Laban efforts

To Accuse	Laban Effort	Action Drives			Affinity
Condemn	**Punch**	Strong	Sudden	Direct	*Bound*
Challenge	**Slash**	Strong	Sudden	Indirect	*Free*
Check	**Dab**	Light	Sudden	Direct	*Bound*
Question	**Flick**	Light	Sudden	Indirect	*Free*
Interrogate	**Press**	Strong	Sustained	Direct	*Bound*
Investigate	**Wring**	Strong	Sustained	Indirect	*Bound*
Uncover	**Glide**	Light	Sustained	Direct	*Free*
Doubt	**Float**	Light	Sustained	Indirect	*Free*

PITFALL

Be wary of using tables, published lists, and analytical breakdowns as blueprints (including these!). These are starting points to help explore, not models that you should aspire to replicate or force your choices into. Find actions and tactics that connect to you as words in practice, not just fancy vocabulary. Any suggestions we make may work for us but they are not definitive!

HANDY HINT

If you need something other than one of the six actions, but cannot think of the word, you can combine basic actions, i.e. to accuse/dominate, to seduce/celebrate, to accuse/beg. All that matters is that it makes sense to you and that it offers something to the interaction with the partner.

Exercise: The Quiet Place

In this exercise, the partners can decide on a fictional surrounding that would require silence or would make it very difficult to have the conversation in any other way than whispered; for example, during a religious service, on a packed train, during a party, in the audience during a play, etc. The actors will then perform the script as if they were in that circumstance, incorporating the obstacle of the surroundings into the interaction.

Due to the lack of vocal expressivity, the tactics can change dramatically and so will the intimacy aspect of the scene. The subject and language used will also become highlighted, since it is shared in a public place. Intensity and highs and lows of the scene, and the subtext and strength of objective, can also be discovered in this exercise, as well as aid the actors in using every word written.

HANDY HINT

Write your tactics in pencil and be prepared to erase and replace as rehearsals start. As with many of the research elements, these need to be seen as fluid and adjustable suggestions, not set in stone or overriding what is happening in the moment with your partner.

PITFALL

We often find some actions/tactics easier than others and they will become our 'go-to' or 'default' actions. It is important to practice and work with the other actions/tactics repeatedly so that your range of actions increases, since the character's default or go-to actions might not be the same as yours.

Exploring Status and Games

In all interactions we encounter the idea of *status*. Status can be distinguished as social or interactional. For example, social status can be determined by someone having a higher position than someone else; for example the headmaster having higher status than the teacher, or the surgeon having higher status than the nurse – within their professional environment – because society has granted that status in that environment. Social status is more straightforward to determine through text analytic research into the characters in the scene. Interactional status on the other hand determines the control or power between people in a situation, not relating to their social status – something that might require more nuanced and practical exploration by the actors involved.[3]

Status is determined by actions, especially in terms of interpersonal status, and needs to be given or taken away by others because without others, status does not exist. We can demand status, but the very act of that means we do not have it. Equally, by relinquishing control to someone else and making it clear that they have your consent to do what they please, your status can rise. Status is therefore very fluid and can be flexible and movable throughout a scene. Relationships can also be seen as mutually agreed status games, which both partners understand and play their part in. The same goes for romantic, familial, and professional relationships. Including games of this nature in the rehearsal process will also often result in actors becoming increasingly observant of each other, since every move, intonation, and eye movement become part of the game-play – and the external concentration in itself will evoke impulsive and spontaneous actions.[4]

Exercise: Status Shifts

Run your scene several times, each time changing who has the higher status in the interaction. Make a note of where the scene flows and where it stagnates and loses relevance; use these notes to understand where the status might shift in the scene (if at all), where status is freely given, and where it is contested. Even if the scene reads one-sided in terms of status, challenging this notion can provide the scene with nuances and new perspectives, and allow for new choices and tactics to be explored. This exercise is also useful for non-linear or non-traditional dialogue exchanges, since it creates a foundation from which to explore relationship dynamics.

Exercise: Follow the Leader

In this exercise the leader will start to move around the space with the intention of getting away or not listening to the follower, whilst the follower will be trying to get the leader's attention. The whole time the script will be performed between the partners in this follow-lead circumstance, and once the whole script has been performed the actors will switch who the leader is and repeat the exercise.

Once both ways have been done the partners can discuss where the leading felt accurate and what tactics came out of that particular intention, but also where it felt wrong to either lead or follow and – as in the status shift exercise – where it perhaps lost a sense of what was happening. Once you have noted the findings, the partners will again perform the exercise; however this time the leading and following can switch at any moment as the characters see fit. If the leader decides to follow, the follower will have to start to lead and vice versa.

This exercise helps the actors explore status, dominance, and powerplay. Does it fluctuate throughout the scene? Does it have one clear change or does it stay the same throughout the whole interaction? By pinpointing these, the exercise helps the understanding of changes and gearshifts in the scene, presents new ways to read or interpret the scene, and underpins the objectives and when they might change.

Taking it Further

This exercise can also be done as a 'game of tag', which could allow the gameplay dynamics within a relationship to be brought to the forefront.

HANDY HINT

Note that the places where it feels *wrong* to do something one way can often give you the most information.

PITFALL

Avoid making decisions about status on your own. As stated earlier these elements are relative and only work in conjunction with the other person(s). If they are not on the same page, decisions like these could be problematic.

Living Research *Through Observation*

Relationships are established on the behaviour displayed within the interaction of people, and tactics, as per the earlier exercises, can help provide subtext to the textual interaction through the use of nonverbal communication.[5] We pay significantly more interest to someone's behaviour and intention than their actual words, for, as it is famously expressed, 'Actions speak louder than words'. Someone's behaviour often directly affects us emotionally, which in turn becomes the instigator of our next action/tactic, as well as determines our relationship and connection.

Observation of the other characters is thus instrumental in finding ways to communicate with each other on stage, because how you interpret someone else's behaviour in a certain situation influences your performance choices. The following exercises have been adapted from and based on Sanford Meisner's approach, which hones the actor's listening skills and ensures that attention is placed on the other rather than ourselves. The exercises are based in the text, but still require the actor to observe (*read*) their partner's behaviour in the moment and integrate character research into the present interaction. These exercises are practical acts of research that can help establish relationship, history, tactics, and subtext in an interactive way.

Exercise: Reading the Offer

The actors are facing each other on chairs with script in hand. The actor with the first line will pick out the first thought (does not have to be a full line, but rather the thought), look up, and deliver it to their partner with the intention that the textual research has provided.

The other actor will then observe out loud their partner's behaviour in delivering the thought. This could range from physical behaviour ('You looked me up and down'), emotional behaviour ('You are angry'), their tactics ('You are attacking me'), or even subtext or objective ('You want me to leave').

The partner will listen to the observation but will not respond to this but rather carry on with the next thought, or if the line has finished, the next actor will do the same with their line.

Example:

ACTOR ONE: (scripted line) 'Where were you?'
ACTOR TWO: (reading the other) 'You look concerned.'
ACTOR TWO: (scripted line) 'Out.'
ACTOR ONE: (reading the other) 'You just shrugged as if you didn't care. You're not meeting my eye contact.'
ACTOR ONE: (scripted line) 'Where?'
ACTOR TWO: (reading the other) 'You're accusing me.'

After doing this with the full script, make sure you make notes about discoveries and discuss with your partner. This exercise is particularly good for understanding relationship dynamic and avoiding set ways of responding, due to having to really pay attention to what your partner is giving you. Further, it helps develop the actor's ability to affect the other actor with their chosen tactics and understand when the chosen tactic is not coming through, as well as find the thought changes and when you may play several different tactics in one line due to those thought changes.

HANDY HINT

Make sure you are both looking at each other when a thought/line is spoken – avoid eyes on the script. Speed is not the goal here, detail is.

Exercise: Finding the Reaction

As in the previous exercise, the actors are sitting facing each other in the same way, delivering each thought to each other with intention. However, instead of the other actor voicing their observation of their partner, they will instead repeat the thought/line back to them – with their own opinion on what has been said. Then the text will move on to the next thought whether it be actor one again or shift to actor two (try to change the 'I' to a 'you' within the line to still make it true to the text).

Example:

ACTOR ONE: (scripted line) 'Where were you?'
ACTOR TWO: (repeated with opinion) 'Where was I?' (scripted line) 'Out.'
ACTOR ONE: (repeated with opinion) 'Out?' (scripted line) 'Where?'
ACTOR TWO: (repeated with opinion) 'Where?' (scripted line) 'Just out thinking.'
ACTOR ONE: (repeated with opinion) 'Just out thinking?' (scripted line) 'It's late.'

Make sure the repeated line is infused with the opinion of your character, not just an imitation of how the first actor said it. This exercise is particularly useful to identify responses and impulsive reactions in your character and understanding how the next tactic is a reaction to the other actor's actions/behaviour and words.

HANDY HINT

Make sure the lines are split up into thoughts because we will have many different reactions during a longer line, and it is useful for the other actor to really hear everything that is being said and be given a chance to process each piece of new information.

Taking it Further

As an add-on to this exercise, once you are aware of the different thoughts, under-line/highlight the *trigger thought* – whatever your partner says that causes you to say your next line, or ignites your reaction. This could range from one word to a whole sentence. Once you have established this you can play the scene incorporating those words (repeating them) as part of your own line (this is different to the previous exercise in which you repeat the whole line before your own; here you only repeat what it is in that line that you are actually responding to). Apart from helping you understand what ignites the responses, and keeping the interaction fresh, this exercise will also help you identify the moments when the response is not coming from the immediately preceding line. The investigation will then begin as to why you say what you say, which could include one or more of the following:

- Responding to behaviour rather than words
- Not hearing the line – accidentally or deliberately
- Choosing not to answer
- Changing the tactic
- Responding to an image or memory
- Responding to an earlier offer/line

Once you have found those moments, research can go into why you say those lines and whether you need something from your partner to help that response.

Exercise: Reading the Reaction

This exercise follows the previous exercise with the same premise of actor one delivering their line/thought and actor two hearing the thought and repeating it with their opinion on it. However, here after actor two has repeated actor one's line with their own opinion, actor one will now observe their partner's behaviour during their reaction – what they did when they repeated the line.

Example:

ACTOR ONE: (scripted line) 'Where were you?'
ACTOR TWO: (repeated with opinion) 'Where was I?'
ACTOR ONE: (reading the other) 'You looked at me like you were really fed up.'
ACTOR TWO: (scripted line) 'Out.'
ACTOR ONE: (repeated with opinion) 'Out?'
ACTOR TWO: (reading the other) 'You are staring at me.'

Again, make sure you do this with the whole scene and take notes of and discuss your discoveries. This exercise also helps us understand the emotional effect the partners have on each other, the dynamics in the relationship, and how they read/misread each other's intentions.

Taking it Further

These exercises work very well in pairs but can also be extended to include scenes with several actors. In those instances, actor one will say their line/thought and all the other actors will read actor one's behaviour (exercise one), repeat actor one's line with their opinion (exercise two), and in the last exercise actor one will interpret each and every response.

PITFALL

It is easy to disconnect from the circumstance when reading the other person, rather than observing them *as your character in the given circumstance*. You will get the most out of the exercise if you stay in character when you observe their reaction; it will easily feed into your next line, rather than creating a pause which requires you to find the moment anew.

Exercise: Working the Lines

In this exercise the actors will stand up facing each other with scripts in hand. Again they will deliver their lines to each other thought by thought., After each thought the other actor will repeat the thought back to them (with their own opinion on it), but instead of moving on, the thought will continue to be repeated between the partners, constantly responding to the other, but also allowing a certain amount of playfulness in the lines, making sure they have included several ways to play each thought before moving on to the next.

This exercise will allow for exploration of tactics, a sense of presence and freshness, and avoid the text being set in one way. It can open many avenues for the actors to go down and give the actors a bigger set of circumstances to explore depending on the subtext that comes out of the repetitions. It will also give the actors a sense of history, because one conversation will allow for several conversations that the partners might have had, replacing other kinds of improvisation without the need to move away from the text.

Taking it Further

You can also include observations of behaviour into the repeated dialogue, as in the following example:

ACTOR ONE: (scripted line) 'It's half one in the morning. Where did you go?'
ACTOR TWO: (repeated with opinion) 'It's half one in the morning. Where did I go?'
ACTOR ONE: (reading the other) 'You're smiling.'

ACTOR TWO: (repeated with opinion) 'I'm smiling.'
ACTOR ONE: (reading the other) 'You don't care.'
ACTOR TWO: (scripted line) 'Nowhere.'
ACTOR ONE: (repeated with opinion) 'Nowhere?!'

The exercise ensures that the responses come out of the dialogue and not something you planned. It can also act as research for the stakes of the scene – understanding what could be lost or gained by not getting the objective. It can also act as improvisations research, going down routes that the character might not want – hence justifying the tactics in the scene, giving the actor a glimpse and physical memory of what they do not want to happen.

HANDY HINT

The example does not indicate a specific structure, or how many times a line or observation should or could be repeated, it is just an example of how the exercise works. However, if you are losing track of the situation or objective, make sure you go back to the text sooner rather than later, because the text will act as a road map ensuring you stay on track.

PITFALL

Do not differentiate in the energy that you use with scripted lines and obser-vational lines. They should all flow as part of the conversation.

Taking it Further

Any of the foregoing exercises could be explored sitting on the floor in a back-to-back position, allowing the behaviour to be observed through physical and aural sensations like tensions, temperature, movement, sounds, tone, breath, and even silences. When we communicate, the *way* someone says something carries a lot of information. When we focus only on the visual perception, auditory perceptions can sometimes be ignored since the visual can be so powerful and detract from our other senses. By placing attention on someone's tone of voice and vocal intention we can create a fuller evaluation of the inner life and inten-tion. Similarly, if the scene is intimate, or uses physical touch, allowing those senses to be awakened through a physical connection can help the discoveries of the character's sensation/reception of the other person.

Investigating Vocal and Physical Relationships in Context

Close relationships are often visible due to how they are vocally and physically manifested; and this might also be affected by the context. Think about when your drunk friend starts saying stuff loudly in the pub that you are embarrassed by, or how you feel when you misjudge how much information your boss wants to hear (or to tell you!). We continually adapt our vocal and physical choices in order to follow our intentions and to achieve what we want from a situation; the same then is true of how characters might interact in performance.

Much of the time, the physical and vocal choices are the expressions of the subtext. Nominally we should be relaxed and at ease in an intimate relationship, but if we are not, then we can begin to seed that the apparently intimate relationship is less benign. Similarly, if we are close and intimate with a character, we don't need to constantly signpost this; if romantic partners constantly hold hands and touch we are more likely to view this as too demonstrative and obvious. Habitual relationships often downplay the signifiers. We can be casual when we don't need to explicitly signal the relationship, and much of the time familiar understanding supersedes social or cultural mores. Core to the actor's research here is to reconcile information that may context the evidenced position (nineteenth-century women generally had lower social and political status compared to men) with the textual specifics (Hedda Gabler manipulates others by exploiting her status indirectly).

Appraising Vocal and Physical Options

It's possible that the playwright (or the publisher) provides some qualitative information here – the stage directions that tell you *how* a character delivers a line which suggests their opinion on it. However, these are rarely fixed blueprints; *angrily* requires more detailing as a choice in performance. Start from your own text analysis, but allow this to be augmented by live discoveries in the rehearsal studio.

Here are some vocal aspects to investigate:

* *Volume and energy* – in respect of proximity and location, as well as content. There are expectations we have about *normative* levels. What happens if these are played around with? Secrets should be whispered, anger should be loud, etc
* *Intonation and inflection* – rising/falling tone. Inflection can often be an indicator of emotional connection. We expect more colour and polarity when we are profoundly emotionally engaged. What is the impact of flattening this, constraining the expression?
* *Adjustments in respect of the given circumstances* – who is there to hear us, where we are; questions of privacy, or social etiquette; and status-related adjustments. We don't want to lose face when we are in public; we don't want to reveal our weaknesses when there are external observers.

- *Accuracy of pronunciation* – including stresses, rhythm, as well as vowel/consonant sounds. Are we using the *right words* in the *right way*? How do we change these according to the person to whom we are speaking?
- *Objective or intention* – We all can adopt *phone* voices, we get direct and sustained when making a complaint, we select different words confidently or not when we are certain of our ground or whom we are talking to.

Here are some physical aspects to investigate:

- *Proxemics* – How close do people place themselves to each other? Proximity might suggest intimacy, but it might be an attempt to threaten or seduce, a failure to read social codes/given circumstances, or an accident. What questions of proximity support the scenic action?
- *Gestures* – Some may reinforce speech acts (nodding in agreement), some may be declarative (you hold the hand of your lover), some may reflect status (you wave away the servant/employee), some may be impulse-driven (you reach out to comfort someone in distress).
- *Movement* – We might move to get/achieve/obtain something, avoid something, attack something, or to occupy ourselves, or we might stay still for any of the previous.
- *Posture/tension* – We might expect that we are tense and held under pressure, relaxed when at ease.
- *Spectators* – Who is watching and how does that affect the physical choices? This includes both audience within the scenic action and the actual audience.
- *Directionality* – Where physically is the action *landing* on the other person? Is it focused or indirect? This might be useful to consider in thinking about aiming actions at specific body areas (e.g. the emotional punch to the gut, the appeal to logic to the head) but also detailing how eye contact is made.

Negotiating Physical Challenges: Intimacy, Combat, Possible Danger

The intention and impulse to hurt, defend, etc has to be found, but we must not actually harm anyone. The same goes for intimacy; it is the need and the dynamic that is required, without physically going further than is comfortable and needed.

In the practical rehearsal environment, as actors you should expect that specific requirements for stage violence/combat and intimacy (sexual or otherwise) are explored under the guidance of a combat or intimacy director who will also be responsible for researching the accuracy of the physical engagement as well as the safe evolution of the actions required to manifest it.

However, locating the impulse and the intention for the character is the job of the actor, and is likely to require some research, particularly if the action is at an extreme level that most people do not habitually experience.

First and foremost, the research for moments of intimacy or physical violence require explicit investigation with the other participants as to how BOTH parties wish to discuss and explore this aspect of the relationship. This is non-negotiable in any context, and any relationship-based exercise which relies on some information being withheld from one party (actor in real life, not character) for alleged reasons of wanting *raw, honest, spontaneous* reactions is NOT ACCEPTABLE.

Exercise: Object Substitution

The impulse to hurt or to lash out can be hard to connect to physically. Everything about our upbringing generally trains us to restrain these desires. If you are exploring this within a relationship, experiment with objects such as cushions, pillows, or boxing bags, and allow yourself to secure the intention without fear of harming someone else.

Similarly, if you need to investigate impulses of romantic or sexual nature, find an object or an activity that is straightforwardly sensuous when you interact with it; for example, silken or velvet fabric, soft fur textures, gorgeous chocolates/foodstuffs that you can savour. Intimate, sensual touch does not require personal sexual substitutes or display. The research is to find a connection to language and impulse-led intention here that works for the character, relationship, and scene.

Dynamics and Tempo

Explore different dynamics for acts of violence; refer to the Laban efforts for ideas here. The scale, direction, and speed are all worth investigating in order to research, interrogate, and connect the action. Is it small, specific, and targeted (knowing where to hit someone where it hurts) or huge, uncontrolled, and unfocused (not caring who is on the receiving end). Using the text work you have done in respect of finding provocations or triggers, explore pinpointing what initiates the intention; is it a shocking explosion, or a slow, cumulative burn which escalates though a scene?

The same approach can be applied to intimate action, as it is outlined in the text. Some intimacy coordinators use animal mating references in order to investigate the potential qualities of an intimate encounter, and the characters who are participating; is the encounter frenzied, passionate, clumsy, overwhelming for one party, or perhaps slow, tentative, tender, and mutual? This can be extremely useful to separate your own self from the experience, and then consider the choreography of intimacy as something which is constructed from textual evidence and connected to the scene and story – not personal exposure or driven by your own sexual identity.

Exercise: Finding Specifics and Suggestions

The imagination can often supply more vivid details than explicit violence, nudity, and sexual behaviour. If the impulse and intention are connected and specific to the participants, then the smallest physical interactions can be loaded with menace or seduction. If both participants are comfortable, then it can be very useful to focus on NON-SEXUAL physical interactions to explore details: for example, using the hands as the only body parts which connect and are touched, and the range of ways they can be interacted with and how tentativeness can evolve into confidence. Similarly, hair brushing, facial or shoulder massage, eye contact exercises as well as using objects as proxies can help evolve ideas for direct physical encounters.

In the 1993 film of *The Age of Innocence* (Scorsese), the climax of one particular relationship is manifested through one actor removing the glove of an another and kissing her wrist. While the nineteenth-century world in which the characters exist clearly provides specific constraints, the moment works because the actors can so clearly imbue this innocuous action with an immense erotic charge and intention.

PITFALL

A character may be uninhibited, violent, explicit, and forward in ways that you are not. This does not, in any situation, require you to explore that behaviour personally in order to act it. Your research should be focused on taking you to the intention and impulse imaginatively, and not through actual experience.

Filling the Gaps

Improvisations Within Script

These exercises are designed to identify gaps in research, explore objectives, and highlight character impulses and responses. The number of characters that can take part is only dependent on the number of characters in the scene, but as a rule, only use one specific question per exercise and make sure all actors ask the questions several times during the scene.

In each of these exercises the scene will run as scripted; however, at any point one of the actors can intercept by asking the other/another character these questions:

1   'What do you mean?' (This question will highlight subtext, relationship, background, inner monologue, and previous circumstances.)
2   'Why do you say that?' (This question will particularly home in on the character's responses and instincts, scene objectives, and super objectives as well as tactics, but can also find elements in previous circumstance that needs exploration.)
3   'What do you want?' (This question will help pinpoint units and unit objectives within the script and the moments they change.)

The actor will then have to, staying in character and the moment of the scene, answer these questions until the actor asking the question is satisfied with the answer and responds with their next line.

HANDY HINT

Try to ask the questions following lines after which it makes sense to ask them.

PITFALL

Try to avoid simply repeating the line, or repeating it in a different way, but really answer the question in your own words.

Building Embodied Relationship History

If you have identified characters with a relationship of some duration, it can be very useful to find embodied memories of the relationship prior to the action of the text; or around scenes as they occur in the action – previous circumstances or indeed *backstory* to the relationship, as distinct from the work you would do here in respect of the character as an individual.

If you look back over the mapping scenic action exercise you should have notes about what events/discoveries have to have occurred within the course of the text, and the frame of reference exercise and character biography may also bring up useful ideas for identifying potentially significant moments to investigate.

Primarily these moments should be explored as character relationship improvisations, allowing both/all actors to participate and explore their insights into the action and live experience of those moments.

Here are some improvisations to explore:

- Detailing shared memories or events that are referred to in the text, such as the row that means they haven't spoken for two years
- Exploring moments that must have happened even if they are not mentioned, e.g. when the couple met
- Identifying tangible details, for example if the characters have shared places, spaces, or objects, establish these together; picture of the childhood bedroom, visiting locations they went to, etc, to evolve an image album for the relationship (it can be useful to allow each individual character to do this, so the memories are specific and personal, as long as key information is consistent)
- Performing shared activity to establish physical ease and closeness: it can be useful to physically do an activity together in character – even if this isn't dramatically constructed or verbal – such as tidying up a small shared space, preparing a meal, etc (explore what it means to physically navigate together, without the activity requiring emotional context or significance)
- Practicing variations of hotseat-exercises using the previous questions as a model, changing the questioner, the tense and interrogating each other after the improvisations (it can be useful to explore having a neutral questioner as well as the other party in the relationship, because this then can offer different insights as far as impulse and intention are concerned)
- Playing 'Mr and Mrs' – This isn't confined just to romantic couples, but can be used to explore interpersonal dynamics in any context (lists of suggested questions are readily available on line). While the questions themselves are unlikely to provide substantial answers in respect of playing the scenes, they will ask you to consider the relationship in non-linear ways, and consider different ways of engaging. This can be particularly useful later in the process, because it can make sure you don't get stuck in single dynamics of playing the relationship.

Any of these can assist with offering different shifts and nuances for each character internally; people often have very different recollections of events in real life. Something completely innocuous for one person might be significant and impactful for another. Any work you can do outside the rehearsal of the scenic action can deepen and specify the relationship, and keep it alive in rehearsal for performance.

HANDY HINT

Don't overcomplicate the work off the script; use the questions that emerge from your text analysis and practical work in rehearsal to drive these. They are suggested in order to detail the choices for the play itself and don't need to be perfected – these are RESEARCH activities, not rehearsal. If they don't work, or offer anything useful, move on.

Constructing Relationships

If you are working on a text in which the evolution of inferred character/presence and relationship has had to come entirely from work in the studio, and not from the text itself, you are likely to find that conventional routes into *backstory* provide less insight and useful information.

Assuming that the work in this chapter has allowed you to develop some connection between the embodied presences/the voices of this text, you have established when the speaker changes, and potential intentions and actions for the lines of text; however, there are still creative elements to continue to research in order to keep the interactions live in the moment.

Here are some suggested activities:

- Imposed relationships –Work with the other actors to *play* the lines according to ideas of nominal roles. What happens if you characterise an exchange as parent/child, boss/employee, lovers/co-conspirators? These might be coherent with the text or in opposition to it.
- Context switches – Referring to the quiet place exercise earlier in this chapter, consider how relationships within the text shift if you impose a specific location or place on the exchange, or change who is listening to it.

Exploring these activities can mean that the investigation stays imaginatively open, but most importantly you will stay connected to the need to establish coherence between action and intention when this isn't automatically given by the presence of structured conversation.

Into Reflection

The nature of researching a relationship on stage requires the activity to be mutual and collaborative – there need to be at least two people involved! It is impossible to make unilateral choices when the point of focus is shared. This doesn't mean that ideas or insights that emerge from individual work are redundant, but more that each actor must be able to interrogate these in the light of the mutual impact. It may be that certain discoveries are more useful to reformat in respect of individual inner work, if what they present isn't helpful to the other participant. Following a relationship research activity consider whether insights obtained inform personal, internal, character work, or whether they have directly informed the relationship in respect of the scenic action.

Much of the research into relationships will be trial and error, since it can only be interrogated in practice in working on the scenes and considering what works or doesn't in the communication of the text; and so useful acts of reflection will be to document insights readily and swiftly from practical exercises. It's worth putting into your practice scheduled moments of consolidation. Share the discoveries and make them explicit, and aim to document this. Make the research work MEAN something in the short term, even if subsequent exercises mean you reject this.

Further Reading

- *An Actor's Craft* by David Krasner
- *Games People Play* by Eric Berne
- *Different Every Night* by Mike Alfreds
- *Laban for Actors and Dancers* by Jean Newlove
- *Meisner in Practice* by Nick Moseley
- *Impro: Improvisation and the Theatre* by Keith Johnstone
- *Words Into Action* by William Gaskill
- *The Mastery of Movement, 4th Edition* by MacDonald and Evans

Notes

1 Alfreds, M. (2007) *Different Every Night*, Nick Hern, London, page 174.
2 Krasner, D. (2012) *The Actor's Craft*, Palgrave Macmillan, New York, page 124.
3 Theatre director and teacher Keith Johnstone was the first practitioner to fully coin this principle within acting – something that has since become a staple in both textual and improvisational scene work. Johnstone argues that status transactions are continuous, and that every movement and inflection implies a status and that no action is ever motiveless, Johnstone, K. (1981) *Impro*, Faber and Faber, London, page 33.
4 Johnstone's book *Impro* has suggestions of status games, of which elements can be used in a rehearsal process. Equally, Eric Berne's book (1964) *Games People Play*, also suggest that human interactions are full of set games; his idea of the *three ego states* (the Adult,

the Child, and the Parent) and how these intersect/inform or clash/create conflict in relationships would be a valuable addition to an actor's relationship research.

5   Experts in interpersonal relations have determined that nonverbal communication makes up around 70–80% of what is involved in communication, leaving the words we use – although the starting point and anchor for our investigation – at 20–30% in terms of meaning. Nonverbal communication includes facial expressions, body movement and posture, gestures, eye contact, touch, spatial relationships, and vocality.

Guy Stanley

6

CHARACTER INTO WORLD – EXPLORING GIVEN CIRCUMSTANCES

Defining the Challenges and the Objectives

The character and the character's relationships exist within the premise of the imagined world of the text. As our environment changes and influences how we behave – for you to fully exist within that environment and be responsive to the imagined truth that the audience will see – you will have to research what that *world* is like, and establish the *given circumstances* in which the scenic action occurs. The most obvious questions to answer are regarding time and place, surroundings, and previous circumstances. This section will consider what information is important to find out, and how you can approach doing that.

Various forms of the questions of 'Where is it?' and 'When is it?' are integral to Stanislavski's approach (and several other practitioners including Hagen and Meisner), but they can seem like simple questions when in fact they encompass a lot of information. Director Katie Mitchell speaks of 'the ripple effect' when researching given circumstances.[1] This means that if you throw a stone into a pond, little ripples will form from where the stone entered the water; likewise you can start with the location of your scene, for example a bedroom in a house. The small ripples will symbolise how the questions will grow outward from that piece of information. Which house? Which street? Which neighbourhood? Which town/city? Which county? Which country? The same will go for time, ranging from year to time of day, because it will affect how you play the scene.

Your research into the time and place will help you understand what it meant to be in *that location* at *that time*. For example, the circumstances of a bedroom in nineteenth-century Russia are obviously different from those of twenty-first-century London, but they would also be different across town and country; if you

DOI: 10.4324/9781003226130-7

were a man or if you were a woman; if you were old or young, rich or poor, etc; thus, being specific in your research is the key to finding relevant information.

Even if you are exploring a text set in a twenty-first-century world, it is still vital to engage with the same questions. Think about your own bedroom; you are likely to have placed furniture how you want it in the space, added objects or pictures that have functional or emotional resonance for you, have a level of *tidiness* you find acceptable, and you may even have added scents or fragrances, painted walls, or selected fabrics in colours and textures that appeal to you. But you may also be in a rented space where some of those choices aren't available to you, or where the physical constraints constantly chafe. In shared spaces, for example the lounge, there will often be a *good* chair or spot on the sofa, perhaps where the best view of the TV is – who gets to sit there? How does that get negotiated by the people in the space? Think about visiting a new partner's space for the first time; we'll have a very different physical relationship to that space when we don't know where the toilet is or what the *rules* of that space are, compared to the ease with which we navigate it when we are comfortable and familiar.

As human beings we pay an extraordinary amount of attention to our surroundings, and we form strong multi-sensory associations, habits, and tastes alongside them, even if these are not conscious decisions. Places *smell*, *sound*, and *feel* certain ways, which affects our behaviour. We adapt our spaces to reflect aspects of ourselves – whether this is hiding the embarrassing teen fiction you like as comfort reading (or dirty laundry) when an unexpected guest arrives or spending time to create specific atmospheres or aesthetics by carefully choosing what you place on view – because how we connect with space is in part a manifestation of our character. However, we also adapt our behaviour and characteristics all the time in tiny ways to adjust for being in different spaces, different people entering the spaces, what activities we do in spaces, and our previous experience of spaces. Our sense of what truthful action is can often be filtered through a strong sense of the norms of an identified space, which in and of itself is often rooted in very specific cultural or social conventions.

Space and time are often intrinsically linked; and this intersection also impacts our behaviour, both in real life as well as in the context of a character in a play. The time of year might affect the temperature of a space, and how important it is to be close to a source of heat in a room. We change our clothing, our physicality, our language, our activity according to a judgement of *appropriateness* for time and space. The time axis affects many physical aspects of a space such as daylight and temperature, and previous circumstances connect with the emotional aspects such as *the room I got dumped in*, or *the room I was proposed to in*. Time-specific evolution of social conventions changes our perception of the function and meaning of spaces. For the nineteenth century, the kitchen was a space for servants, so Miss Julie's arrival in this space is an invasion; yet in the twenty-first century the kitchen, may be a convivial and unifying centre for an affluent family household.

It's also likely that you may encounter texts whereby the given circumstances of time and space are more abstracted or stylised, ambiguous (the *present*), or which actively avoid specifying any locational detail that can be investigated straightforwardly or fully manifested in, for example, a naturalistic box set as a performance space. However, in performance you will still need to be *acting* in the given circumstances of the playing space and time, and so similar questions as to how space affects the action of the text will need to be considered, and the text will have to be carefully mined for those clues or ideas that might spark the actor's imagination.

It's also possible that you will be working within a designed performance environment where the physical indicators of time and space are fully realised but not consistently literal (such as Bunny Christie's design of *The Curious Incident of the Dog in the Night-Time*), simply suggested (basic structural forms), or entirely absent (black box); in these cases the research may need to be extrapolated from different sources to answer less tangible questions. Many of the following exercises are worth considering even if you are working with limited information or need to answer via conjecture rather than researched analysis. This approach will be more fully considered in Chapters 7 and 8.

So, the key objectives for and skills we need to develop in our exploration of given circumstances:

- Identify specific previous/given circumstances in time and space from textual information and research activity.
- Recognise how these specific given circumstances might affect the detail of embodied choices we make as the character in action.
- Adapt to how textual circumstances may change and develop across the time and space axes of the action.
- Appraise how our embodied choices need to connect imaginatively to the temporal spatial world of the performance space (which might be different from the world of the text).
- Recognise and comprehend how character references intersect with the context of given circumstances.

Prep and Tools for the Job

- Your notes from the textual research from Chapter 3 (given circumstances and context, time/space axes, dramatic present)
- Your notes for (or your completed) character biography and character frame of reference from Chapter 4
- Photocopies of your scenes that you can annotate (or reuse those copies you worked on in Chapter 3)

- Your notebook – and it can be useful also to have additional paper available if you need to, for example, map out the physical space/set you are working on
- A working space with routine objects (your bedroom is fine)
- Pens and highlighters
- Reference materials – most of the time a Google starting point is fine, but it can be useful to bookmark good sites which encompass historical, socio-political, or cultural information and have been fact checked or scrutinised in some way (BBC sites, museum websites, published journalism on mainstream sites like the *Guardian*)
- Video documentary sources can also be fantastically useful, but again be very critical if you encounter these via unmoderated platforms such as YouTube.
- Relevant books – Go on, they're worth it! If you're working in a specific historical frame, then there are often good and readable histories and analyses of time periods (right up to present day). *The Time Traveller's Guide* series or Liza Picard's collection of books detailing the lives of Londoners in different historical periods[2] we have also found to be very helpful for older time periods. It's also worth looking for biographies if you're working with named individuals, or eyewitness accounts of specific events.
- Access to any relevant objects, furniture and spaces, pictures, or references from the designer/model box

Into Practice – Exercises and Activities

The Dramatic Present in the Text – WHEN is the Now?

Review your notes from Chapter 3 and pick out any clues or data as to where the scene(s) occurs in time: time era, year, season, month, date, day of the week, time of day, temporal qualifiers/adjectives (late, early, unseasonal, Christmas, *medieval*).

It can also be useful to consider the cultural references characters make as clues to time specificity. If a character is talking about watching *A Handmaid's Tale* on TV, we must be in 2017 or after, or if there's a reference to a specific historical event (VE day, 9/11) we can begin to narrow down the field of possible dates. This may also apply to other references; for example, books can be dated from publication, and music similarly; smartphones were not in wide use before the 2010s. There may also be *spatial clues* which emerge from references and indirect suggestions, and which impact ideas of time. If a character talks on the phone from the UK to the States, we have to be after 1927 (and probably later!); if there's a TV mentioned in a routine family context, we're likely to be in the 1950s at the earliest. (See the section about socio-cultural references, towards the end of this chapter, for a more detailed approach to this type of research.)

Exercise: Detailing Time

Aim to end up with a list of notes from the text which frame its position in time, consider how far you can answer the following questions, and start thinking about where that information might be acquired from:

• How does the time affect the physical world of the text? What is mentioned?
• Does it come from an actual/real time period with references like *Victorian*, or 'after the Boer War' (even if the story is made up)?
• Does it affect characters' language, behaviour/action, events, status, and power?
• What references, activities, occupations, or hobbies do the characters have?
• How might these impact clothing, speech, physicality, interaction, or relationships?

For example, it might be relatively straightforward to identify a historical period and from there begin to investigate further. if we're in 1880s Norway, we have a starting point from which to explore what clothing, social conventions and habits, etiquette, or activities our characters may engage with. What music, art, or culture did they encounter? Where did they live, worship, go on holiday, go shopping? How did they grow up, get educated, get married, get sick, die? What was the expectation of being a man or a woman, an adult or a child, rich or poor?

Key political events shape our lives, and there may be some significant events referenced within the text that might have shaped those of your character. Who was in power? What were they like? How does it affect the world of the play? Are there strong and specific ideals and ideas that shape the characters or the scenic action (Nationalism, Socialism, Communism, Populism)?

While acquiring a broad-based historical understanding is to be applauded, it can be a more efficient use of research time to really focus on *what directly intersects with the text* – the details of the life of a peasant in 1880s Norway may not be useful if your text is entirely engaged with middle-class intellectuals in Oslo. Similarly, while this period saw considerable political democratisation in Norway, and a growing desire to secede from the union with Sweden, this drive doesn't necessarily impact the world of the characters in *Hedda Gabler*. Aim to use the bulleted questions from earlier to keep your research activity focused and specific to details that can build the understanding of how to engage with the requirements of the specific text.

HANDY HINT

It can be worth bearing in mind that often drama is based on characters who conflict with their given circumstances in some way and so finding where and how this conflict exists in their action and differs from the norms of the time can be a useful way of locating specificity.

Concentrate on identifying visual/tangible references as well as facts and explore how you can physically and practically investigate these. As mentioned in Chapter 4, if female clothing is restrictive (corset and long skirt), find equivalents to work with that constrain your movement and aim to accustom yourself to existing physically within this. At a similar time period it's likely that men's clothing would be restrictive as well, with rougher fabrics, many layers, no Lycra, and formal tailoring, and so questions of clothing are not gendered. Your character is used to this (whether they like it or not!), and so you should aim to find that level of physical familiarity as well.

You may be working in a time period outside a historical narrative (the future, or fantasy), in which case your references may need to be wider-ranging and more speculative; but you should still aim to root your understanding of these given circumstances in something tangible. For example if we are in a post-apocalyptic future, what kinds of clothing are most likely to endure for some time? Probably hardwearing jeans, leathers, or felted wool rather than your ASOS crop top. You might anticipate that the apocalypse has disrupted energy supplies, and so more layers are needed for warmth rather than fashion, and less laundry might occur. Fast fashion is unlikely to endure, so clothing is perhaps more likely to be mended than replaced. From this kind of thinking it's possible to evolve visual references and practical ideas that can inform your embodied choices, even without direct reference points.

Timespan and Previous Circumstances

Review your notes for (or your completed) character biography and your mapping of scenic action (Chapter 4).

Some texts are set over a longer period, in which scenes can play out over several days, months, years, or even decades. Time alters us both physically and emotionally and depending on the events that have taken place within the time span of the text, the actor must find out how the time passed has affected their character, as well as their relationships and way of life. Of course, a long time passing has implications on the character's physicality since age affects us visibly; however, even one year of either hardship, fortune, or significant life events will change how someone presents visually to the surrounding world. It will also alter their tactics, wants, and needs, and which characteristics are on display.

Exercise: Evolving Circumstances

It can be useful here to create a timeline, or list, of what has occurred between the scenes, such as housing situation, work situation, family situation, friendships, health, financial situation, etc. Once you have listed those changes, it gives you a platform to gather information and visual clues to aid your imagination in inhabiting those changes in circumstance, and begin to understand how your character has been affected by them. Use the list to answer the following questions:

- In what ways are the circumstances across scenes different and specific? (spaces and times)
- How do these differences impact the character's actions/reactions, communications, desires, wants, needs, and relationships?
- What new information affects the circumstances even if the time and space stay the same?
- How does the character change through time?
- How does the character change in space?
- Where are they coming from and where are they going when they leave?

Exercise: Previous Circumstance Improvisation

It can be useful to explore character improvisation exercises to investigate those events you identify within your biography/timeline as being significant in the action of the play; and it's also helpful to do so in the context of the given space. You may wish to add or remove different objects when working on improvised exercises that exist at different points in the timeline, so you can have a clear sense of how the space has changed through time as well.

Entering the Now

Similarly to the evolving circumstances, we also have to understand what has happened immediately before a scene. This can range from days before the scene to minutes, and it all influences how the scene will play out. A character will act differently if they have been running from somewhere before the scene starts than they would if they have been to a spa day and just entered their own room. But depending on what the scene is about, a previous circumstance days before the scene can have a deep effect on the behaviour in the room. For example, if two characters meet for the first time since having an argument – or kissing for the first time – that previous event will inform the scene, as will what they have done immediately before the scene, so both are important to establish.

Exercise: Immediate Circumstances

Look to create a diary entry, or hourly timeline for the immediate circumstances, to understand how the scene will be influenced by these events and how your choices can derive from this information. Choose how you chronologically order those events and at which time increments.

You can keep it objective, as in a *list*:

10 am: I go shopping, I see a friend from the past who stirs up a lot of emotions in me. I leave the shop quickly.

11 am: I arrive home, I throw the shopping on the floor, I sit in my bedroom thinking.

12 pm: I leave the house to go and confront my friend, I am nervous.

Or you can make it subjective, as in a *diary/journal entry*:

> *This morning I was in the shopping centre just getting a few things and as I turned the corner in the aisle I saw her. What was she doing back? Why hadn't she told me she had returned? I wanted to speak to her but I froze and ran out of the shop. I got home and ran up to my room, I felt in a daze, questions upon questions in my mind. Seeing her completely threw me for a loop, all the old images and feelings coming back. I need to see her, I need to understand . . .*

Exercise: Personal Preparation

Understanding what has happened immediately before the scene starts will also allow you as the actor to determine which type of preparation you would need before entering the space. It can be helpful to use a physical exercise like running on the spot or doing push-ups, if the character might have high inner tempo or physical fatigue upon entering. Similarly, images or pieces of music will also aid the emotional connection to the immediate circumstances, as will daydreams and imaginative scenarios in your head – and the research you do (coupled with your own process and preferences) will present you with the most appropriate preparation for your character.

Try to work from the detail you have extracted from the text regarding the character's disposition, tempo, physical attributes, and emotional qualities, to really ensure that the preparation is rooted in the text and that you find a connected way to prepare for the action of the scene as you have evolved in practice.

HANDY HINT

It can be useful to set up your rehearsal script so that you have the script on one side of the page, and space for notes and reflections on the other side, so that the information you are gathering is always connecting back to specific moments in the text.

The Dramatic Present in the Text – WHERE is the Now?

Review your notes from Chapter 3, and pick out clues or data about the following:

- The country
- The city
- The building/outside space
- The room
- Furniture and objects identified as being present
- What/who we see and hear in the scene
- Whose space it is
- What doors/entrances and windows there are
- Any place names
- Spatial qualifiers or adjectives such as *home, cosy, stark, cold, bright,* etc

There may be locations or places mentioned in conversation which narrow down your geographical area (or temporal). Also note that *place names* change as do the associations people have with places – *Moscow* in *Three Sisters* does not carry the same ideas as Moscow in the twenty-first century.

Exercise: Detailing the Space

Make a list of notes and consider how far you can answer the following questions:

- What is the function of the space? Is it literal (a kitchen, a salon, a garden)?
- Does the text suggest an imaginary space where unusual rules apply?
- Are there single or multiple spaces suggested in the text that are visible simultaneously (e.g. past on stage right, present on stage left, four rooms of the same house)? What are the relationships between these? Do they physically connect?
- What are the physical/visible details of the spaces – large, cramped, derelict, affluent?
- What do the spaces feel like? What are their characteristics – moods, textures, atmospheres?
- What objects/furniture are there in the space? What values/emotional references do they have? What functions?
- Whose space is it? Is it public or private?
- What relationships do characters have with their locations and each other within them?
- What do they do there? Are there activities/behavioural codes which are *appropriate* (or not!) for the space?
- Are there visual or spatial elements which physically confine or free the character?

• Are they physically at home or awkward, free or limited, scared or comfortable? Does this change?

As with questions of time, aim to keep the focus of your spatial research closely connected to the text. If your context is a 1950s poorer community in urban London, and nobody mentions anywhere beyond it, then what Scotland or Mayfair was like then won't necessarily help you. However, if the characters reference locations beyond the dramatic present location, it will be useful to consider what values they ascribe to it – which may be different from the actuality of the location. For example, the dream of escaping from the city to the *country* can often be based on idealised speculation (peace, space, closeness to nature) rather than actual reality (tractors, animal smells, isolation, no transport, poverty).

Identify and look for images and facts that capture the detail of the locations – geographically and internally – as well as the mood and values of the locations. For example, if the action takes place in the 1950s in one of London's poorer communities it can be useful to detail not just the interior space (what kinds of furniture) but also the streets around the space, and what happens in those streets Is entering this space a relief and an escape into private space, or something else? In most cases if you are in a domestic scene, even if there is deprivation and poverty according to a contemporary perspective, it is still a *home*. What elements of the space make it *homely* to the characters?

It can be useful to explore three dimensional spaces, as well as images, and the spatial map in the appendix may be useful to cross reference here. If there are named locations in the text that you can visit in person, try to do so and map out your response to the physical space *in situ*. It's also handy to take your own personal photos where appropriate.

HANDY HINT

The Museum of the Home offers some useful practical details about the UK home throughout history, with some *rooms through time* available online.

Framing the Space

If you are working on a fully realised production, then a substantial amount of information will have been established by the director and designer in pre-production, and is likely to be shared with you via a model box, costume designs, mood boards, floor markups, etc early on in the rehearsal process. However, there will still need to be aspects of visualisation that will need to come from your research.

While historically you might expect – in a naturalistically conceived production – a box set with all relevant details and dressing present, in contemporary productions this level of detail might be visually much more distilled and conceptually stripped back – and yet an audience still needs to recognise from your choices the specificity of the real given circumstances in time and space. Even with a fully realised box set, what lies on or beyond the fourth wall, or outside the window, beyond the door, are still questions that need to be answered with something other than *offstage left wings*.

To establish those unseen elements of the space, consider questions such as:

• What surrounds the location?
• What other rooms are there?
• What's below and above you?
• What's outside?
• Where do the doors go?
• What can you see from the window?
• When you look in the mirror, what parts of the room are reflected back to you?
• When the door is open what can you see that is concealed when it is closed?

If you are working in a studio rehearsal scene study setting this becomes more acute, since you are less likely to have much of a tangible design to work with. You may also be in a studio where all walls must be imagined, and where you have only functional furniture and props to work with. So, what is present on all the other walls? Some of this will be indelibly practical: we're in a kitchen, so where's the sink and the oven? But some elements may be more emotional: the important photos are on the wall, but there are more of you than your brother; the fridge is plastered with kids' drawings, but you don't have children; your mum is still using your gran's teapot even though it leaks and doesn't match.

Mapping Invisible Walls

If possible, work with scene partners to agree the interior walls and what's on them, and map out the space (think *Cluedo* board or images positioned around the space), so even if you are working without any tangibly physical design elements you have a shared idea of what you are believing to be physically present, and how the visible space connects with other unseen spaces, before exploring individually your character's relationships to those and how those can invoke impulses and choices.

Even more important, depending on the space and the direction of the scene, might be to realise the *fourth wall*, or – in non-proscenium staging (*traverse, thrust, in the round*) – the sides of the playing space facing the audience. Most of the time all props or elements on these sides will be imagined, so the actor must rely on their inner connection to their research, in order to engage with this space in an appropriate way.

In most naturalistic settings we would refrain from directly engaging with the audience; however, we should not refrain from using or facing the *fourth wall* during the performance, since it will impact the audience's connection to the scenic action. As actors we have to endow this side of the space with our imagined reality, whether that be the wall(s) of a bedroom, the rest of the park, or a vast deserted landscape.

There are times when we as actors have to engage actively with the side facing the audience, such as using an imagined prop such as a mirror, or an imagined window.[3] In these instances, your research will involve what the character places attention on, so that you avoid *actively seeing* the audience – and because the audience will only see the actor and not what the actor is looking at, it is important that you have a strong connection to the imaginary object/view and what it represents. Similarly, there are times when we use the audience even though the fourth wall is *not* broken – for instance, you are talking to a group of people or an audience in the imaginary world. In these instances we need to *endow* the audience with the properties of the imagined spectators or extend the invisible walls outwards.

Exercise: Practical Placement and Status

It can be useful to experiment practically around establishing the positioning of furniture, characters, and entrances/exits, especially if you are working on a studio-based rehearsal scene study project.

By engaging with the following questions, you can start to get a sense of the status placements in the space, and how that might affect your choices:

- Whose territory is this space?
- Who has status in it? How is that manifested spatially?
- What are the physical positions of status in the space? Is there a focal point?
- Does the spatial organisation demonstrate a hierarchy – socially or emotionally?
- Who subverts or invades the space?
- Who is comfortable and at ease?
- Is it a private or a public space?

Experiment with placing characters (and furniture/objects) in different areas of the space, according to what you have identified as being the necessary details (chairs, a sofa, a table with drinks) and consider how physical variations in proximity, focus, and placement affect the relationships within the action. A space invader might be dominant or hesitant. This can assist with really building the physical sensation of being in a specific space.

Evolving Practical Familiarity

It's also useful to think about the familiarity your character has with a space – not just in terms of status, but also in respect of ease of movement around it. We move around our own homes and familiar spaces with confidence, we don't need to pay much attention because we *know* how many steps there are between the table and the door, where our keys are, and where that door leads. We know the habitual sounds of our environment, what we can see and hear from it, whether we feel safe. This allows us to manage how much attention and aware-ness we need to maintain in that space, our actions within it, and our desire to remain or depart.

Try to work out physically in a space what the level of your character's famili-arity is, whether they need to pay extra attention to the space, or can move with confidence around it, or whether they feel constrained or uncertain. Once it has been established where certain elements of the space have been *set* it's important to keep these consistent.

Exercise: Learning the Physical Space

This can often be best explored in your own practical time (not in rehearsal) allowing you to take the time to embed the knowledge of the territory, so when you move to the kitchen you can move without a conscious decision, or when your character reaches for the coffee cups in their own kitchen you don't have to remember where they are!

Things to play with and note/agree on with scene partners include:

- What things belong in the space (small objects but also furniture)?
- Where do they live in the space?
- What can you see from different positions in the space?
- How long does it take to move around the space (pay particular attention to things like levels/stairs)?
- Which parts of the space can be overheard from others?
- What can you see from different part of the space?
- What can you reach and touch from, e.g. different chairs, or a table?

Aim to generate both a practical actor's knowledge of the space (i.e. don't trip over things in reality as you) and what the character's physical knowledge of the space is.

It can also be useful to play your scene as a physical journey, focusing on how you navigate the space as you attend to the impulse of your actions through the scene – without trying to use the words. This can assist with clarifying the impulses that underpin the units of a scene, and finding a connection with the intention of a physical action.

Exercise – Investigating Character in Space

Looking back at some of your notes from this chapter (and previous) it's worth investigating, in detail, why the space affects your character. For example, it might be possible to identify that they are uncomfortable or uncertain in the space, or that they lack status or familiarity; however, this might lead to playing a generalised level of awkwardness.

- Consider what your characters expectations are before entering the space. What it will be like?
- Who will be/is expected to be present? What's the relationship with them?
- Are these expectations met? It's often the case that these shifts are relationship-based (think about how quickly even as grown adults we revert to 'stroppy teenager' when we return to a parental home).
- What has affected the expectation if it hasn't been met? It might be that the aesthetic has changed, that picture that was always there has been replaced, or perhaps that your character hadn't anticipated quite such dreadful poverty, ugly style, or visible luxury and is trying to conceal a response to the space.

It might also be over the course of a scene that the behaviour of others in the space conflicts with a sense of self, strongly held values, or ideas about social interaction that your character has, and this increases discomfort in the space (or the reverse). When we are in a situation of emotional discomfort, we often find our attention is displaced onto external, environmental details, because it allows us to focus on something tangible and separate rather than complex and painful. This can provide a rich seam of information to inform inner monologues, especially if your character is rendered silent in their discomfort.

Object Relations

We all tend to personalise our spaces with the objects, from the simplest function to the most personal emotional symbols. Our individual frames of reference are vast, multi-layered, and complex in their interdependence – and this capacity to *endow objects* can also be a key aspect within performance language.

Human beings invest a lot of energy into their object relations. Objects can carry literal, metaphorical, symbolic, and emotional value – think of the seagull in *The Seagull* or the boots in *The Three Lives of Lucie Cabrol*. They can often be handy short cuts into establishing the core of a scene, especially in more stylised/physical performances; for example, a bamboo cane held to be a fence rail becomes an umbrella with a change of grip. But even without a constructed metaphor, we allow practical objects to carry layers of meaning and intimate detail – a wedding ring, a photograph, an empty chair – simply by how we interact with them.

From your notes on the text, you may have identified objects with which your character has a specific relationship which carries more than literal meaning. However, we also place varying values on objects which are less potentially symbolic. Consider the very real anxiety many of us feel when we are without our phones in the twenty-first century. A smoker will always know where their cigarettes and lighter are. If we feel a strong desire to leave a place we are likely to pay more attention to the door or be aware of perhaps the location of our keys, our wallet, or our travel card because they are necessary to make our escape. For the following exercises refer to the reading objects map at the Appendix and use the notes to expand your research practically.

Exercise: Personal Props and Objects

Taking great care not to clutter yourself with objects for no reason, it can be useful to work out what personal objects you character would routinely have with them, and where these might be located – in a pocket, in a handbag, etc. Prioritise those objects which are *specified in the text*, work out where these *live*, and how you interact with them. It can also be useful to think about the habitual detail of how we handle those objects. If you can distil that habit into your performance, it will add substantially to the audience's comprehension that you have come *home* – whether or not the space itself is fully designed as a flat.

Exercise: Special *Object Inner Monologue*

While obviously some objects may have generally ascribed value (jewellery/heirlooms) or culturally agreed meaning (a first edition of a book), much of the time there is no inherent or fixed value other than what we endow them with.

If within the text your character does engage with objects or pieces of furniture that have specific meaning, try to create an inner monologue or back story for how the object came to be yours, in your possession, or significant to you. If there is not a tangible object that you will be working with (for example, props department isn't giving you a gold crown), aim to find a substitute or at least a clear visual reference to work from.

Sensory Investigation

As noted earlier, we human beings pay a great deal of attention to our surroundings. Our sensory engagement with the world is our first defence against danger and allows us to recognise sensory triggers that equally indicate safety, comfort, and security. In a more advanced society, the dangers might not be as literal or present as earlier in our evolution, so instead much of this activity is focused on arranging our physical circumstances to our comfort and avoiding triggers that render us uncomfortable. But this still engages all our senses.

It is important to note that this section does not assume that disability does not exist, or where it does it must constrain what the actor can explore. Where sensory impairments present, most of the time equivalent information can be obtained and provides equally valuable perspectives on the potential imaginative exploration and experience of different given circumstances. For example, considering the physical environmental textures which may assist people with visual impairments offers equally vital information about the necessary qualities of a space in performance, which may also affect its visual design. The sensory experience is highly individual and may very well prioritise differently according to individual preference and need, and so this section should be considered according to sensory engagements appropriate to the individual, rather than as a fixed prescription.

Assuming you have amassed over the course of previous exercises a range of information about the visual and tangible elements of the scenic time and space, gather these references together, and consider if there are any gaps in your emerging visualisation of the physical work of the text. Aim to plug these where possible, but looking at your material as a whole, consider how these references might suggest different ideas to explore emerging from the following questions. Again, it is important to stress that there may not always be an integral insight here; you are not searching for a right or definitive answer – simply amassing a range of different ideas that may be useful in practice.

Exercise: Sensory Exploration of the Space

Engage with one location at a time. It can be useful to use separate sheets of paper for each space, and answer these questions:

What might this space/time smell like?

What environmental smells are present? Gas, wood, or coal heating smell more than central heating, old stone houses may be damp, pre-car travel was reliant on horses (with associated manure), drainage/sewers, animals/pets, non-fragranced cleaning products, oil or candle lighting, smells of cooking/spices, garbage, intended scents/incense, room fragrance, human bodies, electrical heat, books, dust, fresh flowers, or plants.

Much of the time smell can be highly evocative. We get a sense of place and memory from the smell – your old primary school, the swimming pool, the perfume of a friend, the smell of *home*. Often, we can use smell as a clear trigger for comfort or the reverse – an unpleasant smell can make us immediately feel physically uncomfortable or nauseated in a space. *Ask yourself: how might the potential smells affect your character's physical sensation in the scenic space/action?*

What might this space/time sound like?

What environmental/diegetic sounds are present? Traffic noise, animals and birds, creaks and groans of pipes, the boiler or the fire, people's voices outside, next door, other rooms, weather outside, sounds of activity (machines, knitting needles clicking, the chink of crockery), phones, alarms and notifications, intended sounds like the radio, music, the TV.

We often encounter sound as a prime emotional memory trigger – songs can catapult us back to memories – or for functionality (the alarm clock, the timer) and we often find that certain sounds provoke ease – white noise, sound therapy, ASMR. However, sound can also be profoundly discomforting, especially when and where it is unexpected or its source cannot be identified. Lack of sound can be utterly peaceful, or terrifying silence. The hum of conversation next door might be a reassuring sense of community, or intrusive noisy neighbours. *Ask yourself: how might the potential sounds affect your characters physical sensation in the scenic space/action?*

What might this space/time feel like?

What is the physical experience of being in the space/time of the scene? Hot or cold temperature; humidity or dampness; empty and sparse or cluttered and claustrophobic; clean or dirty; safe or dangerous; comfortable textures or hard and rough edges; dark or light; easy to move freely in or constraining, restricting, awkward.

Many of these ideas don't carry fixed values. One person's elegant minimalism is another's impersonal 'show-home'; clutter might be cosy and informal, or chaotic and overwhelming. We might very well enter a new space that we find profoundly welcoming or become frustrated and overwhelmed with our own personal spaces. *Ask yourself: how might the potential physical environment affect your character's physical sensation in the scenic space/action?*

What might this space/time taste like?

It's not always the case that this will be a valuable line of enquiry. Not every play requires you to eat or drink within the scenic action. However, it can be useful to consider this when occasions suggest it.

Think about the rituals and emotional significance that might surround food and drink, like the comfort of the cup of tea, the medicinal warmth of the whisky, the family meal. What tastes are luxuries, special, or rare? Which are familiar, necessary, bland, or vile? What are the comfort foods? *Ask yourself: how might the potential food and drink consumption affect your character's physical sensation in the scenic space/action?*

Socio-Cultural Context and References

The world of any text exists in a context (specified or not), and as well as exploring the details in respect of time and space, it can be useful to consider the socio-cultural context on its own terms. This can allow us to really comprehend the value or meaning of cultural references the characters make within the text and offer the actor sources via which a connection with the world can be developed, like listening to music from a particular era or reading the books a character reads.

Look at what's happening in art/painting, photography, dance, film, TV, fiction and literature, poetry, music – all the kinds of things that you encounter in your world and your frame of reference, the characters might find in theirs, even if they are vastly different in nature, content, or accessibility. Our references might be to ideas, cultural artefacts, literature or other works of art, social events and groups, consumer goods, language, people of renown (or notoriety), or places. Older texts will often refer to similar things from *their cultural reference point* like Shakespeare using allusions and metaphors steeped in classical mythology and renaissance philosophy, or the truly terrifying quantity of casual or *comedic* racism and homophobia in TV texts from the 1950s and 60s. What we like or know, what we talk about, what we refer to, and how we do so are often a reflection of our experience in our own given circumstances as well our tastes and inclinations.

Often these references are aspirational. We want to like and know what we perceive to have socio-cultural currency (we want to be *cool, right-thinking, grown-up*, etc) and so we will engage with those references because of what they may signify or represent. Think about how we use clothing, music tastes, or what we read in order to adapt ourselves; or think about how we conceal *guilty pleasures* because their cultural currency has eroded as we got older or the world changed.

Often, we mishandle references in trying to express them aspirationally. Consider different generations struggling with new *youth slang* or technology; or talking passionately about something you love, only to realise the other person has never heard of it.

Exercise: Building Character Cultural References

Reviewing your scenes and the notes from the work so far, identify (highlight or circle) if there are any particular references your character makes.

- What are the references you find in the text?
- Is there a pattern? For example, lots of literary references, or music?
- Do they seem coherent with what you know of the character and their given circumstances (time and space), or are they unusual and distinctive?
- What do the given circumstances established so far suggest about the ease of access to cultural references your character has?

- What is the character's relationship to the reference? What do they mean to the character?
- Are they knowledgeable and familiar with the references, or more aspirational and tentative?
- Might these references nuance character objectives in any way?
- What references might be useful to explore practically as character exploration (such as music to listen to, films worth seeing, places to visit in person)?
- Are there any references that need careful interrogation because the context of the performance values them differently than the context of the writing/scenic action?

Again, you may find a variation here between different texts and the amount of detail available in response to these questions. Similarly, you may find that much of the relevant information has already been identified via earlier exercises with analysing the text and creating the character biography; but answering these questions may further refine your notes and choices explored in respect of the character and relationships chapters. For example, if you can identify that there's a lot of aspirational references used, this may assist with tactics within a relationship – the character may wish to impress, to put down, or reassure the other character. Similarly if you identify a pattern of knowledgeable, intellectual references delivered with certainty you may be able to nuance objectives and characteristics – perhaps they are ambitious, intelligent, with a desire to succeed or discover.

Filling the Gaps

A great deal of investigation of given circumstances is already focused on filling in gaps – quite literally when we are looking at building invisible walls! However, you may find that the spaces suggested in the text (if any) require additional activities in order to i.e. find a stylised sense of space, or movement through it.

Changes of Perspective

Shift where you are physically researching/reading or rehearsing. It's amazing how you can find new insights by changing the literal space in which you are working; for example, sit under the table for a child's-eye view, or run a scene in public space that may textually be located in a private one. You can change the dynamic of a scene by upending the obvious movement around a space, navigating other people within the space, or in a different, more cluttered space.

Pace and Place

Think about a sequence of actions you habitually do such as getting up in the morning. Identify the specific physical actions that make this. Experiment with the pace at which you do them, the scale of the movement/energy needed to achieve each action, repeat elements exactly, reverse the sequence, or do the actions out of sequence; again, music prompts can be useful to assist with this. It can be relatively quick to find an abstracted stylisation of movement sequences that comes from connection to the habitual physical engagements we have with space, rather than wafting around being arty.

Sounds and Symbols

Review all of your notes from the sense of sound exercise. What sounds are likely in that space (again, literal effects or suggested by objects in the space?) For example, are there clock ticks, traffic, alarms (and also silence), muffled arguments? How might using these sounds inform the scenic action/stakes? What's the pulse or rhythm of the scene? How can these be played with if you speed it up or slow it down? How might these potential sounds connect to what you have noted about the *inner* of the character in that moment? How might they be used to build up a stylised sense of the moment in time and space? You might think of suggesting time passing with a distinctive audible clock tick.

Creating Conceptual Space

It may be that you have little or no information about any notion of space in the text, or that you are working from source stimuli in order to evolve text, and so spaces may not need to be literal. They will however need to be specific. It can be useful to work with the spatial map (Appendix) and reverse the order of *reading*; if you want a space that is austere, cold, and sparse, what can you place into your studio/working space that will carry those meanings? If you are working with, say, a poem, are there spatial ideas in the imagery that could translate into objects, locations, or a physical journey around different parts of a space? In other words, does the through line take you forward/backward? Does the use of antithesis suggest a repeated shift between two sections of space?

Into Reflection

Considering the given circumstances of a dramatic present in the *world of the play* essentially is an immediate engagement with the potential insights gained from the idea of the *frame of reference*. Consequently, it can be worth revisiting the character frame of reference exercise (Chapter 4) as well as the character biography at this point, because you may find that further understanding, refinement, or discovery can be made having explored the aspects from this chapter in more detail.

Similarly, it can also be worth revisiting your *own* frame of reference exercise (Window on the World, Chapter 2), and consider how some of these more specific exercises may sharpen your capacity to detail and mine your own lived experience. Could you detail a specific period of time in your life in this way? What stands out as important information?

Sifting through your own rich cultural references and exploring what your engagement with them is, whether critically, contextually, or purely on the basis of what imaginatively inspires you, is also worth exploring further. As noted in Chapter 1, the capacity to engage critically across a rich range of media, and to be inspired by but also draw insight from your life experience is a useful skill – as a human as well as an actor. You may find it useful to journal or curate your cultural encounters more informally and expand this activity within your reflective practice with a view to diversifying how you engage with reflection and recognising insight as it comes, as outlined in Chapter 1.

Some exercises suggested in this chapter also connect with practical skillsets that have applicability on a personal development basis and may also intersect with some mindfulness practice; for example, the capacity to be able to sit in a present moment in a specific space and allow your conscious mind to focus on all the environmental sounds and sensations. The practice of this can be useful in developing the ability to vary and focus your attention, to be present, and to grow the speed with which you can engage with these exercises within your evolving process as an actor.

Further Reading

- *The Director's Craft* by Katie Mitchell
- *The Art of Acting* by Stella Adler
- *Respect for Acting* by Uta Hagen
- *A Challenge for the Actor* by Uta Hagen
- *The Shaping of Us* by Lily Bernheimer
- *The Language of Space* by Bryan Lawson

Notes

1 Mitchell, K. (2009) *The Director's Craft*, Routledge, London, page 22.
2 Liza Picard's collection of books include titles such as Picard, L. (2004) *Elizabeth's London: Everyday Life in Elizabethan London*; Picard, L. (2005) *Victorian London: The Life of a City 1840–1870*; Picard, L. (2013) *Dr. Johnson's London: Everyday Life in London 1740–1770*; Picard, L. (2013) *Restoration London: Everyday Life in the 1660s*; Picard, L. (2017) *Chaucer's People: Everyday Lives in Medieval London* – all published by St Marton's Press, New York.
3 Uta Hagen distinguishes between *primary* and *subliminal* use of the fourth wall, which you can investigate further in Hagen, U. (1991) *A Challenge for the Actor*, Scribner, New York, page 154.

Guy Stanley

7

THE WORLD OF THE PRODUCTION – CONTEXTS OF CREATIVE CHOICES

Defining the Challenges and the Objectives

Any textual worlds only exist through choices made within the context of their production. A written script is not the performance; the performance can only emerge when the verbal forms on the page are translated into embodied action – via the choices made by the creatives in the production company – in a specific place and time. This is often vastly different from the place and time of the scenic action, or potentially also the place and time of the writing of the script. This chapter aims to consider how an actor should engage with identifying and connecting their research activity with contextual factors that frame the creation of performance of any text, and consequently inform the potential meanings that an audience may read from encountering this.

Increasingly the actor might operate as both an interpreter of an existing text (or a new one written by others), and a potential creator, director, or generator/producer of text/performance. Some of the approaches explored in this chapter may bear the most fruit if you are exploring work in the second category, and we include them because there are often points of intersection in specific projects that may directly inform the actors creative choices in that first context, even if this isn't on every text or production. The next chapter will consider research for creative generation more directly.

Our own given circumstances, as actors in the twenty-first century, have a huge impact on many elements of the process of creating performance. As audience members we respond to and comprehend stage action through the prism of our own frames of reference; while we may enter into a pact and suspend our disbelief when we engage with drama, those factors which allow us to do so need

DOI: 10.4324/9781003226130-8

to be profoundly connected to our understanding of our own reality and specific socio-cultural values.

What arrives on stage as the performance is a series of *signs* that, brought together, create potential meaning and comprehension in the mind of the audience. However, these signs don't just encompass the visible, audible, physical elements on stage which denote action and location; within this are also more elusive elements in respect of cultural references, intertextuality, and metaphors. The creation and manifestation of these may not be explicit text; but their interpretation must be *read* in the context of the audience references. For example, *Avenue Q* is a highly popular puppet-based musical reflecting adult themes; as a parody of *Sesame Street*, part of its impact and *meaning* emerges from the audience knowing the TV show and recognising the contradiction that exits between the action on stage *not being* like Sesame Street while also *being like* it – as well as entertaining an audience that has never seen the original. As an actor, it's going to be useful to research the detail of the TV show as a text, so you can be specific about which of your choices within this text either are *like* or *not like* the reference material.

This contextualisation also expands to considerations of the *style* of a text. While much of this book prioritises research activity that support the presentation of character in the context of realist modes and naturalistic processes, this is by no means the only approach as an actor you may need to explore. The realism/naturalism mode of creating and reading performance is very central in respect of Western twentieth-century performance tradition (though by no means universal here), but texts which intersect with this mode also vary widely; Ibsen is not much like EastEnders, though both orbit this mode. There are many texts which operate through other modes of performance which also require research of an actor; these may ask for technical specificity or stylistic precision that is obtained through other processes – considering perhaps in-ear recorded verbatim pieces, up to farce and pantomime which require different forms of character, relationships, and circumstances over and above text-driven psychological investigation.

Writers (and artists in any medium) evolve their work from their own reference points and circumstances, respond to the world as they have engaged with it, and express themselves through the available media, while acknowledging the aesthetic conventions of their time (they may reject or reimagine these!). As with any source (see Chapter 1), their own biases, values, and experiences may infuse their work with both conscious and unconscious effects on it. Considering how the world of the writer intersects with the world of the play can often provide useful insight into nuancing our understanding of the latter in respect of your expressive choices.

Our world changes *gradually, then suddenly*,[1] and it's not always easy to perceive the gradual changes or recognise those seismic ones that will have lasting impact. It's often only possible to see the shifts and patterns retrospectively, and yet by the time we are looking backwards, our own frames of reference will have changed *how* we are looking for or valuing those patterns. We may often need to consider texts which are indelibly *of their time* and use language, characters or attitudes that are problematic to engage with without interrogation in our twenty-first-century context. For example, it's not unusual to find post-war UK/US texts that were (and remain) radical or progressive in matters of social class or politic, but that trouble us now in their representations of race, gender, and sexuality. While it might be said that actors will primarily be engaged to explore a text selected by, say, a director or a producer, it still remains vital for the actor to be able to consider, as an act of research, the potential impacts of the text in the context of their contemporary production.

Drama in performance, as a human cultural form, is inherently narrative; it's an act of embodied storytelling, and storytelling is intrinsic to our sense of ourselves as a species. Intrinsic to us individuals with episodic memories which allow us a sense of identity, but also as families, generations, and nations whose prevailing narratives define and establish all of our activities and interactions. Storytelling gives us a sense of agency by recognising causality and consequences of connected events. But these narratives are not fixed or absolute; they change as the world does, are often worthy of challenge and review, and can co-exist in counter-positions to other narratives and narrators, constantly shifting in significance. The actor on stage (or screen) is the central teller of the story, and so they are never separate from the impacts of the narrative – you are the voice and body of the story – and so the act of research, fundamentally, is to fully inhabit that story artistically. However, in the twenty-first century as we interrogate and seek to include and embrace a richer range of stories within our work, the actor should also be particularly attentive to their identity and frame of reference as a storyteller.

Whether you are seeking greater authenticity through attention to researching a lived experience, or appraising when your voice, mind, and body may not be the most authentic vehicle of representation, navigating the boundaries between performance and experience primarily is a personal and continual act of research for an actor (see Chapter 2). However, because the work is indelibly *collaborative* and *representational*, there is always a need for an actor to comprehend the interpersonal boundaries of working intimately with others and to research the ethical impacts not just of thematic content and material explored, but also the processes for obtaining and developing material in practice. Whatever the detail of the *worlds* explored imaginatively on stage or screen, we must always explore these worlds from the frame of our own, with the associated values and responsibilities that brings.

PITFALL

It is important to highlight here that although some of the research in this chapter might seem more intellectual and analytical in its approach, the actor still uses this type of research practice to nuance later practical choices and scenic interactions in the context of specific productions. Apply these approaches selectively according to the specifics of the text/project you are working on, and always think about how it connects to your work in practice. If it doesn't connect, don't get bogged down by it!

So, the key skills and objectives we need to develop investigating the context of production:

- Identify and appraise the intersections between the potential worlds of the text in context.
- Recognise and explore how contextual references and considerations may have impacted the text.
- Investigate how formal and stylistic demands in a text may affect research for practice.
- Explore how the context of production may need to affect choices we make for performance.
- Comprehend and operate through appropriate ethical processes for research, rehearsal, and performance.

Prep and Tools for the Job

- Your trusty notebook
- All your notes and ideas so far (in many cases you will already have noted relevant information in some way, such as a cultural reference, or a query over what something means)
- Pens and highlighters
- It's useful to bookmark some general reference sites. There are several suitable ones which provide quick introductions to various practitioners (contemporary and classical), styles, and modes of performance such as *Essential Drama* [www.essentialdrama.com], the *British Library* [www.bl.uk], *Theatre Links* [www.theatrelinks.com], and *The Drama Teacher* [www.thedramateacher.com]; and these can be good starting points to refine your investigation. However, be critical of what you find online; there are many sources who write with passion rather than precision
- *Drama Online* [www.dramaonlinelibrary.com] provides an excellent range of practice and contextual texts, as well as plays.

- Similarly, it's helpful to bookmark locations for reviews and commentary. Many newspapers and online sites will have archives going back many years, and sites like the *British Theatre Guide* [www.britishtheatreguide.info] integrate reviews, commentary, podcasts, and interviews.
- Over the 2020 lockdown, a great deal of material was generated online. We particularly like Dan Rebellato's *Playwrights in Lockdown* series of writer interviews.
- *Equity* [www.equity.org.uk] provides a useful resource for members (you can join as a student) in respect of ongoing ethical professional practice (intimacy guidelines, etc), and other organisations such as *Spotlight* [www.spotlight.com] may also have relevant up-to-date information.
- It can also be useful to develop your own sense of the chronology of theatre performance and practice historically. Again, some good online resources via the *V & A* collections [www.vam.ac.uk], the *British Library*, and *Drama Online*, but for a highly readable book option we really like *The Time Traveller's Guide to British Theatre* (Sierz and Ghilardi); and on video, *Crash Course Theatre* (available on YouTube [www.youtube.com]).

Into Practice – Exercises and Activities

Establishing the Contextual Frames

Depending on the individual text you are working on, this may be a varied area to explore; and you may also find that much of this investigation will largely be informed by the director's creative vision. A contemporary text set in a realistic representation of a single reality is most likely to have the simplest quantity of frames.

It's also worth remembering that there may yet be other *worlds* to consider; for example, a writer places their narrative in another space or time, and we then stage the play sometime after its original production. Arthur Miller's *The Crucible* makes explicit parallels between New England Puritanism in the seventeenth century and 1950s McCarthyist America. When we produce that text today, central thematic preoccupations (*witch hunts*, personal truth, moral absolutism) are still resonant with the fears and troubles of our own *world*, and so need to be explored from an actor's point of view in respect of all three potential *worlds* of enquiry; these expand when we add concepts and adaptations.

For example, Shakespeare wrote intrinsically from his Renaissance/Elizabethan/early Stuart context, but rarely located the world of his scenic action in his own lived reality (plays were set in Ancient Rome, Athens, Bohemia, somewhere in English history, etc). Neither did he give literal representations of scenic given circumstances (it's an *idea of Rome*, not a meticulously physically researched one) nor explore these via a *realistic* style (blank verse, soliloquies, no box set, etc).

In many cases, twenty-first-century productions will then translate that rather nebulous *world* to another place and time, whether historical or conceptual, and yet they'll still also need to ensure that the context of twenty-first-century production is attended to, which may be a children's *version* or for the RSC! Add in a *play within a play*, and the research elements become complex to say the least.

HANDY HINT

Many of these framing and interpretative questions can only be fully answered through the rehearsal process, and in conjunction with the creative team (director and designers). The actor's research priority is to focus on the information that allows you to play your scenes, but stay sensitive to how these frames may shift the nuances and impacts of your action.

These frames may require an additional layer of research, sometimes vital in refining and detailing your choices as an actor and sometimes less so. It's a useful skill to be able to judge when you need to explore these in more detail, as well as the kinds of questions that are useful to apply to relevant sources in order to do so.

Our potential frames might be:

- World of the textual scenic action – the given circumstances, the dramatic present (which may not be naturalistic or realistic)
- Worlds within the world of scenic action – the dream sequence, the play within a play, multiple time frames/spaces, stylistic sequences
- World of the conceptual translation – the adaptation, the updated setting, the director's interpretation – which may reference but not literally represent the given world of the textual scenic action
- World of the writer(s)/maker(s) – their frame of reference that has shaped the creation of the dramatic present in the text, which may also include adaptation from other media and divergent original staging (for example, 'all-male cast')
- World of contemporary performers/actors – their personal frames of reference, cultural/production values, medium/physical playing space
- World of the audience – their socio-cultural values and contexts, which may connect with but also differ from those of the actors

Research Questions to Consider

- Are there different levels of *world* to consider with the text? What are they?

- What is the purpose of multiple worlds within the scenic action? (Have a look at plays such as *The Pride*, *Rockets and Blue Lights*, *Time and the Conways*, the 'Somewhere Ballet' in *West Side Story*, and *Earthquakes in London*.)
- Do these *worlds* differ stylistically? In what ways? What are the connections or similarities?
- How do those different frames provide additional meanings or ideas for your choices?
- What parallels have been drawn when the different world is a conceptual translation? (Why are we setting *Romeo and Juliet* in Colonial India, or *Three Sisters* in 1960s Nigeria?)
- What connections are there between the world of the writer, and the world they have created? (See the next section, 'The Frame of the Writer/Original Performance'.)
- What connection or differences exists between the writer's world and/or the scenic world(s) and the time of production for the actors and creatives?
- How might that shift in frames affect interpretation and potential meaning of the text?
- How do these connections or differences reflect or connect for the audience?
- How might these parallels or connections potentially impact my choices in the scenes?

What to Investigate

Classic texts will often have lots of criticism published about them, but read these critically because they are often more about the play as a literary text rather than a piece of performance. Look for study guides, commentaries, or theatre histories; often, published versions of the text will have notes by the author or critics included which can be very helpful. *DramaOnline* also has a good range of critical and contextual material.

Have you seen the play performed? Look at the programme, or potentially online resources, production websites, or resource/rehearsal packs. Often these will have notes by the author or director included.

Was it reviewed? What was the response to it? Many papers have an online database of past reviews or comments (the *Stage*, the *Guardian*, *whatsonstage.com*, etc); also consider questions of interpretation and framing within these.

How have previous productions explored the potential frames? What interpretations, conceptual or otherwise, have been explored? How were these manifested? Have there been interpretations in other media, or reimaginings? (For instance, *Prospero's Books* and *Return to the Forbidden Planet* both reimagine *The Tempest*.) It can be useful to look for production shots, design materials, or even marketing materials, as well as the resources detailed earlier.

PITFALL

While it's useful to explore previous versions and interpretations, watch any other live or filmed versions critically, because often they are much altered for the specifics of their medium and their own production concepts and context. You don't want to copy previous performance choices, or get set on ideas that are irrelevant in a very differently conceived production.

Is it original work or is it an adaptation? Read the original source text if it was an adaptation. What did they change? What was the effect of this? Can you anticipate any impact on your potential choices?

If you are working with several worlds within the text – for example two or more distinct time/space frames for the scenic action – then each of these will need to be processed through the given circumstances exercises of the previous chapter as your character intersects with them.

If you are working within a conceptual translation or setting, then film, fiction, artwork, or other work unrelated to the specific text can be a good way to get a sense of the values and details of those other times, alongside the specific detailing of the previous chapter's exercises for the given circumstances of your own scenic action (for example, other films set in the same period, even if the story is completely different).

Many of these questions intersect and conflict with each other, and also connect in respect of other lines of enquiry we've talked about in this book. Take for example the musical *Hamilton*. Although rooted in historical events and given circumstances, yet not *accurate* at all in respect of casting those historical identities or the staging, add historical costume and contemporary music, and we have a conceptual frame that brilliantly rips up the history books – while simultaneously staying faithful to much detail within them, and arguably doing more to build knowledge of the historical era than many books ever did for the contemporary audience, who find an intrinsically contemporary resonance with their own context by engaging with it.

HANDY HINT

Many of the online resources or company websites (National Theatre, Royal Shakespeare Company, Headlong, etc) can be incredibly useful if you need to prep quickly for an audition situation and get up to speed with ideas around a text you are not familiar with.

The Frame of the Writer/Original Performance

Any text is an illustration of the writer's perspective, and as an actor it can be practically very useful to explore and understand what has formed their particular vision. For example, Chekhov insisted his plays were comedies, which is rarely how we encounter them in twenty-first-century UK performance!

With older texts we may find there's not a huge amount of personal information (Shakespeare didn't do many interviews . . .) and so this may be a more general consideration of what we know of the socio-political circumstances in their time period – rendering some of these questions unanswerable. With more contemporary texts, and if you are working on new writing by a living writer, you may find there are opportunities to discuss these questions personally with them.

Research Questions to Consider

- Who is the playwright? Can you identify any information about their background (class, education, race, sexuality, etc)?
- In their time frame are there any dominant social or political events or ideas that are referenced or connected? For example, were they an avowed socialist, living through war or revolution, or affected by a particular social experience?
- Can you identify any parallels or connections between their lived experience (speculative or known) and the ideas and forms of their writing?
- How do they talk about their writing? Can you identify any ideas they have about how they imagine or conceive the style and form of plays in performance?
- Is there any information about how they have explored creative ideas through their writing? Is there any particular resonance they underlined?
- What intention or meaning did they have in creating the text as they did? Are there any particular parallels or connections they have made explicit?
- How have others valued their writing? Are they recognised for distinctive values or styles, or more obscure and low-profile?
- What constraints may have been operating while they were writing (censorship, discrimination, lack of access)?
- What else did they write? Other plays? Any other kind of writing? If so, are there common themes, styles, patterns, or characters appearing?
- Where were their plays performed and how? Who were the audiences?
- What was the response to them in performance, both at the time and also in respect of subsequent productions?
- What else is going on around their time in writing and performance? Who else is writing and how? Is this writer part of a shared movement or an outlier, a radical reimaginer?
- What else is going on culturally?

What to Investigate

Some established canon writers may have their own biographies, or they may be acknowledged within theatre history books if they are considered classic. These may also detail the constraints and other writers and activities around the specific time. It can be useful to bear in mind that the idea of fixed chronologies or canon significance can be flawed, because some writers come in and out of view according to the frames of reference of those who write the histories.

There are often good contemporary practice analysis and history texts which consider a range of more up-to-date writers and makers in our own context, and a new consideration of older writers, revisited texts, and new adaptations. These can also assist in answering questions raised by considering our own twenty-first-century frame (we have noted some examples at the end of the chapter).

For more contemporary writers, you are also likely to find interviews and articles about their practice and approach, as well as this kind of material within production resources such as programmes, or video pieces and some excellent podcast series.

Depending on the amount of their work that has been published, you may find notes and thoughts around the play within the published editions.

It can also be useful to explore whether there are any resources which come from actors or directors talking about the work, since they may potentially have had greater access to the writer within the production process (or already done some of the investigation for you).

It can be worth considering what else is happening in art/-painting, photography, dance, film, TV, fiction and literature, poetry, music, social media – all the things that you find in your world that shape your frame of reference. The same is true in any other time period. Often there are dominant cultural forces, ideas, and techniques (realism, expressionism, modernism, multimedia, post-modernism, etc.) that colour a whole generation of material. These may also have strong political intersections as well as cultural impact, such as antiracism, feminism, inclusion, or gender equality. How does this relate to the writing in the text? This may also inform some questions in the following sections.

Sometimes all of us are affected by large-scale political and social events, but in many cases writers are channelling a personal creative engagement with these. Most history sites provide a good timeline of key events and impacts, but, as an actor, prioritise thinking about what would have directly affected the world of the writer and how that might connect to the text you are working on. Good resources often include political speeches, pamphlets, TV documentaries and films, other biographies, newspaper articles and photos, and other fictional plays and books.

HANDY HINT

Your job isn't to come up with a definitive history text, and you don't need to know everything. In **many** cases there may be little to investigate which will fruitfully inform your practice as an actor; however, engaging with this aspect will develop your critical acuity and capacity to identify when it is materially useful, or when you may wish to operate as a writer/creator or even a producer!

Investigating Medium

The work of an actor is, perhaps obviously, not limited to a singular medium; on a basic level you are likely to operate across screen, audio, and live performance forms; and increasingly, technology generates new aspects of these: motion capture, green screen, and live streaming to name a few.

While the capacity to make expressive choices as an actor in the given circumstances of production is an exercise of acting skill, technical understanding, and craft, often the varying methodologies of generating drama across different media require different priorities in the actor's research.

Typically, you can expect theatrical performance to emerge from a collaborative, cumulative, and intensive rehearsal process. However, you are likely to find that screen work de-prioritises cumulative discovery in rehearsal, and asks the actor to make and adapt quick, specific choices on their feet on set. Filmed drama often is shot out of sequence, and sometimes without the scene partner readily available, so accessing the connection to impulse and intention or sustaining the through line of dialogue often requires a stronger personal investment in the *world*, and a stronger capacity to sustain the inner life of a character.

Research Questions to Consider

Assuming you have already considered character, relationship, and given circumstances as per the previous chapters, consider the following:

- What do I need to access the connection to the *moment* of the scene quickly, truthfully, and independently? (This might be a piece of music, or an image, or a visualisation, or even a quick physical activity.)
- Have I got a good sense of the immediate previous circumstances in order to hit the stakes, energy, and continuity of the scene, and sustain coherent choices?
- How is the scene being recorded/shot? Have I got access to the shot list, story board, the set, previsualisation (pre-vis), etc?

- What is the frame through which my choices are being viewed? What are the considerations for audio or sound?
- What are the technical constraints? Mics, marks, angles?
- Who else is around me? Who's in my eyeline? Where am I landing my lines?

What to Investigate

Much of the material explored in the previous chapters can be repurposed here, but the aim is to ensure that you can access clear visualisations of people, spaces, and objects that allow you to connect to the scenic action, even if the people are not present, you are working on the last scene first, or you're recording in a radio studio or against a green screen set-up. You will need vivid personal material to ensure you can *see* and *hear* what is necessary to inform your choices, and in some cases this may also need to be augmented with design information from the production team, whether as pre-vis, or as location references.

Working on screen you can expect camera rehearsals which should develop your understanding of the frame in which you are acting, even if the story board and shot list aren't available to you, and what is immediately around you in respect of the set on which you are working. It can be very useful to practice the navigation of shots, manipulating your eyeline, being able to land lines as if on another character even if you are actually working purely with a tennis ball on a stick or a bored clapper loader. This might perhaps be considered technical research.

Investigate your own methods of swiftly getting and staying warmed up physically, vocally, and mentally, without the adrenalin of a real-time performance to assist you; again suggestions from earlier chapters involving music for example may be useful to explore.

Investigating Style and Form

Much of the time we can end up in an area of generalised understanding around form and style, which can then translate into generalised acting. So, it is useful, again most typically in conjunction with the creative team, to spend some time researching and detailing the precise practical impacts of any identifiable form or style within a text.

The art of performance and the writing of drama are not static forms; they evolve and are subject to shifts in style and aesthetic, as much as any art form responds to the world which informs it. While most of us could recognise a naturalistic performance of a realistic text, Ibsen is different from *The Kitchen Sink* British writers of the 1950s, and, while the time period may be equivalent, the *realism* of US writer Lorraine Hansberry's *A Raisin in the Sun* is different again. The idea of realism in the twenty-first century necessarily reflects a changing and diversifying understanding that realities and *realism* can be very different for the different voices integral to contemporary practice; Kwame Kwei Armah's

Elmina's Kitchen and Tom Wells's *The Kitchen Sink* may share some stylistic elements (conversational dialogue), but the reality represented is not homogeneous.

Beyond any notion of realism, many actors will recognise that there are also practitioners, forms, and styles that have relatively common currency in theatre; we call things *Brechtian* and *Pinter-esque* or we recognise a performance as *farce* or *pantomime*, or encounter texts which are *verbatim, physical theatre*, etc.

While this may be a generalisation, twenty-first-century texts often are hybrids, or work within a range of stylistic modes or forms in performance; and in these cases it's even more vital to detail the specific shifts and transitions of forms within a text. It's not unusual to encounter a written text that is a record of a first production which evolved those elements in rehearsal; and so the text provides us with stage directions or verbal descriptions of a physical or a visual sequence within sections of conversational or other forms of dialogue (look at texts and adaptations from *Frantic, Complicité*, or *Shared Experience* for illustrations of this). Exploring how these stage directions can be developed into precise and specific performance choices in the context of your specific production may require practical investigation beyond simply identifying given circumstances, character, and relationships.

Research Questions to Consider

- Is there an identifiable style or form provided by the text (or in notes from the writer)?
- Is this coherent throughout, or is there a range of stylistic or formal elements? For example, a farce is likely to be coherent throughout, even if conversational/*realistic* scenes might be interspersed with *movement/physically articulated* (rather than verbal).
- If there's a range of stylistic elements, how might they impact your character's action?
- Is there a sense of what the artistic intention is by using the range of styles? Do they nuance the meaning or heighten a resonance within the action?
- Do they seem to cohere the piece, or are there intended contradictions?
- Can you identify any specific technique or craft that might need to be investigated within your action (for example, in-ear verbatim, puppetry, technical comedy/business)?
- Does the identified style carry any specific values in terms of characters, or set pieces of action (for example, pantomime holds consistent characters, tropes, and narrative devices)?

What to Investigate

If there is a clear style, form, or practice referenced in the play, then it can be useful to follow these up via reading practitioner or critical texts. However, because you need to be able to investigate in practice, a better route in terms of research can be to find opportunities to encounter practices, forms, and styles through practical workshops, etc.

Styles and forms are complex and mutable themselves, so it can be useful to explore the form via other engagements with it, and in other media. For example, *farce* has some relatively established hallmarks – *Flea in Her Ear* and the film of *Clockwise* might both have elements to consider even though one is a 1980s British film, and one is a 1907 French play.

If the text has emerged through a particular company's working process, resources from that company via websites and the like can often be a good way to comprehend the process through which they arrived at the text; if possible try to see any filmed material generated either within this process, or of other performances they have presented.

PITFALL

Often a style is intended to work in contradiction with the core of the text, using the friction of this to provoke different ideas, but this means the actor has to be additionally careful about not just playing the style. *Poppy* uses pantomime to engage with the colonial legacy of the English/Chinese Opium Wars. *The Importance of Being Earnest* is often only comedic if the truth of the given circumstances underpins the action, rather than demonstrating the self-conscious wit of the style.

Contemporary Context and Ethical Impacts

The production context starts with a piece of writing to be represented on stage/screen, evolved collaboratively as a performance event, that ultimately is presented in the context of an audience. The rehearsal and production environment is in itself a context, which will impact and affect the generation of expressive choices and in which the personal contexts of all involved will need to be considered.

You are likely to carry personal values and references into your work on the text within the company, and while in many cases part of our work is to be able to journey beyond our own personal frames of reference, there is still the need to consider questions of boundaries and challenges; to know what we are challenging and why, and when a challenge is valid and when it is reductive or exploitative.

While again, many of these questions are not solely the actors' job to research and answer, it is important that the actors' voices are part of the investigations and answers. It's your body and voice that is representing these characters in these worlds.

Dramatic performance is often complex, engaging with an array of contemporary problems, challenges, or provocations to the perceived status quo. While performance intended to shock and offend can be misconceived as an artistic objective, it remains the case that challenge and provocation can be core aspects of performance. The questions of who is provoked or offended (and by what *triggers*), who judges what appropriate or suitable content is, who defines what is *okay to say* or to express, etc are by no means straightforward, and are fundamentally contextual. What seems complex or triggering for one person may not be so for another. There is always research to do in respect of appraising the potential impacts of a text, and considering this from a multiplicity of frames of reference. This does not mean that any production should automatically seek to limit its potential scope for fear of negative reaction, but more that due consideration should be made as to how that is explored and expressed in the contexts of research, rehearsal, and presentation. This is detailed further in Chapter 8.

The nature of texts intended, say, for children may offer one set of problems; for example, the vocabulary: swearing, overly complex references they won't get, *age-appropriate* material, etc. These can seem relatively straightforward to attend to; but they do still need to be investigated.

Explicit scenes of physical intimacy, violence, or abuse may be central to textual action in many plays and may raise questions more about the process of evolving these for performance, rather than the nature of what is represented. *How* explicitly scripted action of nudity or sexual activity is presented on stage often comes down to artistic choice, and the question of what is deemed *dramatically necessary* can often be legitimately challenged. However, just finding stylised or symbolic representations might not be coherent aesthetically within the form, genre, or style of performance. What is never negotiable is that any situations in which there is personal vulnerability, exposure, and physical/emotional risk MUST be appropriately researched as to how such activities and scenes can be safely developed in practice.

Older texts often carry *outdated* attitudes, and difficult vocabulary around race, gender, sexuality, disability, religion, etc which may be accurate in representing the values of that time/space, and with contextualisation can be useful illumination of prevailing attitudes in the past. However, there may also be texts you encounter in which a comedic, satirical, or ironic tone makes these areas muddier beyond whether or not they are *historically accurate*, or texts which simply don't intend to represent these aspects *accurately* – but where this doesn't necessarily compromise the work itself and in fact can be central to its artistry (see *Hamilton* again).

Some texts evolve through a focused engagement with specific communities or social groups, with an avowed intention to gather and represent those specific voices and stories, via documentary theatre or verbatim practices. It's not uncommon for actors within a company to be part of that development of the textual material, in which case ethical research practice is intrinsic to the evolution.

However, even if the textual material has been shaped prior to the actor's engagement in rehearsal for performance, there is still a responsibility on the part of the actor to research and comprehend the values and experiences of the communities from which this material has been drawn and represents.

Questions of authenticity, representation, lived experiences, and theatrical truth are complex in and of themselves within our contemporary practice; who has legitimacy in representing a specific identity, how far away from the authentic self should performance go, can there ever be such a thing as gender/colour/ability-*blind* casting, are these desirable or simply eroding different lived experiences, how far can *conscious casting* truly include those who are *othered* professionally? There are no easy answers, and not always clear rights and wrongs – they are always contextual and intricate. Considering your own frame of reference, challenging this, and embarking on investigations beyond this is the personal research that continues throughout your career.

Many of the following questions should be considered by directors and producers, but it's always worth as an actor making sure that you have considered your needs and embodied knowledge and matters of inclusion and representation on your own terms. As an actor there will be texts or processes you encounter which it may be appropriate to investigate, challenge, or question in order to build your own agency and navigation within the process.

Research Questions to Consider

- Are there aspects of the text which strike you as complex or problematic in what they explore or represent, or how they express it?
- Are there aspects of the text which need specific attention within the process and rehearsal requirements in order to meet that complexity? Consider yourself as an actor and your needs within that complexity.
- Are these a question of needing more information to contextualise material which carries outdated attitudes, language, etc?
- Are these to do with personal frames of reference, or more widely observable and applicable?
- Who is the intended audience? Does that affect your judgement of elements of complexity? Who might provide insight here if so?
- Are there elements within the text or production which may require consideration of *triggering* content? This might affect you, other cast members, and audiences.
- Does your lived experience collide with textual representations of it? Is this a question of informed characterisation of a different person in different circumstances, or are there factual elements which may need clarification?
- Does the text directly emerge from and/or express the lived experience of real people? Have their voices and identities been safeguarded appropriately through this? Do you have sufficient information to substantially engage

with understanding and respecting these experiences as an actor representing them?

- Does the text purport to represent real or historical people and events? How do these reflect general contemporary thinking or factual evidence about those people or events?
- Does the text or the planned production of it suggest, rely on, or explore specific casting or representation in performance? Has this been interrogated? Are questions of authenticity and inclusion addressed appropriately?
- With new writing it can also be useful to consider whether or not you have been given the rehearsal version of the script, so you are appraising the planned version, not an earlier draft.

PITFALL

Your identity is vital as a source of your acting. But it is important to be able to transcend and go beyond this; and this may also ask you to inhabit characters that are problematic and repellent in service of a complex drama. Make sure your lived experience allows you to enrich the conversation, not obstruct it – but do recognise that sometimes you may be better to withdraw from a project if there seems little capacity on the part of others to engage with dialogue around this, or if you are not ready to explore issues safely which have direct personal implications.

What to Investigate

If you are finding content problematic and there isn't an immediate personal trauma impacting you that you are aware of, consider specifically *what* it is that may be triggering or problematic, and also consider when you may just need to familiarise yourself with an issue of which you don't have much experience or informed personal understanding.

Try to separate your emotional response or distaste for certain attitudes from the material itself and consider the specifics of the characters' circumstances and relationships. A text like Roy Williams's *Sing Yer Heart Out for the Lads* frankly engages with questions of British racism and racist characters; but as an actor working on this, you cannot play your own rejection of racism within those scenes. When you are uncertain, seek out voices who may have different experiences and insight from yours in respect of complexities; many organisations exist and have websites where a wealth of information, personal testimony, and guidance can be explored to move your response from the personal to a more objective understanding of what authentic truth could be in this situation. You may very well have done this via the character frame of reference and biography exercises already.

It's also worth raising concerns with others who are not directly connected with the process, as well as those who are. Often articulating queries results in a sigh of relief and recognition from others in the process, and the act of discussion with anyone often dispels personal worries or clarifies specifics and potential solutions; working on material which contains problematic content should include collaborative discussion that acknowledges potential impacts on everyone within the process. Consultation with those who have greater understanding of specific groups at an early stage can also be helpful in order to avoid making assumptions; for example, informally or formally running material past primary school teachers or parents for a children's show. This might encompass a consideration of both target audiences and any groups specifically represented as such within the piece.

A central part of the investigation should be conducted through the rehearsal. You are never solely responsible for the potential impacts and challenges of a text for production, and questions of contextualisation of content and collaborative working should be group authored. It can be useful if you are working in a training environment to establish group working practices, by which relevant discussion, support time, and ensuring all voices are heard can be agreed (see Chapter 8). These also underpin Equity's *Safe Spaces campaign* for the professional contexts.

If you have questions regarding a planned staging of a text, or how that text has evolved, the investigation should primarily be via conversations with the director and producers. You should expect information about the detail of intimate scenes, expected nudity, or staged combat/physical stunt work that is required. In general, do this before you agree to the contract. A central part of your research is to appraise what you can safely explore and which boundaries you can traverse, and decline work that you are not ready to engage with.

It's useful to keep abreast of current guidelines which exist within rehearsal processes, such as Equity's intimacy guidelines for stage and screen. Increasingly the role of an intimacy director or coordinator is expected within production processes; however, on a personal research basis it can be useful to explore training and workshops in this area, to allow you to build a good understanding of navigating these aspects safely as an individual. Similarly, personal practice research in stage combat skills can be a useful exploration. This doesn't remove the responsibility on the part of the production company to ensure appropriate staff, production time, and training are available, but it will allow you a greater understanding of when such activities may need to be flagged, and to navigate scenarios with some agency.

Filling in the Gaps

No actor has an encyclopaedic knowledge of cultural contexts, practitioners, styles, and forms – and so there will always be gaps. Every production, in any medium, is a gap to be filled by the business of rehearsing and performing it.

Building your own understanding, whether this is through reading material, viewing performance in any medium or other artworks, or investigating in practice via workshops, can be an important aspect of your research practice as you aim to expand your own cultural frames of reference.

The more you build your own knowledge independently, the more connections and intersections you can identify, the richer your practice can become. It can be helpful to consider exploring these practically. If you think about some of the creative response exercises outlined in Chapter 1, can you explore notions of style and form, or fuse different artistic ideas and concepts within your imaginative response?

Into Reflection

Many areas explored in this chapter will not be required in full with every text, but it can be helpful to consider some aspects as worthy of reflection and research beyond working on a specific text. Building your knowledge of historical shifts in performance, or the impacts of significant socio-cultural events within your own context, will never be a waste of time.

Think of how conversation shifted around the COVID-19 pandemic, #metoo, or Black Lives Matter. It will have impacted you as a human and possibly expanded your own frame of reference, but also will inform the texts you are likely to encounter and the contexts in which you will experience them. Be active about considering how the dramatic material you encounter – in any form or medium – engages with, explores, or represents the world around you, and recognising your own discoveries and development of new frames of reference that emerge from this.

Further Reading

- *Style for Actors* by Robert Barton
- *Acting in High Comedy* by Maria Aitken
- *Modern British Playwriting: 2000–2009: Voices, Documents, New Interpretations* by Dan Rebellato
- *Verbatim Theatre* by Claire Summerskill
- *On Connection* by Kae Tempest
- *The Time Traveller's Guide to British Theatre* by Aleks Sierz and Lia Ghilardi

Note

1 Hemingway, E. (1926) *The Sun Also Rises*, Scribner, New York.

Guy Stanley

8

REPURPOSING ACTOR'S RESEARCH – DIFFERENT APPLICATIONS

Where Do We Go From Here?

We hope you have reached this point with some understanding of how to research creatively, being able to appraise existing ideas and material in rigorous detail, to support and evidence this with a diverse range of sources, while also being able to consider different ways to explore and present findings and think outside the box. We also hope that we have encouraged you to integrate some reflective practice into your work, and this has allowed you to come to richer capacity to appraise yourself and your work, and consolidate discoveries, shape your thinking and choices, and invest and trust in your practical creativity. These are skills that can be useful in many contexts and developed through further study and training. This chapter aims to suggest some potential applications for the research work you have undertaken and will continue to explore, and some ideas for developing your work and your skills further.

Increasingly, the contemporary performance landscape is being shaped by actors who can generate their own material; they can write, direct, or create performance work on their own terms. Beyond the creative generation of material, again it's often quite common now to find actors taking greater autonomy over the producing and presenting of their (or others') work – a skillset that in early careers can be enhanced by also understanding the intersections between this creative research practice and how it can inform funding applications, marketing, design, or educational projects. Alongside the creative application of research is also the need to consider the ethical framework in which practice research sits, whether this is in the context of a university course, or within the profession. Performance generation in any context relies on a nuanced appraisal of the human stories we often wish to explore, and the appropriate levels of attention being paid as to how we tell these stories, respectfully, inclusively, and safely.

DOI: 10.4324/9781003226130-9

Repurposing Rehearsal Research

Over the course of a rehearsal process, and through your own research activity, it's very likely that you will have amassed in some cases a truly impressive amount of material – whether as notes, images, music playlists, imaginative writing, or anything else. While you may be working in a production context whereby many of the following suggestions are undertaken by specific company members, you may also find that you are working in smaller-scale ensembles, or presenting your own production, in which these can add immense value to getting a project off the ground.

Programme notes – As we have mentioned several times, this material can be a valuable source for actors in the future, as well as often being really handy for contextualising the particular choices or distinctive themes and ideas explored within a specific production. It can be a useful exercise to practice writing these, because it can help consolidate your journey, as well as identify what register and details are enlightening for an audience.

Educational/Background resources (print or online) – Again, this is a vital future source for other actors, as well as a real boon for teachers bringing young people to the show. You are likely to find that you have a wealth of detail that has already been thought about as to how it can communicate practically, but which intersects with various subjects and skills. What was it like to live in another time (history)? What affected the environments (geography)? What choices did people have to make (sociology, politics)? How do we tell the story? Interpret set texts (English, drama/theatre studies, music)? You may need to do some additional research to make sure this gets presented in a way that supports education and age-appropriate learning. For example, what part of the history curriculum might it support? Think about GCSE in the UK or High School diploma, or even Junior School. Can you offer fact-based sources? What accessible activities can you suggest for the classroom? But much of what you have done practically in the rehearsal room as well as in research may be useful to consider here. You may also have recorded video material within the process, or find sharing action/event timelines, character biographies, diaries, etc are great additions. It's a useful exercise to practice identifying how these resources evolve value, and what content, tone, and structures work in this format and for different audiences; this kind of work may also be an interesting side business in different contexts.

Theatre practice resources/workshops – While this may get integrated with the previous point, it can also be conducive to look at shaping some of your rehearsal work into resources specific to the drama curriculum. You may have emerged from a devising or physical process that explored particular practices or approaches for which there is a valuable practical workshop to distil. You may also have worked through a clear Stanislavskian process but within a contemporary context, which may offer more than just reading books about him. There may very well be a personal benefit in reflecting on and consolidating your own process, alongside investigating whether there is any benefit in sharing this on a wider basis (online or in person; academically or practically).

Curating Q and A/discussion sessions – This usually occurs in your venue, before or after a performance, but may also be online. These can be valuable to an engaged loyal audience, especially in regional theatres. You might anticipate questions and discussion about the particular production choices – specific themes, choices, or processes – and there is often a fascination with how actors create their role. These can be useful methods also of understanding feedback and response to your work (as an actor or a maker, see the following), and often having to articulate your process can be helpful in clarifying your thinking and discoveries. It's also worth thinking of these as preparation for when you book your big Hollywood movie and have to go on chat shows . . .

Taking it Further

- If you are looking to repurpose your research, especially in print or online, be aware that there may very well be copyright clearances and permissions to obtain if you use other people's text, photos, video, images, or music.
- If work or material is collectively generated, and much is, in this context, it's important that everyone's consent and permission is obtained for usage.

Practice Research and Developing Performance

While this book has focused on research for practice as an actor, there are many intersections between this and the potential practice research of creating performance or creating work yourself for production. As noted earlier, increasingly the actor is viewed as a generative as well as an interpretive artist, capable of creating content, not just turning up to act in it.

Many of the skills and objectives we've tried to identify in each chapter also intersect with those of the writer, maker, or director; the exercises can be repurposed to create character, relationships, and situations, as well as explore within an existing text. The analysis of texts and sources as suggested can offer just as much information and insight to the maker/creator as to the doer. That said, we do not wish to suggest that there aren't particular and distinct skills within the work of the writer, maker, or director. The art and craft of these disciplines is varied but specific, and often requires additional mindsets, activities, and critical viewpoints to the actor.

You may very well find over the course of exploring some of the exercises in this book, that you end up with some great material that you just know *has legs* and potential for further development, or which others have told you they're excited by. We're delighted. So now let's think about how to take that further.

Scratch and sniff – There are various theatres and organisations that offer scratch nights, impromptu quasi-open mic types of events at which works in progress can be shared. Test your work, get feedback from people who may be supportive and constructive, but who aren't emotionally involved with you or the piece – whatever stage it's in.

Evolving a writing skillset – The capacity for shaping nuanced dialogue, creating characters, structuring scenes, *telling* a story through moments are all hallmarks of good writing, and these are skills to be developed and refined. Seek out places where you can take your understanding to the specifics of these; many theatres and institutions such as the Arvon Foundation offer short-form (and longer) writing programmes, and there is a wealth of resources via, for example, the BBC Writersroom. Take some time to develop your understanding of this as a writer practically. Very rarely is anyone's first script solid gold – even those who go on to be recognised for their work. The more opportunities you can find to test in practice and get feedback on your work, the more substantial your understanding can become.

Evolving a making skillset – You may have spent some time within a degree course on devised projects, but there are always additional skills to explore here, particularly if the course you have done is primarily acting/text-based. There are various companies which do offer workshop-based training for devising and making (e.g. *Frantic*), but it can also be useful to explore other routes in here such as clown or mime approaches, which may assist with non-text-based ideas and practice. You may find workshops around festivals which introduce this method of working, alongside more specialist practices such as Lecoq and Gaulier. It can be useful to really consider your practice in this area as a skillset to work on before engaging on a full-scale devised project – evolve the skills, and then apply them.

Research and development workshops – On occasion you will find organisations who will offer funding or space for these, but even if you have to fund and resource yourself, go through a process of practical interrogation. Plan this – and many of the exercises in this book may assist. Try to avoid leading R&D hoping the actors will just bring something in – help them to do so! What are the moments/scenes/units? Where/when are we? Who are the characters? What are the relationships? What is the story? How is it told? Share where you get at the end of this, however fragmented and chaotic, with people who can be objective.

Make your idea substantial – Much of the research you undertake as an actor is framed by the text, which is the result of the research that has already happened through the work of the writer. Often we find the creative material we have evolved through a rehearsal process is working from givens in the text, but these are not absolute, and we're still imaginatively filling in the gaps. It's relatively easy to construct plausible dialogue in an interesting situation; but this is rarely sufficient to give real theatrical substance to an idea. You will need to do your writer's research, which will require you to go further; you are going to need to detail all your characters, not just one you might be playing. Take time to consider potential *frames* through which this idea might be encountered; different perspectives, different given circumstances and settings, different styles (see previous Chapter 7).

Testing your work – There are various theatres and organisations which also run competitive programmes and awards for new writing (*Bruntwood, Papatango, Paines Plough*, etc). These can be great opportunities, though some may also offer constraints as to, for example, duration, cast size, topical engagement, etc. It can be a useful exercise to reframe a piece according to constraints, but there is also a critical act of research implicit here in respect of shaping material for form and context. If your work doesn't fit, cutting eight scenes and two characters may not necessarily help if it takes the heart from it. Research where your work might fit, or work to create something within the constraints of where you wish to send it.

Taking it Further

- Very few plays ever spring fully formed and perfect from the head of a writer. Your first draft is never perfect, however inspired it feels. Make your peace with that and expect to edit without rancour.
- Positive feedback is often about potential, not the precise script. Don't read positivity as specific endorsement of a fixed product.
- There's a huge benefit from seeking feedback from those who have different creative engagements with performance such as designers, directors, producers, etc, not just actors or writer/makers.
- Sometimes great ideas just don't develop. Sometimes a moment passes. Sometimes the process is more useful than the outcome. Sometimes someone else will do it better than you. It is always valuable to consider and recognise if this might be the case.

Establishing Ethical Collaborative Practice Research

If you are looking at translating some of your research practice as an actor on a text, or within a devised process, into a format for creating new work, it is important to consider the ethical aspects of doing so. As mentioned in Chapter 7, the ethical practice of a safe rehearsal room regarding intimacy, inclusion, and equality are important areas to consider as an actor. If you are looking at creating work these and other ethical consideration should be fundamentally part of taking your research further.

Whether you are inside or outside an institution, whether there is a *research ethics* policy or not, there are key areas of activity that your research for creating a performance piece should consider: human participation at the ideational stage of research, and human participation at the rehearsal stage of research. Many theatre companies now will evolve ethical principles which govern how they wish to generate material; the ethical and inclusive treatment of actors (and other collaborators) in rehearsal and on set should always be mapped against the accepted values of the industry bodies such as Equity, Solt/UK theatres, and BECTU (the Broadcasting, Entertainment, Communications and Theatre Union).

The process of *making work* as a performer is multi-dimensional, and there are no standard formats and processes; in fact much material generated comes through innovative and non-standard processes. For example, the context of lockdown generated a large amount of hybrid live/digital work for which there were few fixed protocols.

If you are working collaboratively to create the performance text (i.e. devising as a group, rather than using a text written already by someone within the group (or outside it), it should be regarded as good practice to establish a collaborative practice research agreement for the project, which considers any relevant ethical questions, as well as agreeing on the principles and methods of group-authored practice research. This can be particularly useful if you are working informally, and voluntarily, without a professional production team or company running the process – or if in fact you are the production company!

If you are working on a professional contract, these may be a useful checklist to look for in a contract (though many won't necessarily be detailed in this way) or in discussion with the company.

When evolving collaborative practice research agreements, we have found the following useful areas to consider, though not every project will necessitate all areas in the same amount of detail:

- *Practical professionalism* – Establish your company's approach to attendance at sessions, timekeeping, breaks, warmups/cool-downs (emotionally as well as physically), health and safety, practically running sessions, planning activity/timeframes, weekly goals/targets, etc, and how you are going to keep to this, but also adapt and adjust as needed. How are you going to manage the functional administration, communications, and schedules?

- *Ethical research* – Establish your company's approach to interviews (verbatim use or otherwise), workshop activity with third parties, data management and retention, confidentiality and anonymity, rights to withdraw, provision of information to all especially regarding sensitive/triggering subject matter, recognition of potential content impacts in the room, and any relevant support for appropriate exploration of this.

- *Interpersonal intimacy and physical practice* – Establish as a group how you are comfortable working safely considering respectful boundaries, representation of sexual/intimate acts, physical touch, combat, nudity, additional physical activities (e.g. acrobatics). Is a fight director or intimacy coordinator required?

- *Inclusion and engagement* –Establish as a company any adjustments/support workers you may need to accommodate needs, ensuring all individuals can participate and contribute. How will you support if there are challenges in practice? How will you integrate *all* voices not just *loud* voices? What strengths do you all bring? Can you ascribe some activity/roles accordingly?
- *Agreeing on independent activity* – Establish expectations on self-led work. What will individual contributions look like? How will you divide tasks equitably but appropriately? How much time is enough? Can this be flexible? How does independent work come into the studio? How will you handle deadlines, weekly updates, shared docs/resources, etc? What is the level of detail and substance you want as a group?
- *Practical development* – How are you going to work (e.g. scripting, improv)? What research activity will you do? How will you allocate this? What practices are you going to integrate? How are you going to explore these appropriately (i.e. avoiding invasive exploitative practices, however *raw*)? What additional creative inputs are you planning? How are you going to identify resources? How will you agree when/if any of these change? How much time do you want to allocate to talking? How will you consider the allocating and sharing of other practical roles (e.g. rotating director, dramaturgy, script writing, or allocating tech, movement/music roles)?
- *Artistic decision making* – Establish how as a group you are going to shape the idea to evolve. What does the imagined destination look like to all of you? How will you manage *dropping* an idea to select another one? Do you need a majority to do so? Will you reject at the discussion stage, or only after trial in practice? How will you make sure everyone feels connected to the journey of travel? How will you manage if you feel that the idea isn't what you wanted originally? How will you negotiate *killing your babies* artistically, and those of others?
- *Accountability and conflict resolution* – How will you resolve disagreements (majority rules, identify a *director* role)? How will you manage if someone isn't *pulling their weight*, or only invests and contributes when it's their idea on the floor, or if boundaries are crossed unexpectedly/accidentally? How will you give feedback to each other in the room on their/your work, and discuss matters when group members disagree? How will you support and enable the work, but also challenge, interrogate, and hold yourselves accountable for the journey and the destination?
- *Future development* – Who owns the material and text that emerges? How is the writer/creator identified? Is it the group, or does someone end up named as the writer? Do all the company members have the power of veto over next steps? Can different people take the same material further independently of each other? Are all the participants/contributors guaranteed the same role in any subsequent opportunity with the piece, or might you recast?

Engaging Ethically With Sources and Subject Investigation

There is also an ethical aspect regarding using source material, whether this is legally managed through copyrights or whether there are greyer areas around working with directly supplied personal material. Whenever ideas and material emerge from somewhere other than just your head, it is important to appraise and research what may need additional consents or discussion, and how this may vary at different stages of your process, and depending on whether the research is being conducted by you as a writer primarily, or as a director, or as one of a group of devisers.

Very few ideas leap fully formed into our brains without being inspired by or responding to some form of stimulus. However, it's not always immediately obvious, even to ourselves, which stimulus fires the neurons of creativity, or how our imaginations evolve these into works of art. A great many pieces of performance text would be impossible to precisely appraise on the basis of what ideational or imaginative *research* directly informed them. However, there are also some research activities which are straightforward in needing to be acknowledged and managed, as well as some very grey areas, where using someone else's *story/experience* that you came across anecdotally or informally may require additional consideration.

Subject Research from Non-Human Sources

Subject research from sources which are published or distributed (in any media) and freely available, in general may not need permissions and consents. For example, you may need to look up facts about how you register the death of a parent, or you read/watch a lot of films, fiction, and poetry about bereavement, but then create a unique character/situation yourself who experiences this. As long as you create/write the text with no actual individuals (living or historical in some cases) identified, quoted, or represented within the text, which will be a *fictional construct from ideas drawn from imagination* and a range of source materials, then you are not using human subjects as sources and so there are no ethical aspects to consider.

However, any use of third-party copyright materials within the text (e.g. quoting lyrics) rather than just as stimulus will in most situations require permissions from copyright holders, and potentially usage fees. Texts, or elements of the text, or performance *which use/are directly adapted from existing published fictional or non-fictional material in any media will be subject to copyright*. This includes music, video, images, etc, as well as textual sources; and it's worth noting that using such material online has very different restrictions from those in the live context.

Similarly, if you wish to represent a particular individual (famous or otherwise) or event it can be a good idea to consider whether any individual or related party (family, etc) should be notified or considered within your research process. Under any circumstances in the twenty-first century, it is good practice to consider this as an ethical element of research, and also to be aware of legislation around libel and defamation when and where you are writing or producing for publication or a public audience. If you are representing something as an accurate and truthful depiction (i.e. not a clearly fictional artistic construct) then your research into demonstrable factual evidence for this must be bulletproof – and not just artisti-cally – if any party could take issue with this in respect of reputational damage, or a right to privacy. If in doubt, take legal advice.

If your practice research is being shaped within an educational context, e.g. it's your master's thesis, it's also worth bearing in mind that in most cases you are likely to need to formally write your research, and so your institution's guidance for citation, referencing, and bibliographies should be considered alongside your subject investigation. It's good practice to note all the sources that form part of your process even in a professional context; these can be useful to keep track of for future development purposes if you are doing a staged R&D (research and development). They can be useful to retain in order to inform the wider creative team and your actor's work and they may potentially be good references to revisit if you need to evolve marketing or educational materials for the performance of the piece. (See the following section 'Taking Research to Practical Production'.)

Human Subjects In and As Research

Beyond subject investigation from existing sources, it is also relatively common for practice research to *engage with human participation and human sources within the process*; to inspire, or inform a script/text at any stage of research and develop-ment, even if any individuals are not actors or intended to be physically present within the presentation of the piece (i.e. they aren't necessarily just those cast in the final performance project).

The following areas cover most ways in which you may need to consider ethical practice within your ideational stage of research. It should be noted that sessions conducted should also be considered in the light of the collaborative practice detailed in the previous section, and/or the rehearsal practice detailed after this. These areas identify those activities which should generate an informed consent process, which should be recorded in writing, and agreed to in advance of participation; in a professional context this would often be detailed in a con-tract, and so consent agreements even in an educational setting should be viewed as operating similarly.

- Subject research conducted *through creative human participation in improvised/ R&D/workshop scenarios from provided stimuli/direction* and outcomes from which are refined into a fictionalised text. (Participant consent is required if these sessions are separate from any formally identified rehearsal for perfor-mance sessions, wherein they are cast as actors, and this should encompass limits on this; i.e. they might do the R&D but there is no guarantee of first offer of casting.)

• Subject research conducted by researcher *through interviews/questions in any form/media with identified individuals/groups specifically selected* for their knowledge or experience of the thematic ideas. (Participant consent is required in respect of method/process of engagement, questions asked, recording, use, anonymity, individual depiction/representation as character, direct identification, use of actual voice recording in performance, context, generation of verbatim text via editing, and ability to withdraw.) You should also consider the inclusivity of your methodology, and the narrative agency and rights of veto particularly if you are selecting *subjects* for insight into specific lived experience or protected characteristics.

• Subject research which is based on *unpublished personal material or individual/ personal experience provided to a researcher personally and obtained for this research purpose specifically*, however informally. (Participant/Copyright owner consent may be required in respect of copyright, recording, use, anonymity, individual depiction/representation as character, context, and generation of verbatim text via editing, up to and including personal photos/video and social media inputs.)

• Presentation or textual elements/scenarios which derive from *researcher's personal experience with others and which may have been acquired anecdotally or indirectly, within which individuals may recognise themselves* even if anonymised in presentation in this context. (This is likely to require additional consent in respect of professional or interpersonal courtesy, use, anonymity, individual depiction/representation as character, and verbatim text, including personal photos/video, social media inputs, and family stories.)

Ethical Rehearsal Room Practice Research

If you are rehearsing and then performing your scripted piece, then your practice research also needs to be considered through ethical considerations for participation in rehearsal and performance. You should consider the potential impacts of the rehearsal practice, content, and material on your human participants! In professional terms, these are elements which may be useful to articulate within a contract discussion, or about which to anticipate questions from your cast. As an actor they can also be useful things to shape your discussions about taking on work.

The same is true in respect of working with student actor participants on a project within an institution within a course of study. It may be expected that professional actors will receive a final script alongside the contract, even if there is the likelihood that this will evolve in rehearsal.

We have found it useful to consider the following areas in order to identify matters which may need additional investigation, or information provided to your performers/participants so that they can consent, within both an institution and the professional context. Each of these areas will vary according to the specifics of the project/production, and so your practice should be focused on detailing these areas in reflection of your text/material.

- *Theme/idea or content* – Pay attention particularly to subject matter which may be considered emotionally triggering, complex, or in need of contextualization and support in and around rehearsal.
- *Necessary intimacy, nudity, combat/violence, or physical depictions of traumatising activity* – This is especially important if the intended aesthetic does not easily permit an alternative staging.
- *Mitigations, management, and support structures* in place to support the previous points – For example, this may be intimacy coordination/direction, a fight director, a support or wellbeing staff member, company meetings/exercises to detach or *cool down* from complex emotional work, or other processes for dealing with issues if they arise.
- *Practical process requirements* – This includes physical/contact/character improvisation, text work, and intellectual research/reading of sources What is the expected prep for and activity in the studio?
- *Performer/Participants commitment* – Performers contribute their time and artistic practice through a specified intensive rehearsal and performance period, and may be asked to do provisional read-throughs/development activity within the process. Detail out any other commitments such as fittings, recordings, photocalls, post-show events, etc. Include policies if needed.
- *Performer/Participants may be video/audio/still recorded* by researcher/production team within the rehearsal process in order to inform the development of the performance, the documentation, and potentially marketing materials.
- *Use of other material in any media in the performance* – Depending on the creative development of the piece, some material may be recorded or created by participants within the process and used within the performance or marketing activity. No additional consent should be required if this is specified and agreed upon in advance.
- *Authorship and Intellectual Property* – This piece of research/performance will be regarded as the IP of the named researcher/writer/director, since all participants' contributions are obtained under specific direction, and according to the parameters established via the individual researcher, who retains the copyright. You may wish to augment this if you are working with someone whose story is the central source, or if the process means you should consider a broader collective authorship has operated in evolving and realising the story as a performance text.
- There are no *hazards or risks in participation*, and all performance practice will be conducted according to the expected safe practices of a professional rehearsal room. If there are, then a risk assessment and mitigations should be included.

- *Safeguarding* – No children or vulnerable adults form part of the participant/ performer group. If they do, detail the mitigations and protections you have put in place for these, including signposting to company or institutional policies. What is the process if there is a problem or a complaint about safe and appropriate practice? Where or to whom do these issues get reported? How can they be managed?

While the previous prompts may map onto standard research ethics protocols in an institution, it is vital to comprehend that many of these areas are fundamental to professional contracts you will embark on, or indeed may want to issue if you are producing your own work. Ethical research performance practice is an unambiguous goal, and the fusion between professional and academic practice in establishing this is one we wholly support.

Taking it Further

- The fundamental principles that underpin all of this are to provide detailed and relevant information about what is expected, to offer relevant and appropriate support to achieve this, and to make sure that informed consent is obtained at all stages; the details may vary according to the individual script/text.
- Research practice or performance that is obtained by exploitation, contrived exposure, or manipulation has no validity; there is no idea so good that it has to be predicated on this.
- The artistry is in being able to create visceral, raw, and challenging work without traumatising participants/actors/anyone else. This is the research we want to undertake.

Taking Research to Practical Production

Even if you are not focused on translating your actor's research into generating new performance material, the research work you undertake in and around the rehearsal room and the skills this takes can have a useful application in a production context.

While in many professional cases you are likely to be working within a creative team, for whom there are clear roles and responsibilities – for example you'll be working within a set created by a designer – there will be someone producing or shaping and detailing the marketing. You may also be in a situation in which this is not the case, and a more self-led or collective route is required. These areas will also connect with your own research skillset, though in most cases you will need to do more specific and practical investigation here, because again, these are expert professional skills, functions, and activities.

Funding and Pitching

If you are looking to produce work yourself, it's quite likely that you will find yourself in a situation of pitching for a programming slot, selling a tour, or applying for funding. This work might be written (the ACE application form, or other funding bodies' proposal processes), in meetings in person, or via online crowdfunding campaigns. While some aspects of the process really require meticulous data-driven research (budgets and finances), your creative research skills can also be repurposed and extended to shape your proposal; it's not unusual to produce a concise and engaging 'production pack' which distils key aspects of what is distinctive and appealing about your piece.

Most pitches and applications will ask for a concise outline of what the intended production is, and why it's artistically valid; and usually will ask for some detail regarding the process of development, distinctive interpretations, access and connection to target audiences, and, after the production, an evaluation of successes or areas to improve. Applying the questions from Chapter 7 about contextual frames is likely to be a good starting point here.

As much as anything else, funders often have clear objectives (for example, they prioritise funding youth projects) and venues similarly also have artistic direction, or brand values which shape which productions they pick up. Researching what these are (in advance of applying) can provide you with a clear set of given circumstances in which to shape your choices of what to highlight and detail in your application, and the language, vibe, and register expected in a proposal. Similarly, apply those research skills in really understanding who your target audience is/ might be (their *world*) and how they might connect with your work. What makes a great crowdfunding campaign for your targets? What material or communication is going to attract them? What is their relationship with the production?

If you are pitching for a programming slot in a venue, you can also apply your ability to appraise the space here. Sometimes this can be entirely practical (Will the set fit on the stage?), but you may also want to explore site-specific, found space or immersive environments. In this context, your spatial research is partly artistic as well as practical when you are proposing what you might present in the space and how you might do so.

Taking it Further

- While your creative research is vital for informing funding and pitching activity, this has to be accompanied by more practical research as well. Avoid applying or proposing if you haven't really detailed the finances, feasibility, and practical logistics of what you want to do.
- Producing and all associated roles are complex and demanding; if you are undertaking this it can be very useful to look for training and guidance. We

really like the training and support offers by the ITC (Independent Theatre Council UK) in this area; they will often prove a worthwhile investment.

• If you are producing, at any level, keep up to date with Equity and other union guidance in respect of the work. Make sure you treat your actors (and everyone else) as you would like to be treated yourself!

Shaping the Words

Alongside thinking about taking your research into writing/creating funding pitches, you will also have to think about some words that go alongside this that 'sell' your show to your intended audience.

These might take the following forms across digital or print media:

• Tag line for adverts/posters
• Flyer copy
• Press release
• Social media hashtags/interaction
• Teaser material

• Brochure *blurb*
• Blog/Vlog
• Listings info
• Other web-related material

Typically, these need to be as short and punchy as possible, giving a strong sense of the unique qualities of the show as quickly as possible. It's going to be very useful if the words used regarding the production connect to or emerge from the textual language of the show – meaning that a prospective audience can shift towards the language of the piece, and that their expectations are accommodated. As an actor you will have spent some time investigating this world; it can be a clarifying process to try to distil that rich investigation into concise words and phrases, which are adapted across different purposes. A press release for a national newspaper will need a different tone and content from a social media campaign.

It's worth also considering the marketing *vibe* of the production. In most professional contexts you are likely to find that there is a specific team member given the job of marketing and visualising the show as a performance event. But again, you may be in a situation in which you are wanting to do this for your own work and can be working from the creative research you have already done. You will have explored all the potential worlds connected to the text, whether these are literal or conceptual. You may also, if you are producing work, make these kinds of decisions ahead of going into the rehearsal room, and so research done for the marketing activity might also be useful to share with the actors in the room.

Contemporary marketing obviously benefits from what you can do on the internet, including direct emails, a show website, Instagram, Facebook, Twitter, promotional trailers on social media, YouTube, etc, but it still can be valuable to think in terms of coherent visual/media design that provides the through line throughout the campaign, and really connects to key aspects of the production.

• What should you think about? What are the core ideas that have emerged from your research?

- What is the play *in this production*? (i.e., it might be new version of a classic text)
- What are the key aspects of the play you are trying to represent?
- To whom are you trying to market it? What might their references be?
- What are the connections you are making with the interpretation of the text?
- What imagery really speaks about the play/production (i.e. content, style, imagery, references)?
- Is the sequence of marketing activity eye-catching and interesting in the right way?
- Does it appeal to the audience most likely to buy tickets?

As an actor, what visual sources have proved central to your work on the production? How might your appraisal of these connect with whole text, with ideas that transcend just your character and situation?

You may also find that other research activity you have explored within your process can contribute to this area – whether that's sharing elements of your research within online resources or talking about the process in vox pop/video diary segments – that might build an awareness of the production. What ideas and activities might be exciting to share for an audience to generate anticipation?

It's also worth considering production materials – objects, furniture etc. – You are likely to have phenomenal references that may be of use to a designer, but be aware that many aesthetic decisions about production materials (objects, furniture, etc) will need to be made before the rehearsal period. The designer is likely also to have done considerable research so it can be useful to cross-reference with them if you are looking for image sources, and it's quite likely they will share mood boards and model boxes with you in the early stages of a professional production period. On smaller-scale productions, offers you can make particularly if you have access to the actual objects may be very much valued, especially in a studio scene study.

Sustaining Reflective Practice

As we've outlined throughout this book, research and reflection are intrinsically interrelated. If you are an actor in training it's quite likely that you will be asked to produce various reflective tasks within this, whether this is ongoing journals, actor's project notebooks, or more specific self-reflections. We've avoided trying to model these; reflection, especially creative reflection, is indelibly personal and there isn't a model answer to assess here, only where the process takes you in practice. And that is another book.

But beyond training, this capacity to reflect and research is a central aspect of the professional actor's skillset. Your sustained progress as an artist is going to be driven by your ability to explore the new, be curious about the different, and to understand how your own self can be explored, shaped, and developed in the pursuit of great performance.

Your capacity to reflect on your work within a process, either as an actor or as a maker, can be central to the development of future work. Often being able to appraise what worked or what didn't is a massive personal learning journey, but it may also be part of evaluating a funded project or beginning to build a company brand that continues to make work. What are the values of the work you do? Who is it speaking to? How does it communicate? Your now enhanced capacity to appraise a wealth of source material can always be repurposed to illuminate this.

Reflecting on your process and research can also be compelling to articulate; there's a strange fascination people have for the alchemy of creating a role, how an actor managed to make them believe so very much in a character or a situation, the rich and lateral connections that integrate in evolving performance, the strange and marvellous insights we acquire. Being able to communicate this is often part of the cultural value of performance – be it live or filmed. Some actors have also then been able to extend this into their own writing, such as Antony Sher's *Year of the King*, Emma Thompson's *Sense and Sensibility: The Screenplay and Diaries*, and Richard E. Grant's *With Nails*. We're not suggesting you start hunting for a book deal immediately, but to make sure that your reflection can be celebratory, joyful, and clarifying, not just self-critical, conflicted, and destructive.

However, reflective practice does need to accommodate feedback, to be clear-sighted about your work, identifying when elements need more work or refinement, and when you're not getting yourself to where you need to go. Actors are often so exposed to feedback and criticism, whether it's via rejection from an audition, critical reviews of their work, or random insults in the Twitter sphere. It's important to make sure your reflective practice can keep you clear but close to your own experience, capable of recognising opportunities for growth and change, accepting past errors of judgement, and able to balance both the positive and negative healthily.

Further Study and Application

We hope that you are on course for building a long-term and creative career as an actor, but it's unarguable that for many talented, dedicated actors this proves to be a bumpy road. Many of the areas explored in this book might open different doors, additional side careers, or suggestions for further study.

There's a wealth of creative MAs (Master of Arts) or similar programmes available, which will usually focus on research-driven projects within the course. Obviously, there are those specifically created in the field of performance; perhaps writing, applied theatre, producing, collaborative theatre making or film making. But there are also those which may value this kind of activity within a different field: heritage/museum interpretation, teaching, interior design, dramatherapy/counselling, coaching, public speaking.

We hope this book has given you a range of different ways to research as an actor: to extract every nuance from the materials you encounter, to build fascinating, multi-layered characters in many different relationships and contexts, react in the moment in time and space, to imaginatively explore all our many worlds. It's the work that allows us, ourselves, now, to be present, available, and truthful, to listen and respond to others, in what they say and don't say, to tell stories that connect with the world.

As human beings, there's nowhere where that doesn't have value.

Further Reading

- *Theatre-Making: Interplay Between Text and Performance in the 21st Century* by Dûska Radosavljević
- *So You Want to Be a Theatre Producer?* by James Seabright
- *Open Book Theater Management: Ethical Theater Production* by Rafe Beckley
- *Research Methods in Theatre and Performance* by Baz Kershaw and Helen Nicholson
- *Practice as Research in the Arts: Principles, Protocols, Pedagogies, Resistances* by Robin Nelson

APPENDIX

Creative Critical Mapping

Working With the Maps

These are broken down into three key features:

TYPE OF SOURCE MEDIUM/THE WHOLE SOURCE

HEADINGS OF SUGGESTED KEY AREAS TO CONSIDER WITH THIS FORM OF SOURCE

PROMPTS

Adaptations and Applications

Not every source will generate ideas under every heading or prompt, and there isn't necessarily a right order in which to go through the prompts on the maps.

These are not intended as prescriptions; they can and should be adapted, rejected, and reimagined as suits your particular project, sources, texts, or area of research, and according to your own responses and ways of *seeing*.

We have tried to keep these as concentrated as possible, and so it may also be useful to look at some sources as hybrids which might encompass more than one map. A feature film for example is likely to include visual, audio, and physical material to consider, as well as verbal elements of the spoken dialogue, not to mention the objects placed in the spaces and locations used.

It's also worth considering the impact of the context in which you encounter the source material you are appraising; people-watching in the park can be valuable in terms of reading movement characteristics, but the liveness and spontaneity of this will mean you'll need to focus perhaps on fewer different prompts compared to viewing something physical that has been recorded and can be rewatched.

Source material, as we've noted previously, can often be most useful when we actively try to find friction, opposition, or new perspectives rather than looking for the obvious connection. Peoples' voices might suggest a physicality or a movement, spoken word audio can be intensely rhythmic and physical as well as verbal, space makes us move differently. Many of these intersections are included within the prompts, but we encourage you to build and connect on your own observations!

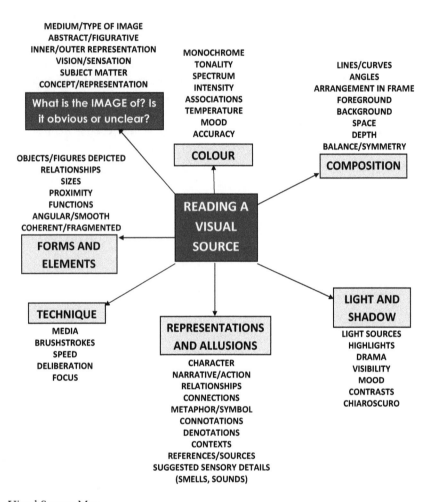

Visual Source Map

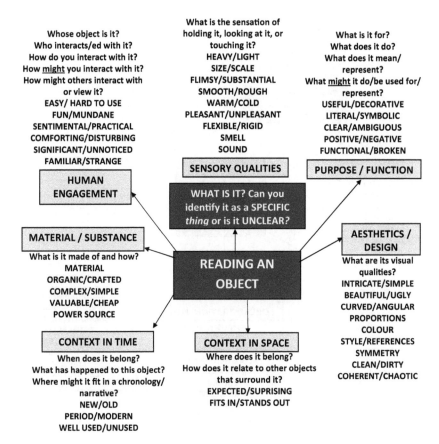

Whose object is it?
Who interacts/ed with it?
How do you interact with it?
How <u>might</u> you interact with it?
How might others interact with
or view it?
EASY/ HARD TO USE
FUN/MUNDANE
SENTIMENTAL/PRACTICAL
COMFORTING/DISTURBING
SIGNIFICANT/UNNOTICED
FAMILIAR/STRANGE

**HUMAN
ENGAGEMENT**

What is the sensation of
holding it, looking at it, or
touching it?
HEAVY/LIGHT
SIZE/SCALE
FLIMSY/SUBSTANTIAL
SMOOTH/ROUGH
WARM/COLD
PLEASANT/UNPLEASANT
FLEXIBLE/RIGID
SMELL
SOUND

SENSORY QUALITIES

What is it for?
What does it do?
What does it mean/
represent?
What <u>might</u> it do/be used for/
represent?
USEFUL/DECORATIVE
LITERAL/SYMBOLIC
CLEAR/AMBIGUOUS
POSITIVE/NEGATIVE
FUNCTIONAL/BROKEN

PURPOSE / FUNCTION

WHAT IS IT? Can you
identify it as a SPECIFIC
thing or is it UNCLEAR?

MATERIAL / SUBSTANCE

What is it made of and how?
MATERIAL
ORGANIC/CRAFTED
COMPLEX/SIMPLE
VALUABLE/CHEAP
POWER SOURCE

**READING AN
OBJECT**

**AESTHETICS /
DESIGN**

What are its visual
qualities?
INTRICATE/SIMPLE
BEAUTIFUL/UGLY
CURVED/ANGULAR
PROPORTIONS
COLOUR
STYLE/REFERENCES
SYMMETRY
CLEAN/DIRTY
COHERENT/CHAOTIC

CONTEXT IN TIME

When does it belong?
What has happened to this object?
Where might it fit in a chronology/
narrative?
NEW/OLD
PERIOD/MODERN
WELL USED/UNUSED

CONTEXT IN SPACE

Where does it belong?
How does it relate to other objects
that surround it?
EXPECTED/SUPRISING
FITS IN/STANDS OUT

Object Source Map

FORM/MEDIUM
EVENTS/NARRATIVE
PURPOSE/FUNCTION
LYRICS/LANGUAGE
VOCAL/INSTRUMENTAL
PREPARED/SPONTANEOUS

PATTERNED/ORGANISED
THROUGH COMPOSED
FORMAL/SEQUENCED
STORY/JOURNEY
COHERENCE
EPISODIC/FREE FLOW
ORGANISATION

What is the TYPE of audio source?

STRUCTURE AND STYLE

SPEED/PACE
SYNCOPATION
TIME SIGNATURE
STACCATO
RHYTHM/REGULARITY
PAUSES/SILENCES

VOCALISATION

DIALOGUE/SPEECH PATTERN
ACCENT/DIALECT/PATOIS
ARTICULATION/DICTION
BREATHINESS
FLUENCY
TONAL QUALITY
EXPRESSIVENESS
CHARACTERS/ RELATIONSHIPS

READING AN AUDIO/ MUSIC SOURCE

RHYTHM AND PULSE

REFERENCES AND SOURCES

SAMPLES/QUOTES
SOUND EFFECTS
PARODY
SOURCES
INTERTEXTUALITY
THEMATIC
MOTIFS
CONTRADICTIONS

INSTRUMENTATION, ORCHESTRATION, MIX

INSTRUMENTS
COMPLEXITY
SCALE/AUDIBLE INPUTS
ACOUSTIC/DIGITAL
AMPLIFICATION
VOLUME
MIXING/LEVELS
FREQUENCY

TONALITY AND HARMONY

MAJOR/MINOR KEY
UNISON/HARMONY
HARMONY/DISSONANCE
TONAL SCALE
MOOD/EMOTION
DYNAMICS
LYRICISM
ECHO/DISTORTION
PITCH

Audio Source Map

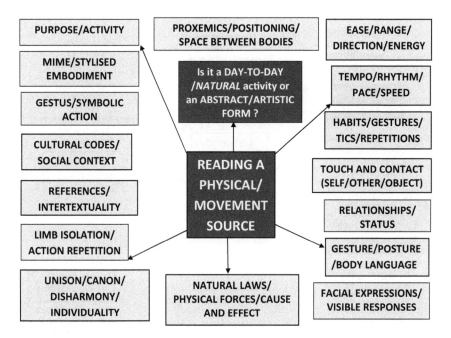

Movement Source Map

Spatial Source Map

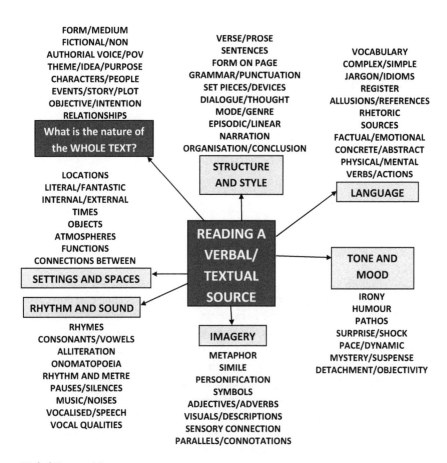

Verbal Source Map

GLOSSARY

Action/Tactic   These are terms for what someone *does* to achieve an objective. We have written both words because we use and refer to both within this book. Actions and tactics are also referred to as active or transitive verbs – something you do to someone else, to get what you want. You may encounter this as 'verbing' or 'actioning' within this text and in other processes. Some practitioners might refer to tactics/actions as 'activities'.

Activities   In this book 'activities' relates to exercises that we suggest, or physical activities within a scene like 'washing up', 'folding clothes' or 'having dinner' – things that you are physically *doing*.

Characteristics   Characteristics are qualities or traits inhabited by the character such as kind, jealous, selfish, childish, positive, helpful, etc. Characteristics can be both *inner* (those we don't show or that are not immediately visible) and *outer* (those we have on display).

Connection   When we use the term 'connecting to' or 'finding the connection' we refer to how successful the actor is in inhabiting the given circumstances of the scenic action, and allowing those given circumstances to affect them.

Given Circumstance   The term 'given circumstance' refers to the imagined situation within which the play/scene/exercise is set. It is what we know in terms of relationship, location, time, and era – the given information. This term can also be used to describe the full situation of the performance; for example, encompassing the fact that there is an audience and a stage and lights, etc. We will mostly be using this term regarding the actor's imagined circumstance within the performance.

Impulse   We relate to the term 'impulse' as something instinctive – when an actor reacts in the moment to a stimulus (such as another actor, a line, someone's action, etc) without it being pre-planned, filtered, or thought out. In order to work with spontaneity, one has to use instinct and impulse and allow them to be part of the interaction.

In the moment   This phrase is used within acting to define the moment when the actor is fully concentrated on the action of the scene and scene partners. Being in the moment means that the actor is reacting to the present imagined circumstance and is entirely engaged with the story, dialogue, and relationship, rather than the surrounding circumstance of 'being an actor'. It is essentially a state of *flow*.

Inner life/Monologue   The inner monologue is used to make sure we are thinking, listening, and evaluating the situation as our character within the set given circumstances. Inner monologue can be thoughts the character is thinking when they are not speaking, or whilst someone else is speaking. Engaging in an inner monologue ensures sustained presence and commitment to the objective, obstacle, stakes, and relationship.

Objective   This means what the character wants or needs in the scene or the whole story. It can sometimes be used instead of *Goal, Intention, Need* or *Motive*. We use this word in terms of what the character or actor wants in a scene or exercise, but at times also for the intention of the exercise itself. The phrase 'super objective' is often used as the reason behind the character's scenic objectives – what the character is ultimately working towards, or the *long-term goal*.

Obstacle   This is what stands in your way, and/or makes it harder to achieve your objective. These can be both outer (like another person or a physical object like a locked door) or they can be inner (like fear or pride).

Previous Circumstance   This is similar to *given circumstance* but it focuses on what has happened previously in the story. This can be actions or events that have been alluded to or that we have witnessed within the text, or an imagined preceding situation informing the current situation.

Stakes   This refers to what is at stake within the scene and determines the urgency in the scenic action/exercise. If the stakes are high, there is a greater urgency to accomplish what you came to accomplish; i.e. you have more to lose.

Units/Beats   A unit is a portion of a scene that contains one theme or subject. In that sense, a unit changes every time a shift occurs in a scene. It also changes as soon as anyone enters or exits, a phone rings, etc. The units create the spine of the scenic action.

Lightning Source UK Ltd.
Milton Keynes UK
UKHW022321070223
416657UK00018B/117

9 781032 123684